Doris Behrens-Abouseif held the Nasser D. Khalili Chair for Islamic Art and Archaeology from 2000 to 2014, and is now Professor Emerita, at the School of Oriental and African Studies (SOAS), University of London. She previously taught at the American University in Cairo and the University of Munich. She has written a number of books on Islamic art and architecture including *Cairo of the Mamluks: A History of Architecture and its Culture* (I.B.Tauris), *The Minarets of Cairo: Islamic Architecture from the Arab Conquest to the End of the Ottoman Period* (I.B.Tauris), *Beauty in Arabic Culture* and *Egypt's Adjustment to Ottoman Rule.*

'As I read on, the sensation grew that the world described by the Mamluk chroniclers was richer and stranger than the one we live in today.'

– *Times Literary Supplement*

'Comprehensive and masterful ... Professor Doris Behrens-Abouseif draws a detailed history of the art of giving in the context of the Mamluk Sultanate, considering all the ins and outs of what became a sophisticated tradition. Thoroughly documented, this stimulating book will become a reference work for students and scholars in the field of Middle Eastern studies and beyond.'

– Frédéric Bauden, Professor of Arabic Language and Islamic Studies, Université de Liège

'Abouseif's command of the primary textual sources is even more impressive than her treatment of the surviving body of art-historical artefacts and the information these supply about late medieval material culture in the eastern Mediterranean.'

– Anthony Cutler, Evan Pugh Professor of Art History, Penn State University

'The importance of gift-giving was enshrined in premodern diplomatic culture, and with the Mamluks at the centre of an enormous web of political and commercial networks ... [Abouseif's] superb command of the sources and her knowledge of Mamluk art once again make for an authoritative work which adds fascinating new material.'

– Bernard O'Kane, Professor of Islamic Art and Architecture, The American University in Cairo

Practising Diplomacy in the Mamluk Sultanate

Gifts and Material Culture in the Medieval Islamic World

Doris Behrens-Abouseif

I.B. TAURIS
LONDON · NEW YORK

Revised paperback edition published in 2016 by
I.B.Tauris & Co. Ltd
London · New York
www.ibtauris.com

Hardback edition first published in 2014 by
I.B.Tauris & Co. Ltd

ISBN: 978 1 78453 703 6
eISBN: 978 0 85773 541 6
ePDF: 978 0 85772 424 3

A full CIP record for this book is available from the British Library
A full CIP record is available from the Library of Congress

Library of Congress Catalog Card Number: available

Typeset by Bright Lantern Publishing

To J.M. Rogers

CONTENTS

Illustrations and Credit xi
Acknowledgements xv
Note to the Reader xvii
Introduction xix

PART ONE: THE CULTURE OF GIFTS

1 The World of the Mamluks 3

2 Protocol and Codes of Gift Exchange 11
Diplomatic Hospitality and Safety 11
The Meaning of Diplomatic Gifts 17
The Monetary Value of Gifts 26
Recycled, Used and Requested Gifts 31

PART TWO: GIFTS IN GEO-POLITICAL CONTEXTS

3 The Red Sea and Indian Ocean Connection 37
Yemen 37
India 46

4 Africa 49
Ethiopia 49
Nubia 52
The Maghrib 52
West Africa (Mali and Borno) 57

5 The Black Sea, Anatolia, Iran and Central Asia 61
The Golden Horde at the Black Sea 61
The Ilkhanids and the Jalayirids in Iran and Iraq 65
The Timurids in Iran and Central Asia 70
The Turkmens 77
The Qara Qoyunlus 77
The Aq Qoyunlus 79
The Dhul Qadirs 80
The Safavids 82
The Ottomans 84

6 Europe 95
Castile and Aragon 95
The Cyprus Connection 102
Venice 107
Florence 112
France 115

PART THREE: THE GIFTS

7 Tradition and Legacy 121
Traditional Diplomatic Gifts in the Middle East and the Muslim World 121
The Fatimid and Ayyubid Legacies 127

8 Gifts for and from the Mamluks 133
Gifts for the Mamluks 133
The Mamluk Assortment of Diplomatic Gifts 135
Spices and Porcelain 137
Mamluks and Craftsmen 139
Giraffes, Elephants and other Animals 140
Balsam, Theriac and other Local Products 146
Religious Gifts 150
Textiles 151

Illustrations and Credit

Plates

1 Façade of the hospital of Sultan al-Mu'ayyad Shaykh, temporarily used as a guesthouse. Photo by the author.
2 The mausoleum dome of the Emir Jawhar al-Qunuqba'i in Cairo, 1440. Photo by the author.
3 Ceramic figurine of an elephant carrying a palanquin with musicians, Syria, thirteenth century. Khalili Collection, Nour Foundation (POT 1285).
4 *The arrival of a giraffe sent by Sultan Faraj to Timur in Samarqand.* Double page of Yazdi's *Zafarname*, Shiraz, 1436. Left: Worcester Art Museum, Worcester, Massachusetts. Bequest of Alexander H. Bullock, 1962 (187). Right: Keir Collection. By kind permission of Ranros Universal SA. Photo by A.C. Cooper.
5 Medieval French jug of rock crystal. V&A Museum, London (15-1864).
6 Brigandine in the name of Sultan Jaqmaq. Museo Nazionale del Bargello, Florence (Azmi 1244).
7 Elements of Aq Qoyunlu silver-inlaid armour. Askeri Müzesi, Istanbul.
8 Helmet in the name of Sultan Barsbay. Musée du Louvre, Paris (OA 6130).
9 Chamfron in the name of Emir Muqbil al-Rumi, early fifteenth century. Musée des Beaux-Arts de Lyon, MBA Lyon (D 377-1).

10 Axe in the name of al-Nasir Muhammad, son of Qaytbay. Askeri Müzesi, Istanbul (8434).
11 Axe in the name of al-Nasir Muhammad, son of Qaytbay. Kunsthistorisches Museum, Wien (HJRK C 113).
12 Mamluk axe. Fifteenth century. Museo Nazionale del Bargello, Florence (1227/M).
13 Armour in the name of Sultan Qaytbay, front, back and detail. Mersin Naval Museum.
14 Armour of Emir Sayf al-Din Inal, 1428–43. Furusiyya Collection, Vaduz (R- 749) front and back view. Photos by Debra Noël Adams.
15 *Vulcan and Aeolus*. By Piero di Cosimo, 1490s. National Gallery of Canada, Ontario (No 4287).
16 *Giraffe with Mamluk groom*. Engraving in Sigismondo Tizio's *Historiae Senenses*. After John Barclay Lloyd, late fifteenth century.
17 *Adoration of the Magi* by Bernardino Luini, 1525. Santa Maria dei Miracoli, Sarrono. Alinari Archives (BEN-F-001304-0000).
18 *Adoration of the Magi* by Bernardino Luini. Cathedral of Como, 1513. Alinari Archives (RAN-F-000002).
19 *Lorenzo di Medici receiving a Mamluk embassy with a giraffe and other animals.* Painting by Giorgio Vasari 1556–8. Ceiling of Cosimo di Medici's apartment at the Palazzo Vecchio in Florence. Alinari Archives (BEN-F-000562-0000).
20 *Feast of the gods.* Giovanni Bellini, 1514. National Gallery of Art, Washington.
21 *Giraffe led by an African groom.* Veneranda Biblioteca Ambrosiana, Milano/De Agostini Picture Library (D 140 inf).
22 *Elephant with Mamluk groom.* Fresco by an unknown artist, 1480s. At the courtyard of Castello Sforzesco, Milan. Commune of Milan, all rights reserved. Photo by Fabio Saporetti.
23 *Capture of an elephant.* Roman mosaics, Piazza Armerina, Sicily. Erich Lessing Culture and Fine Arts Archives (11010360-a4).

24 Mantle for a statue of the Virgin. Fifteenth-century Mamluk silk. Cleveland Museum of Art (39.40).
25 Dalmatic at the St Annen-Museum Lübeck. Fourteenth-century Mamluk silk. Photo by Walter Haberland.

ACKNOWLEDGEMENTS

The idea of a study focused on Mamluk diplomatic gifts occurred to me when I was given the opportunity to present a paper at a conference titled *Mamluk Cairo: Crossroad of Embassies*, which was organised by Frédéric Bauden at the University of Liège in September 2012. This highly stimulating event, which unfolded the breadth of the Mamluk diplomatic network, inspired me to expand my research in a book on gift exchange around the Mamluk Sultanate.

I am grateful to colleagues, students and friends who have given me valuable references and information, or helped me acquire material that is not easy to access: Manijeh Bayani, Rémi Dewière, Sami De Giosa, Carola Di Pauli, Richard Goldthwaite, Julien Loiseau, Lucian Reinfandt, Scott Redford, J.M. Rogers, Maria Sardi and Tania Tribe.

I am also very much indebted to David Alexander for sharing with me his information, including his unpublished notes, and for his kind and prompt responses to my many email queries.

The generous support of Nurhan Atasoy in Istanbul, Marco Spallanzani in Florence and Bashir Mohammed at the Furusiyya collection made my fieldwork an agreeable experience.

I also thank Matthias Pfaffenbichler at the Kunsthistorisches Museum in Vienna, Francesco Civita at the Stibbert Museum, Marino Marini at the Bargello Museum, Bülent Tütüncüoğlu and Tünay Güçkıran at the Military Museum in Istanbul and Ece Irmak at the Naval Museum in Istanbul for their kind and friendly assistance during my fieldwork, and Richard Deunger, Nahla Nassar and Birgitt Borkopp-Restle respectively for the pictures from the Keir Collection, the Nasser D. Khalili Collection and the St Annen-Museum in Lübeck.

I am very grateful to my colleague Takao Ito for drawing my attention to a number of mistakes to be eliminated in the paperback reprint.

My fellowship at the Annemarie Schimmel Kolleg at the University of Bonn in the summer of 2013 greatly facilitated the completion of my research; I thank Stephan Conermann for the invitation.

I am grateful to the Barakat Trust for the grant that significantly contributed to my fieldwork, the production of the manuscript and the illustrations.

Doris Behrens-Abouseif

بركات
BARAKAT
U.K. Charity No. 328664 & No. 1136842

Note to the Reader

The most difficult part in the preparation of this study has been the terminology of the material culture, which cannot be found in dictionaries. The problem lies in identifying unfamiliar technical terms that have been used only in limited periods and areas, and spotting erroneous readings in published texts. The medieval terms for textiles have always posed a problem to scholars in this field; they are regional and period specific and cannot always be identified with the help of dictionaries or with physical evidence. Due to the significance of textiles in gift culture, we are left with many question marks.

The technical terminology of weapons and equestrian items is similarly problematic, albeit less desperate. The abundant Arabic literature of manuals in the military and equestrian disciplines might shed light on some unclear spots in the historical texts, but the investigation required would be far beyond the scope of this study. The tolerance of the reader is requested in this matter. For weights and monetary values I have relied on Hinz's invaluable manual *Islamische Masse und Gewichte.*

I have converted all the *Hijri* dates given in the chronicles, as far as they are precise, into CE dates. In cases when the month is unknown, the date has been indicated as lying between the two years in question.

For the paperback edition the Introduction has been modified, and corrections and a few bibliographical additions have been made.

INTRODUCTION

Since the 1920s much has been written and elaborated on the meaning of gifts in society.[1] The recent florescence of studies of the history of diplomacy initially focused on Europe has stimulated further scholarship on its material culture, which includes not only diplomatic gifts but also the whole ceremonial *mise en scène* of the gift exchange procedure.[2]

The considerable scholarly output on the material culture of diplomacy along with recent studies and exhibitions related to this subject in the context of East–West exchanges made it necessary to add a monograph dedicated to diplomatic gifts in the Mamluk Sultanate, when Cairo was a 'crossroad for embassies', as declared in the title of a conference organised in 2012 on this subject,[3] in a crucial time of Islamic history and a transitional period in global history.

The history of diplomatic relations in Islamic culture has a long tradition, but only recently has attention been dedicated to its material cultural aspects and to the meaning of gifts. Whereas some historians of Islamic art have tended to look at gifts from the perspective of luxury objects, without discriminating between those that belong to diplomatic exchanges and other forms of gift-giving such as bonuses, pious endowments or personal gifts, it is necessary to discuss diplomatic gifts as a topic within its own context and specific code of rule.

The Middle Eastern diplomatic gift culture goes back almost to the beginning of documented history and continues well into early modern time. In pre-modern time the exchange of gifts between monarchs and states was of utmost significance as a medium of communication; it was a state affair rather than a private courtesy matter and like diplomatic correspondence, it was managed by specialised royal offices, whose competences may have changed over time along with the history of institutions. The references to royal gifts in connection with King Solomon and the Queen of Sheba, Christ's birth and the Prophet Muhammad's life attest to the exalted meanings attributed to this practice in ancient societies.

Some important contributions have already been achieved in the study of Mamluk diplomatic gifts, notably in bilateral contexts.[4] This book explores the objects exchanged as gifts and the extent to which their selection was ruled by universal paradigms of inherited alongside contemporary court culture in relation to Mamluk-specific values of self-representation. The discussion will deal exclusively with gifts exchanged between monarchs, and not with gifts at the lower echelon of the diplomatic scale, about which our sources provide no information.

The approach taken here is to consider the entire period of the Mamluk Sultanate between 1250 and 1517. This panoramic perspective aims at the gift exchange and is not meant as a survey of Mamluk diplomacy. This approach being based in the first place on the choices made by the Mamluk chroniclers, who often omit what they found obvious or irrelevant, can only be lopsided, not evenly covering all the ramifications of the diplomatic gift exchange between the sultans and the world around them. As a result of the fact that the chronicles prefer to tell about gifts received rather than those given, especially when Christian rulers are concerned, almost our entire knowledge of Mamluk gifts to European courts is based on European sources. Some diplomatic relations are less documented than others. Little is recorded about diplomatic gift exchange with Muslim Spain and Byzantium, which explains the absence of a dedicated entry for these subjects, while Borno in West Africa is mentioned because of an odd gift that arrived from there to Cairo. In spite of the uneven nature of the material available, it is possible to discern an evolution over time in the design of the packages of diplomatic gifts, which reflects the political and social vicissitudes within the Mamluk Sultanate.

Although Mamluk chronicles are replete with information about diplomacy and embassies that also refers to the exchange of diplomatic gifts, descriptions of gifts are not always available or as detailed as we would hope. The chroniclers usually refer to the main features of a 'gift package', leaving us with many questions unanswered. Neither are the enumerations of gift items always comprehensive. They moreover vary between different accounts of the same subject, as in the case of Baybars's presents to Berke Khan. The Venetian account of the gifts presented by Domenico Trevisan to Sultan al-Ghawri is not identical with the Mamluk version. However, this shortcoming is partly compensated by a number of diplomatic letters copied in Mamluk chancery manuals that refer to gifts, notably Qalqashandi's *Subh* and the anonymous text of the Bibliothèque Nationale (ms. ar. 4440), to which Bauden has drawn attention. Mamluk diplomatic letters often included an appended list of the accompanying gifts presented by the embassy that brought them.

This study needs to be complemented with material from the counterparts of the diplomatic exchange, either archival or narrative sources or objects, as has already being done regarding Mamluk–Ottoman relations.[5]

One of the issues addressed here is the relationship between diplomatic gifts and art, which proved to be more complex than expected. Gifts were less about artistic achievements in the modern sense, than about the rare and the wonderful (*tuhfa*), which very often could be an exotic animal or a commodity of daily use made in a place remote or inaccessible to the recipient. Scrutiny of the relationship between diplomatic gifts and what we define as Mamluk Art has revealed, to my surprise, a significant discrepancy between them, which requires a revision of the definition of Mamluk Art that would give more consideration to the perception of Mamluk society itself of its artistic culture. This may not be exclusively a Mamluk phenomenon. It is mainly with Renaissance Italy that art began to play an increasing role in the European diplomatic gift exchange, without eclipsing, however, the significance of exotica, which the age of discoveries rather continued to stimulate.

Although the history of objects, which has recently become a discipline of its own, can in principle contribute to the study of gifts, the major problem of the present study is the almost total absence so far of surviving objects that can definitely be identified as diplomatic gifts. The illustrations in this book showing textiles and weapons serve only to illustrate what certain gifts may have looked like. Most disappointing is the rarity of Mamluk ceremonial or inscribed textiles. However, most diplomatic gifts were not meant to last forever: exotic animals, scents and spices, textiles and edibles were short-lived. Like the ceremonial celebrations that accompanied the arrival of gifts, they belonged to the ephemeral aspects of the gift culture.

PART ONE

THE CULTURE OF GIFTS

CHAPTER 1

THE WORLD OF THE MAMLUKS

Due to its geographical location between Africa, Asia and the Mediterranean, the Mamluk Sultanate occupied a central position from which it derived much of its power, wealth and prestige. At the same time, its position in world history, and Islamic history in particular, following the hiatus of the Mongol invasion, enhanced the role of the Mamluk Sultanate as the embodiment of a Muslim and Arab revival.

The Mamluks stepped onto the world stage at a most critical time in Islamic history, when the Crusaders from the West had occupied the Syrian littoral and the Mongols from the East had terminated the Abbasid Caliphate of Baghdad in 1258 and subdued most of Central Asia. The Mamluks were the soldiers who, in the second half of the thirteenth century, stood up to both the Crusaders and the Mongols almost at the same time, evicted them from the Holy Land and Syria, and undermined alliance schemes between them. Under the rule of Sultan al-Zahir Baybars (1260–77), who, after usurping the throne from Qutuz, united Egypt with Syria and the holy cities of Mecca and Medina under his central authority, the Mamluk capital, Cairo, became the largest city in the medieval world,[1] and the epitome of the last splendour of Arab Islamic culture. The military achievements and the pious patronage of the Mamluks earned them legitimacy in the eyes of their subjects and the Arab world, although some of their Muslim rivals would not acknowledge this. Although they were purchased, as indicated by the term *mamluk* meaning 'owned or possessed', the Mamluks were not slaves. The status of the *mamluk* was not associated with servitude, but rather with the fact of being a soldier in a military aristocracy that ruled an empire. When Mamluk documents refer to *mamluks* as diplomatic gifts, they mention them separately from the ordinary slaves. The Mamluk regime of military recruitment was based on a system, which already had an established tradition in the Muslim world, of purchasing young males for the army in 'pagan countries'. The Mamluks of Egypt and Syria were either Turks from the Kipchak steppes or Circassians from the Caucasus. They converted to Islam when they received their military training and were issued with a certificate of manumission before they began their professional military career. The first *mamluks* of Egypt were recruited by the last Ayyubid sultan, al-Salih Najm al-Din, to serve as an elite corps in his army. After his death during the battle with the Crusaders at Damietta, which the Mamluks won, they took control of Egypt. From that moment, the Mamluk recruiting system not only served the army, but was also extended to serve and supply the new sultanate and its ruling aristocracy. The Mamluks recruited *mamluks* to serve them and to succeed them. Although it was in principle a first generation aristocracy that did not acknowledge hereditary succession, the fourteenth century was dominated by the Qalawunid dynasty, which ruled from 1279 to 1382. However, the new sultan had to be elected by the great emirs from among his predecessor's *mamluks*. The Mamluks were proud of earning rather than inheriting their status and prestige, and in theory only those who had been purchased were eligible to reach the highest positions in the state. However, some of their Muslim adversaries, such as the Mongols, Timurids and Ottomans, looked down on the Mamluks for their lack of lineage, regarding them as slaves and challenging their religious patronage and their guardianship of the Muslim holy cities.

Although the Mamluks, unlike the Ottomans, were not great conquerors, they managed, right up to the end of their history, to consolidate and secure the integrity of the territory they had shaped at the beginning of their rule. When they faced the Ottoman conquest, their empire collapsed without having first crumbled. At the fringes of this territory the Mamluks maintained suzerainty over smaller kingdoms and principalities. In the north, they controlled Little Armenia and East Anatolia, while Yemen and Nubia belonged to their zone of influence in the south, safeguarding Mamluk interests along the Red Sea–Indian Ocean connection.

The Mamluk Sultanate owed its wealth and prosperity to the blessing of its geographical position: in addition to the natural and human resources of Egypt and Syria, the spice trade between the Far East and Europe, over which they held a monopoly, provided the major source of revenue, comparable in a way to the role of the Suez Canal in Egypt's economy today. Trade and related matters of safety and freedom of passage were, therefore, a major factor in the diplomacy of the Mamluk period, which coincided with the age of a 'commercial revolution' in the world, whose driving force was this very spice trade.[2] The strongly centralised character of the Mamluk state gave the sultans hegemony over foreign trade in their realm, increasingly so in the fifteenth century, thus fastening the link between diplomacy and commerce. As much as diplomacy, pilgrimage was intimately linked with commerce. Issues regarding Christian pilgrims travelling to Palestine and Muslim pilgrims going to Mecca were frequently involved in the diplomatic relations of the Mamluk Sultanate. Its control of Jerusalem, Mecca and Medina compelled Christian and Muslim states to cultivate diplomacy with the sultans and to win their favour with lavish gifts. Moreover, the presence since Baybars' reign of a symbolic Abbasid caliph in Cairo, who was often requested to issue letters of investiture to various Muslim rulers, added to Mamluk religious and, by the same token, diplomatic prestige in the Muslim world.[3] The Mamluk sultans were very well aware of their leverage in the world, as was forcefully displayed in their lavish receptions of foreign embassies in Cairo, which aimed at cultivating the image of a power of worldwide significance.

The number of foreigners and embassies arriving at the Mamluk court enhanced the prestige of the sultan in the chroniclers' view. The Ayyubid sultan al-Malik al-Kamil (r. 1218–38) was praised for attracting a unique gathering of embassies at his court from Khawarizm, Georgia, Hims, Hama, India, Europe (*faranj*), Shiraz and al-Andalus,[4] and years later Ibn Shaddad dedicated a whole chapter in his biography of al-Zahir Baybars to listing the scholars, refugees, princes and diplomats who came to his court.[5] Maqrizi writes that in 668/1268–9 almost all neighbouring countries sent envoys to Baybars,[6] and in his obituary of al-Nasir Muhammad, he praises this sultan for the gifts he received from the rulers of the Maghrib, India, China, Ethiopia, Africa (Takrur), Nubia, Byzantium, the Turks and the Franks.[7] The pride the Mamluks took in their worldwide connections is also reflected in their pious patronage of academic institutions, which were meant to host scholars and students from the entire Muslim world, and in the markets of their cities, in particular Cairo, Damascus and Aleppo, which boasted goods from all over the world.

Al-Zahir Baybars, the first great Mamluk sultan, combined the virtues of a military hero, who celebrated triumphs against the Mongols and Crusaders, with the wisdom of a statesman who, for the sake of stability and commerce, cultivated diplomatic relations with the East and the West including former enemies. After several successful military campaigns against the Crusaders, he exchanged embassies and signed truces with the remaining Frankish rulers in the Levant as well as with the Hohenstaufen and the Angevin kings of Sicily, with Castile, Aragon, France, Genoa and Byzantium. The sultan obtained authorisation for Mamluk vessels to cross the Bosphorus, and later Qalawun signed a treaty with Constantinople that secured the slave trade that supplied the Mamluk state with the vital manpower of *mamluks* via the Crimea. The Byzantine emperors also interceded in favour of the Christians in Mamluk lands and the churches in the Holy Land. Amicable relations with Byzantium continued under al-Nasir Muhammad.[8] These good relations did not preclude, however, the conquest of Constantinople by the Ottomans in 1453 from being highly celebrated in Cairo.

Baybars also fostered an alliance with the Mongols of the Golden Horde, as soon as they converted to Islam, in order to neutralise their Mongol rivals who were ruling Iran and at the same time to secure the purchase of *mamluks* through the Black Sea.[9] His next significant successors, Qalawun (r. 1279–90) and his sons al-Ashraf Khalil (r. 1290–3) and al-Nasir Muhammad (r. 1293–1341 with two interruptions) continued and consolidated this diplomacy.

Following a period of tense relations with the Mongol ruler of Iran, the Ilkhanid Ghazan (r. 1295–1304), al-Nasir Muhammad, whose long reign enjoyed a period of stability and prosperity, signed an entente with Abu Sa'id (r. 1316–35) that served the interests of both sides by consolidating and promoting trade, taking advantage of the reopened Silk Road. A period of intensive diplomacy followed between the two sultanates. After the break-up of the Mongol Empire, which had been favourable to commercial activities between the East and the West, Mamluk hegemony on the transit trade between the Far East and the Mediterranean was reinforced.

The Pope's ban on trade with the Mamluks in the post-Crusade period could not have a decisive impact on their commercial relations with Latin European states, who were able to circumvent it. Among the Italian states, Genoa and Venice were major trade partners of the Mamluks alongside Aragon, all three being the major players in Mediterranean trade and navigation.[10] The shift in the technological lead during the fourteenth century towards Europe led to a dramatic increase of European textile export to the Levant, thus favouring the import of other Eastern goods to Europe. In spite of the regular post-Crusade raids on Mamluk coasts and piracy in Syrian and Egyptian waters, notably by the Catalans, which provoked harsh reprisals against the commercial and religious interests of all Europeans, embassies carrying gifts were regularly sent to promote European exports and regain the sultans' favour.

After the elimination of the Crusaders from Syria and Palestine, the main threats to Mamluk territory came from their Muslim rivals, the Ilkhanids, followed by the Timurids and the Ottomans. While diplomacy with Europe after the Crusades was mainly about trade and pilgrimage, diplomacy with Muslim powers included issues of legitimacy, power and territory.

The fifteenth century opened with a military and economic disaster for the Mamluks, caused by Timur's raid on Syria in 1400–1 and the temporary vassalage of Sultan Faraj. Timur's ambitions in the western Muslim world were pursued, albeit in a different style, by his son Shahrukh, who pursued a vivid diplomatic correspondence with Sultan Barsbay (r. 1422–38) and his successor Jaqmaq (r. 1438–53). Shahrukh's embassies arrived regularly in Cairo asking for the permission to donate the curtain (*kiswa*) of the Ka'ba in Mecca, which is traditionally renewed on a yearly basis. This request was rejected by Barsbay, who perceived it as a challenge to Mamluk supremacy over the sacred sites of Islam and by the same token to the Mamluks' religious leadership. Barsbay's successor, Jaqmaq, showed more leniency in the handling of this matter. The conquest of Cyprus by Barsbay in 1427 was a significant and last addition to the area of Mamluk domination. The island, which held a key position in Mediterranean trade and was a bone of contention between Aragon, Naples, Genoa and Venice, remained tributary to the sultanate till the Ottoman conquest. This led to the involvement of the Mamluk sultans in issues of Cyprian throne succession.

Barsbay also gave special attention to Indian trade, and under his rule the port city of Jeddah, governed by a Mamluk emir, replaced Aden as the major port of the Red Sea.[11]

The Timurids in the east and the Ottomans in west Anatolia and southern Europe contributed to the increasing pressure on the Mamluk Sultanate, which in the later period could be defended only at very high cost. Following the disintegration of the Mongol and later Timurid empires, the Turkmen states of the Qaramanids (1256–1475 in southern Anatolia), Dhul Qadir (1337–1521 in south-eastern Anatolia), the Qara Qoyunlus (1351–1469 in eastern Anatolia and western Iran), the Aq Qoyunlus (1396–1508 in eastern Anatolia, Mesopotamia and western Iran) and the Ramazanoglus (1378–1608 in Cilicia) added to the complexity of the Mamluk diplomatic map with new suzerainty bonds and intermittent alliances that were often troubled by rivalries, betrayal and conspiracies. Cairo at that time saw a regular traffic of Turkmen embassies.

Trade with China went through the Indian Ocean, India and Yemen along the same routes as the spice trade, so that there was no need for regular diplomatic relations, although some attempts to establish direct contacts are recorded.[12] There were, however, diplomatic relations and gifts exchanged between China and the Rasulids of Yemen.[13] The spice trade and the Muslim connections in the Indian Ocean, including the pilgrimage to Mecca and issues of pious foundations, required diplomatic contact and gift exchange with the sultanates of India in Bengal, Delhi and Gulparga.[14] The rulers of the Tughluq and Lodi dynasties of Delhi, the Bahmanids and others used to send embassies carrying precious gifts and exotic animals to Cairo, requesting the investiture diploma from the Abbasid caliph to legitimise their rule.[15]

Owing to the significance of the Red Sea as the major channel to the Indian Ocean, the Mamluks controlled it, as had their Ayyubid predecessors, and prevented non-Muslims from navigating its waters without authorisation. Along this route, Yemen was a vital link in the chain of the spice trade and the connection with China, and its rulers had to abide by Mamluk rules and send gifts that were in fact tributes.

The Timurid and then Safavid threats imposed temporary alliances between the Mamluks and the Ottomans, as did the Portuguese advance in the Red Sea and the Indian Ocean a century later. An intensive exchange of embassies took place between the two courts almost to the day before Sultan Selim I overthrew the Mamluk Sultanate. Ottoman ambitions regarding the heartland of the Muslim world, in particular after the Ottoman conquest of Constantinople in 1453, had become obvious to the Mamluks, who fought at a high price to defend their territory until they finally lost the battle in 1517.

CHAPTER 2

PROTOCOL AND CODES OF GIFT EXCHANGE

Diplomatic Hospitality and Safety

Following ancient inherited traditions, Mamluk diplomatic protocol dictated that the sultan should provide hospitality and maintenance to the embassies that came to meet him. The reception of embassies was a highly onerous matter for the host, who had to provide a residence for the ambassador and his retinue that could be quite large, as well as maintenance and presents including robes of honour for the ambassador and his retinue and sometimes also cash. Diplomatic ethics of hospitality, disregarding religious differences, implied reciprocation and thus served mutual interests. 'Ceremony symbolised the mutual respects of the parties.'[1]

The offering of personal presents to the envoys was a custom practised worldwide.[2] In medieval Venice, however, the envoys had to turn over such gifts to the state to avoid there being a conflict of interest and suspicions of bribery.[3] The reception of the Yemeni embassy in 1353 cost Sultan al-Salih Salih 200,000 *dirhams* (*c.*50,000 *dinars*); it included, besides maintenance and robes of honour, a per diem of 500 *dirhams* for each member of the embassy.[4] This kind of largesse might not have been the common practice, but in this case it corresponded to the outstanding value of the gifts that the Yemenis had brought with them on that occasion. An envoy from the Hafsid ruler of Tunis in 1391 received a per diem of 100 *dirhams*, which was considered to be very high for his status.[5] The Venetian embassy of Domenico Trevisan received for its maintenance 44 sugar bread loafs each weighing 4 pounds, 5 containers of honey, 2 containers of fine fat, 40 sheep, 50 pairs of chicken, 20 geese and 2 bags of rice.[6]

The rules of diplomatic hospitality, which also warranted immunity and safe-conduct to the ambassadors, were not exclusive to the Mamluks or to Islamic culture, but rather followed diplomatic conventions that went back to Roman, Byzantine and Sassanian traditions,[7] which continued to prevail worldwide at the time of the Mamluks and beyond. Probably following the Byzantine tradition of impressing the Barbarians, European medieval courts treated the arrival of an embassy as a solemn event, and later Renaissance courts enhanced and cultivated diplomatic receptions with sumptuous apparel, ceremonial banquets, music and fanfares and other spectacles.[8] In the seventeenth century the Medicis used ballets and theatrical performances as a medium to promote their political and diplomatic self-representation.[9] Diplomatic hospitality fulfilled the major purpose of impressing foreign ambassadors so that on their return to their own countries they might convey their impressions to their patrons; it was a visual and material means of carrying out diplomacy, as were robes of honour and gifts.

Our picture of the Mamluk court would have been much poorer without the accounts of European members of embassies who were impressed by what they experienced. The account of the Castilian envoy Clavijo immortalised Timur and the image of his court, which shows how the literary portrait of a prince can be conveyed to a remote and strange world over centuries.

Clavijo reports of the hospitality granted to him from the moment his embassy arrived in Azerbaijan; he received copious food and drink, luxurious lodging and transport. In the capital,

Samarqand, the embassy was received every day of its stay in a different lavish residence and invited to sumptuous festivities, with luxuriant banquets served accompanied by overflowing wine, which was intended to display a glorious picture of Timur's court. Similarly in Venice, the Mamluk envoys were usually greeted by the doge on the regal golden barge the Bucintoro.[10] Entertainment there included a procession, a shopping tour, receptions and the attendance of festivities and concerts.[11] Lorenzo di Medici likewise greeted Qaytbay's embassy in Florence with great pomp in the decorated loggia of the Signoria.

The Mamluks were aware of the propagandistic effect of diplomatic paraphernalia, and therefore staged carefully choreographed ceremonial spectacles for foreign ambassadors. The streets were decorated for the occasion, candles were lit along the way and musical performances accompanied the diplomatic procession, attracting a large crowd into the streets to greet the visitors.[12] The presence of the crowd, which is always mentioned by the chroniclers, may have been programmed as an obligatory element of the reception scenario. The official celebration took place at the Citadel, with a military parade, elaborate audiences and banquets at which all the sultan's *mamluks* displayed their finest outfits.[13]

There, the members of the embassies were usually invited to attend the *khidma*, which was the customary public audience of the sultans combined with a military parade. Ibn Taghribirdi was dismayed at the fact that Sultan Jaqmaq did not respect the tradition of inviting foreign ambassadors to attend the *khidma* in the Great Hall (*Iwan*) of the Citadel.[14] Following a tradition that went back to the Fatimid period,[15] parades, spectacles and events were specially staged or scheduled to take place during the diplomatic visit.[16] For example, the envoys of the Golden Horde attended the circumcision of Baybars' son.[17] Al-Nasir Muhammad arranged spectacles for the Ilkhanid envoys and excursions to the Pyramids, where they were given a grand reception in a ceremonial tent. The visit to the Pyramids is regularly mentioned in this context and was part of the routine of diplomatic hospitality in medieval Egypt. Sultan al-Ashraf Sha‘ban invited a European embassy into his encampment while on a hunting excursion, where they were given a solemn audience in a ceremonial tent and lodged in the same compound. Al-Ghawri (r. 1501–16) invited the Ottoman envoy to a banquet in his newly built palace on the Nile shore of the island of Rawda,[18] and other envoys to watch polo tournaments or other equestrian games.[19] The Venetian embassy of Domenico Trevisan in 1512 was accompanied by its own orchestra, members of which, dressed in red and gold, trumpeted the arrival of the diplomatic cortège at the palace where they were lodged.[20]

All accounts, even the ones that are hostile to the Mamluks, like that of Pedro Mártir, emphasise the magnificence of the royal palaces at the Citadel. Pagani praises them as being more beautiful than the doge's palace in Venice. Sultan al-Ghawri in particular dedicated great attention and zeal to regal representation. His large ceremonial complex at the hippodrome beneath the Citadel, with residential and representative structures and pavilions built around a pond amidst gardens with imported trees carrying cages of exotic and singing birds, was the first monument he erected after his accession to the throne, preceding the foundation of his mosque. Al-Ghawri also designed a new throne for himself that was a polychrome marble structure built to replace the bench used by his predecessors.[21] The garden complex at the hippodrome soon became well known abroad, as it becomes clear from a satirical poem compiled by a Safavid court poet to ridicule the Mamluk sultan and his affinity to myrtle and narcissus, which must have been known to grow there.

For the reception and maintenance of foreign envoys, normally an emir with the title of *mihmandar* was in charge, unless the embassy had a specially high or extraordinary status, in which case the Majordomo or the Chief Chamberlain would be in charge.[22]

There was a hierarchy in the lodging of embassies. Sometimes they were hosted in the residential structures attached to the various hippodromes, which were connected to pavilions and gardens and overlooked equestrian exercises and spectacles. Protocol dictated that the great hippodrome beneath the Citadel, which was attached to the sultan's court, should be reserved for the highest ranking envoys, such as those of the 'khans of the East',[23] who would be greeted by the Chief Chamberlain (*hajib al-hujjab*). There was a Palace of Hospitality called *dar al-diyafa* in Cairo, which was for receiving embassies. It stood at the foot of the Citadel, and must have been erected at the same time as the Citadel itself when it was founded by Salah al-Din between 1176 and 1183, or shortly thereafter. Its exact history is unknown.[24] In 819/1416 Sultan al-Mu'ayyad Shaykh (r. 1412–21) ordered its restoration after it was abandoned by Barquq and his son Faraj.[25] Shortly after the restoration, the Ottoman ambassador was lodged in its premises.[26] After Mu'ayyad's death, the hospital he had founded in the vicinity of the Citadel was turned by Barsbay into a Palace of Hospitality to host embassies, but soon afterwards he changed his mind and turned it into a Friday mosque[27] (Plate 1). The chronicles, however, usually report that embassies were lodged in the residences of state officials, emirs or high-ranking bureaucrats. In special cases they might be lodged in a quarter within the Citadel, the sultan's residence.

The palace, where the Venetian embassy of Domenico Trevisan was lodged, had been built, according to Pagani, by Sultan Qaytbay for his wife and decorated with marble and gold inlay of better craftsmanship than that of the Cathedral of San Marco. It was furnished with large carpets that made it a delight to dwell in.[28] Foreign embassies often carried cash and goods with them to trade on their way, either on their ruler's account or for themselves, and sometimes merchants joined the mission.[29] This would also explain attempts on more than one occasion to rob them, and their need for protection by the hosting authorities. Part of the hospitality that a monarch was supposed to grant to foreign embassies was warranty for their security and the safety of their possessions and the goods they carried. The breach of this security placed the host in a most embarrassing position, as for example in 1444 when the mob of Cairo, in alliance with some soldiers, angry about Sultan Jaqmaq's decision to grant Shahrukh permission to donate the curtain (*kiswa*) of the Ka'ba that year, took to the streets to attack and rob the Timurid envoys. The sultan was extremely embarrassed and went out of his way to punish the perpetrators and appease and compensate the envoy and his retinue.[30] The Timurid embassy was not the only victim of robbery in Mamluk territory; another incident 70 years later embarrassed Sultan al-Ghawri.

The chroniclers also report noteworthy cases of Mamluk diplomatic hospitality towards European royal persons, who took refuge at the sultan's court in the second half of the fifteenth century. In 1459 following the death of John II of Cyprus, his illegitimate son James came to the court of Sultan Inal, where he spent a long time campaigning for support against his half-sister Charlotte's aspirations to the throne, and he enjoyed Mamluk hospitality for more than a year.[31] Years later, Ferdinand of Aragon, the king of Naples (r. 1458–94), who hoped that his illegitimate son Alfonso (born c.1462) would accede to the throne in Cyprus, sent him to Qaytbay's court. After an aborted attempt to land in Cyprus, Alfonso found refuge in Cairo, where he spent several years.[32]

Although it once happened that a Mongol envoy was killed by Sultan Qutuz (r. 1259–60) and another was tortured by Sultan Barsbay, diplomatic hospitality followed a code of honour that was valid for all circumstances, just as gifts continued to be exchanged even in critical and confrontational situations. After he was captured during the conquest of Cyprus by Barsbay, King Janus was paraded in the streets of Cairo in a most humiliating spectacle and imprisoned. However, once his ransom was paid, Barsbay gave him a robe of honour, an allowance for himself and his retinue, and a horse with golden textiles that carried him in a procession to a residence allocated to him in Cairo. Janus was allowed to spend some time in the Egyptian capital, moving freely and visiting churches.[33]

The Meaning of Diplomatic Gifts

As other Muslim rulers of their time, the Mamluks viewed the exchange of diplomatic gifts as a matter of political significance. Its function and meaning were perceived to be apart from the traditional generosity that rules the personal present (*hiba*), which has always been mandatory in Arab and Islamic culture as a deliberate act and praised in contrast to avarice, which was condemned as a vice. Generosity and avarice were not involved in the context of political gifts being given by a higher standing donor to an inferior, this being rather a form of remuneration that was expected as an entitlement.[34] Likewise, the exchange of diplomatic gifts was a political and institutional practice in which generosity and avarice were not involved, rather decorum versus the lack of it. The diplomatic gifts discussed here pertain to the category of 'Maussian gift' and its further elaboration in the paradigms defined by A. Caillé's view of the gift being a means to enable the transition from war to peace, being a deliberate and yet obligatory and a self-interested yet liberal act.[35] As in European diplomacy at that same time, the gift was 'a crucial means to cultivate relationships and promote allegiances within a dynasty or between rulers or governments' and the act of presenting the gift was part of an elaborate ceremonial.[36] A diplomatic gift was a vehicle of communication, intended to convey subtle messages as a memento, like, for example, portraits of the donor in Renaissance Europe.[37] The Islamic *tuhaf* (sing. *tuhfa*), or marvels, which were an essential part of diplomatic gifts, were meant to occupy a place of honour in a royal treasury or a *wunderkammer*, and thus be part of the recipient's regalia. The term *wunderkammer*, or 'chamber of wonders', which means a repository of *tuhaf*, is rooted in an oriental tradition of a treasury filled with *tuhaf*.

Diplomatic gifts fulfilled at the same time an obligatory function. The Mamluk chroniclers consistently refer to gifts, even in their most brief reports on the arrival of an ambassador in Cairo, conveying the notion that the gift-giving was an essential part of a diplomatic visit to the sultan. Power, legitimacy and self-representation required the Mamluk sultans to consolidate their position in the world and enhance their image with ceremonial pomp of which the culture of gifts was an integral part. Beside self-representation, diplomacy and diplomatic gifts also served immediate and strategic interests. In a shrewd and pragmatic statement, Sultan al-Nasir Muhammad emphasised the strategic significance of diplomatic gifts to his Inspector of the Army (*nazir al-jaysh*), in response to the latter's misgivings about the considerable funds spent on lavish gifts for the Ilkhanid ruler Abu Sa'id, with the words: 'Keep quiet Qadi Fakhr al-Din for God's sake! If you knew what I know you would not say so.' The sultan then argued that the amount he spent on this gift, which was minimal compared with the budget of his leisure excursions, saved political, strategic and military costs on a much higher scale.[38]

Beside the significance of gifts as a medium of communication between kings, as presented in the 'Mirror for Princes' literature, the fascination with royal gifts was expressed in the literary genre of *tuhaf wa hadaya* (marvels and gifts), where history mingles with legends and poetical fantasy to delight the reader with curious and marvellous things about the lifestyle of kings in the remote and near past. It is interesting to note that diplomatic letters refer to gifts mostly with the double term *tuhaf wa hadaya* and they acknowledge the 'marvelling effect' they have on the recipient, using the verb *athafa* of the same stem as *tuhfa*. *Tuhaf*, literally meaning marvels, referred to exotica and art objects of rare or outstanding craftsmanship as well as to fabulous jewellery. Ibn Khaldun observed that kings used to fascinate (*athafa*) one another with the outstanding products of their countries to cultivate friendship and mutal support.[39] Similar to the *tuhaf* effect in Islamic culture, historians of medieval European culture refer to the symbolic significance of luxury objects as tokens of acknowledgement from one ruler to the other.[40] The notion of rarity was intimately associated with premodern royal gifts in Europe as well. Charlemagne's contemporary biographer Einhard reported that Harun al-Rashid, who ruled most of the world, offered Charlemagne his only elephant, which was white. The rarity of the gift is doubly stressed by the white colour and the uniqueness of the animal at the caliph's court. By indicating these attributes of a gift from the mightiest monarch in the world, the biographer enhanced Charlemagne's status in world history. The same notion of a 'wonderful' diplomatic gift is also found in Persian texts, where beside the Arabic *tuhfa/tuhaf* the term *tansuqat* (sing. *tansuq)* is also used.[41] It is also interesting to note that in the seventeenth century the word *tuffas* was used in Dutch, coming from Persian, meaning gifts and curiosities.[42]

The protocol of Mamluk diplomacy is discussed in chancellery manuals and in literature of the 'Mirror for Princes' genre, which relies heavily on ancient traditions of Persian and Greek lore, being documented with examples of the great kings of antiquity. The Persian legacy in particular shaped Islamic material culture of kingship, and this was also the case for the Mamluk Sultanate.[43] The major items of diplomatic gifts (textiles, slaves, animals, gems, gold and jewellery, spices and perfumes), the custom of displaying gifts at their arrival before the monarch in the presence of his courtiers, the distribution of part of the gifts to the royal entourage, and the praise of gifts in poetical forms belong to ancient traditions that persisted in Islamic culture and at the Mamluk court. In his *Siyasatname*, the classic 'Mirror for Princes', the Saljuk vizir Nizam al-Mulk (d.1092) wrote a chapter about the etiquette of receiving embassies and the guidelines for dealing with them, in which he recalled that the duty of honouring ambassadors went back to ancient traditions.[44] The author of a Mamluk treaty of the 'Mirror for Princes' genre (dated 1309), Ibn al-'Abbas, also includes a chapter on the reception of diplomats and gift exchange. In this chapter he refers to the importance of a king displaying his magnificence with all necessary ceremonial pomp and his obligation to provide both hospitality and maintenance to the members of diplomatic missions. The gifts received should be displayed before the monarch, including the wild animals and textiles, whereas the slave girls should not be displayed publicly but in private apartments. The principle of displaying diplomatic gifts was also a tradition in the German Roman Empire, where it was meant to advertise the honour received before a large audience of officials.[45] The gifts received from other courts were equivalent to a tribute paid to the ruler. Diplomatic show was not merely aimed at a foreign audience, but it conveyed a message to the local audience as well.

Ibn al-ʻAbbas also comments that some gifts can be riddles encoding threats as aggressive as a weapon.[46] Ibn Shahin al-Zahiri, a Mamluk emir and once governor of Alexandria, writes in his book on kingship – which likewise draws on ancient traditions – about the skills and etiquette of diplomacy, the duty of the monarch to display pomp in diplomatic audiences, to host foreign envoys with largesse and dignity and to offer suitable presents. He comments that gifts represent the status of the giver.[47] Another Mamluk treaty on kingship includes a chapter on gifts referring to Sasanian courtly traditions of gift giving; the author mentions that the listing and assessment of gifts by the *diwan al-khassa*, the administration of the Privy Estate, is necessary for the evaluation of reciprocated gifts.[48]

From these statements it can be concluded that gifts, alongside the written and the oral message, constituted a decisive component in a diplomatic mission. Although not all accounts of embassies mention gifts, it can be assumed that diplomatic gifts belonged to a universal rule in the world of the Mamluks, going back to ancient traditions. Because of their routine character, they were not always found worthy of mention by the chroniclers. The envoy of the Spanish court of Ferdinand of Aragon and Isabel of Castile, Pedro Mártir, was severely reprimanded for not having presented a gift to Sultan al-Ghawri. On the spur of the moment Pedro Mártir explained that there were different rules at the court of his masters.[49] This was not the general rule in Europe though; in Venice the arrival of an embassy without a gift was noticed as an oddity.[50] The exchange of gifts belonged to the rituals of diplomacy in Roman and Byzantine history and the tradition was maintained in medieval and Renaissance Europe.[51]

Gifts are mentioned regularly in Mamluk diplomatic correspondence. In a letter to Sultan al-Nasir Muhammad, the Ilkhanid ruler of Iran, Ghazan, emphasised the Mamluk sultan's obligation to send him *hadaya* and *tuhaf*, to which al-Nasir replied that when he receives gifts from Ghazan, he will respond with yet better ones and when he receives *tuhaf* he will reciprocate with yet more marvellous ones. Al-Nasir obviously expected his counterpart to make the first step.[52] Diplomatic letters refer to gifts to acknowledge their receipt with thanks and appreciation and mention, as a trope, their 'marvelling effect'. Sometimes individual gifts were praised in a flowery hyperbolic style covering several pages, composed by poets associated with the Chancellery.[53] A letter from an unnamed Mamluk sultan to the Rasulid sultan of Yemen, al-Mujahid 'Ali (r. 1321–63), lauded at length (two pages), and in most poetical and highly elaborate terms, the horses of various colours, white, black, yellow and brown, the elephant whose trunk 'strikes like a polo stick, and moves like a snake, and swings like a dancer cajoling the audience with her sleeves' and the giraffe, which 'in all her grace, like dawn between stars, like lightening crowned by the halo of clouds, penetrates the hearts as swiftly as it passes through windows and doors'. The laudation goes on about the tiger, the zebra, the civet and the scents received.[54] Another letter from Sultan Barquq to the Hafsid ruler of Tunis 'Abd al-'Aziz al-Mutawakkil celebrates in similar terms the horses he received for the variety of their colours, white, black, green [*sic*], red, and yellow, each colour being individually praised, and informs the donor that his horses have been ridden by pages in royal processions.[55] The poet Abu Nubata used to compile poetical prose for Mamluk circles in praise of gifts of horses, mules and birds of prey.[56] This must have belonged to the same poetical genre used in diplomatic correspondence. It is therefore likely that poets like Abu Nubata were commissioned by the Chancellery to compose such texts to be inserted in diplomatic correspondence. Diplomatic letters also refer to the gifts sent or reciprocated by Mamluk sultans, sometimes listing their content in an appendix to the main text. The tradition of appending the list of gifts dispatched with a letter goes back to Abbasid diplomatic correspondence of the tenth century.[57] Diplomatic letters on both sides emphasise the significance of gifts as a symbol of friendship (*mawadda*) and goodwill.

In his manual on chancellery, Qalqashandi mentions the importance of a secretary being knowledgeable about gemstones, their qualities and value, and about animals and birds, and scents and spices in order to be able to compose verse and eloquent texts when referring to gifts in diplomatic correspondence.[58] He then dedicates several pages to documenting the major features of these gift items that might be relevant to diplomatic correspondence.

The Mamluk chronicles use two terms to describe diplomatic gifts: *hadiyya* (*hadaya*) and *taqdima* (*taqadim*). These terms were usually accompanied by the attribute *hafila* or *saniyya* or *jalila* meaning lavish. The term *taqdima*, unlike *hadiyya*, is also regularly used to refer to a gift of tributary kind, such as what Mamluk governors of Syria or Jeddah and other dignitaries offered, and were expected to offer, to the sultan, but never expected to receive. The reverse – that is, the sultan's gift to a subordinate – is defined as *in'am*.

In Mamluk narrative sources the terminological lines are blurred between diplomatic gifts and gifts in suzerain–vassal relationships, which were more of a tribute. Among these were the gifts from the kings of Nubia, Yemen, the Turkmen rulers of the Dhul Qadir, Ramazanoglu, Qaramanid and Aq Qoyunlu dynasties and after their conquest in the fourteenth and fifteenth century respectively, Cyprus and Little Armenia/Cilicia. In his chronicle, Ibn 'Abd al-Zahir speaks of gifts 'imposed' on the ruler of Armenia.[59] These were expected to amount to a million *dirhams* in silver and kind that included textiles, 50 horses and mules and 10,000 horseshoes with their nails.[60] Similarly, the Rasulids of Yemen were ordered to send gifts (*taqadim*) to the Mamluk court that were set at the value of 6,000 *dinars*, otherwise they would risk military reprisals.[61] The frequency of this remittance is not clear; normally they were expected on a yearly basis. In 1339 ‘Ala al-Din Eretna, a ruler in north-eastern Anatolia, sent a special gift that consisted of a large tent or pavilion (*khirqah*) worth 300,000 *dirhams* (*c.*15,000 *dinars*),[62] made of silk brocade on the outside, adorned with a sable bordure and furnished with silk carpets, alongside 30 Tatar horses, 24 falcons of three different types (*sunqur*, *saqr* and *baz*) and 60 silk garments accompanied by a letter of apology to appease Sultan al-Nasir Muhammad, who was considering a punitive expedition against him for not having the Friday prayer (*khutba*) performed and the coinage struck in his name.[63] Other vassals, like the Turkmen rulers of Anatolia, did not offer substantial material gifts to the Mamluk court, but their symbolic gifts seem to have been tolerated in view of the strategic significance of these states, which secured a buffer zone on the borders of the Mamluk Sultanate and kept its rivals, the Ottomans in Anatolia and the Mongols and their successors in Iran, at a distance.

Vassals’ gifts were always reciprocated with robes of honour (*khil‘a*) that in the fourteenth century went together with ceremonial bejewelled belts (*hiyasa*),[64] horses with ceremonial trappings, weapons, textiles and sometimes cash. Besides the rulers of subordinate status, the members of foreign embassies also received personal robes of honour along with other gifts. Similar practice is reported about the Timurid court.[65] When Muslim rulers requested a diploma of investiture from the Abbasid caliph of Cairo, they received a *khil‘a* at the same time. When the Bulgarian Tsar Ivan Alexander sent a message to al-Nasir Muhammad in 1331 requesting a banner and a sword as a token of Mamluk support against his enemies, he was given a lavish robe of honour, a brocaded ceremonial cap with golden clasps, a golden belt, a golden sword and the yellow silk Mamluk banner.[66]

The Mamluk sultans themselves did not receive or accept diplomatic *khil‘as*, which were, as rightly observed by G. Hambley ‘a ubiquitous symbol of bonding between a superior and an inferior'.[67] Such a gift was considered a serious offence. When Timur in 1403 sent a *khil'a* among his gifts to Sultan Faraj, the historian Ibn Hajar described it as a symbol of the Mamluk sultan's vassalage, and indeed this is how Timur qualified Faraj after his raid on Syria.[68] Similarly, when Timur's son Shahrukh sent a *khil'a* and a crown to Barsbay with a letter explicitly asking him to let the *khutba* and the coinage be in his name, the Mamluk sultan was enraged as never before: he tore the *khil'a* to pieces and ordered the envoy be beaten up and waterboarded, which almost killed him and for the same reason he was seriously offended when, in 1432–3, he received a *khil'a* from the ruler of the Aq Qoyunlus, Qara Yoluq 'Uthman.[69]

Some gifts were war trophies, like weapons, prisoners of war or severed heads. The canon and other weapons and two European prisoners in their military outfits sent to Sultan al-Ghawri by the Hafsid ruler of Tunis in 1511 announced his victory over the Franks (*faranj*), probably meaning the Genoese, on the island of Djerba.[70]

Just as the Chancellery dictated different formulations for diplomatic correspondence with Christians and Muslims, there was also discrimination in the selection of diplomatic gifts. On the occasion of a negotiated truce between the Fatimids and Byzantines, it was reported that the Fatimids followed a rule according to which reciprocated gifts to Christian monarchs should not exceed two-thirds of the value of the gift received from them, one-third being withheld as a Muslim privilege. This rule, which does not seem to have been generally applied, may have been recalled in times of confrontation and truce negotiations.[71]

The opulent gift package of al-Zahir Baybars to Berke Khan was of particular symbolic significance as it celebrated the Golden Horde's conversion to Islam and their alliance with the Mamluks against the Ilkhanids of Iran. Similarly, Jaqmaq's gifts to Mehmed II, which included a Qur'an manuscript said to have been penned by the caliph 'Uthman, celebrated the holy war led by the Ottomans and their expansion of Muslim rule in south-east Europe.

Gifts, being part of the diplomatic dialogue, were exchanged even in times of extreme conflict and warfare, and they were sent along with hostile, belligerent or conciliatory messages. Diplomatic and gift exchange went on with the Crusader kingdoms between battles and during sieges, sometimes accompanying prisoners to be ransomed or exchanged. When the French king Philippe Le Beau sent an embassy in 1329 with a letter to al-Nasir Muhammad demanding he relinquish the Syrian coast and Jerusalem, the sultan felt so provoked that he insulted the envoy, but this did not prevent him from fulfilling his duty to take charge of the embassy's maintenance.[72] The most lavish gift package to the Mamluks ever mentioned in connection with the Safavids was accompanied by a most provoking letter from Shah Isma'il to Sultan al-Ghawri. Although Ibn Iyas described this embassy as the 'beginning of enmity between al-Ghawri and Isma'il', al-Ghawri did not fail to throw a grand reception and offer lavish robes of honour to the ambassador.[73] Al-Ghawri and the Ottoman sultan Selim I continued to exchange gifts even after the Mamluk sultan had moved with his army to Aleppo to meet Selim I on the battlefield.

It did also happen that the gift itself was as offensive as the message that accompanied it, as observed by Ibn al-'Abbas when he compared certain gifts to riddles and weapons. Such a gift was sent to al-Nasir Muhammad by King Alfonso of Castile and consisted of a sword, a Venetian gown and an object that resembled a coffin. It was interpreted as an obvious menace, and the response was a black rope and a stone meaning: 'You, dog, should be either leashed or stoned'.[74] In 1432–3, Barsbay was infuriated by a gift from the Aq Qoyunlu Qara Yoluq 'Uthman that consisted of a mirror, a sheep and a robe of honour. It was interpreted as follows: the mirror compared the Mamluk sultan to a woman, the sheep implied submission and the robe of honour the suzerainty of the Turkmen donor.[75] When al-Zahir Baybars sent arrows, a quiver, and armour to the Mongol khan Abaqa, it was taken as an insult,[76] and similarly when Timur sent a sword, a mail armour and a quiver to Barquq in 1394, the gift was interpreted as carrying the same sense as the menacing written message that went with it.[77] Gifts of weapons, however, were not necessarily a belligerent message.[78] Weapons were among the most important gifts offered by the Mamluks, and some of them were part of the ceremonial outfit.

The Monetary Value of Gifts

Diplomatic gifts were not viewed as personal gifts to the sultan, but as the property of the Public Treasury or rather the *bayt al-mal*.[79] Owing to the centralised nature of the Mamluk state, the chroniclers report only those gifts offered to the sultan, but it cannot be excluded that personal gifts to high dignitaries were also involved. Gifts to the sultans were traditionally registered in state archives that were kept for centuries. The monetary value in *dinars* of every gift package received was recorded, as well as the value of the reciprocated Mamluk gifts. For example, a gift from Shahrukh, the son of Timur, was estimated to be worth 'only' 3,000 *dinars*,[80] while a gift from the Ottoman sultan was worth 5,000 *dinars*.[81] In 1510 the ruler of Tunis sent horses, weapons and textiles worth 10,000 *dinars*.[82] The fact that gift packages were usually accompanied by a descriptive list of the items they contained suggests that this was to be used for the record, for the evaluation of the gifts by the recipient and hence their reciprocation, and also as a means of verifying their safe and integral condition at their destination.[83] This is not only a Mamluk phenomenon. The Byzantine court also used to register and evaluate gifts and there was also a comparable practice at the Abbasid court.[84] The Aragonese court likewise kept inventories of diplomatic gifts and used to apply a royal sign to the gifts sent by the king, and this may well have been the case elsewhere as well.[85] Besides the monetary value, the Mamluks also carefully recorded weights and numbers, as they appear in some detailed lists given by the chroniclers. The Venetian records of Mamluk gifts mention the weight of drugs and spices in *ratl* and reveal that this is how they have been marked by the sender. The custom of assessing and recording the monetary value of gifts seems to have been a common practice everywhere at that time, as can be understood from the fact that the Mamluk chroniclers were informed about the value of gifts exchanged between other foreign states, as, for example, in the report of a gem worth 84,000 *dinars* offered by the ruler of Mardin in 1261 to the Mongol court.[86]

An ambassador from Ethiopia had to face an angry reception when he arrived at the court of al-Ghawri in 1516 with gifts that were valued at a mere 5,000 *dinars*. He was severely reprimanded for the shabby present and shown the registers (*qawa'im*) with the figures of previous gifts sent from his country to the Mamluk sultans, including the dates and monetary values of them. The register indicated that in 1312 the Ethiopians sent a gift to al-Nasir Muhammad worth 100,000 *dinars*.[87] When in 1516 the Dhul Qadir vassal sent camels and mules to Sultan al-Ghawri, the latter, after consulting his emirs, rejected the gift for being too small.[88] The Mongol gifts were not highly regarded by the Mamluk chroniclers,[89] and neither were those of the Turkmen principalities. Al-Sayrafi and Ibn Taghribirdi described gifts sent by Uzun Hasan as 'mean (*hayyina*), as is customary with the Turkmen princes'.[90] However, a gift from the Master Hospitaller of Rhodes, accompanying a conciliatory message to Barsbay, was described as a great gift (*hadiyya hafila*), although it was worth only 600 *dinars*, which is the lowest on the scale, but was probably suitable for the donor's status.[91]

The high costs of hospitality, robes of honour and reciprocation were compensated by the material value of the gifts received, which could be substantial, as is demonstrated by Sultan al-Mu'ayyad Shaykh's order that all diplomatic gifts from Venice, Yemen and the Ottoman court, and all other diplomatic gifts he received, should be sold to finance the foundation of his mosque.[92] Unfortunately, we are not told who bought these gifts.

The great significance attached by the Mamluk sultans to gift exchange is best demonstrated in the diplomatic crises that took place when things went wrong or their expectations were not met, as for example in the case of the famous gift package sent by Baybars to Berke, the khan of the Golden Horde. The embassy with the precious objects and animals ended up in Constantinople, where the emperor Michael Palaiologos VIII, afraid of irritating the Mongol ruler, Hulagu, who was on hostile terms with Berke Khan, prevented the embassy's passage to the Black Sea. The Mamluk ambassador, Emir Faris al-Din Aqush, was kept for three years in the Byzantine capital, during which time the animals were left to die of neglect. According to Maqrizi, when Baybars was informed of the detainment, he summoned the Greek patriarch and clerics and asked them to excommunicate the Byzantine emperor. He sent an unnamed Greek monk and 'philosopher', accompanied by a priest and a bishop, with the excommunication document and an angry message to Constantinople. The Byzantine emperor eventually released the Mamluk ambassador, who resumed his voyage to the Golden Horde. According to Ibn Abi 'l-Fada'il and Ibn al-Dawadari, it was a raid by Berke on Constantinople in other circumstances that compelled the Basileus to release the embassy.[93]

Another episode during al-Zahir Baybars' reign shows how a diplomatic gift became the cause for the termination of the illustrious career and life of the famous Sufi shaykh Khadr, the sultan's spiritual guide. Abu Bakr Khadr al-Tahrani, a mystic of Iranian origin believed to be endowed with powers of divination, had managed to gain Baybars' confidence to the extent that the sultan consulted him and followed his guidance in all matters, including major state affairs, and took him along to his battlefields. Moreover, Baybars endowed Sufi foundations (*zawiyas*) in Khadr's name in many cities of Egypt and Syria. The shaykh, who had led a fierce campaign of church demolition, became extremely powerful and wealthy, and had a lifestyle that increasingly provoked accusations of debauchery and perversion against him. The straw that broke the camel's back and ultimately led the sultan to throw Shaykh Khadr in jail, where he died in 1277, was the incident of a gift from the sultan of Yemen to Baybars, described as a magnificent and unique *karr* or *kurr*, a kind of prayer rug perhaps, which the shaykh appropriated and gave to one of his women.[94]

Sultan al-Ashraf Barsbay was particularly keen on diplomatic gifts; in 1436 the Mamluk authorities in Jeddah arrested all members of a Bengali embassy because the sultan, who had sent a gift to the ruler of Bengal, was informed that it had been reciprocated with a gift package worth 12,000 red *tankas*. The Bengali ruler had died before his gifts were dispatched, but his son al-Muzaffar Ahmad had sent them slightly later, after adding more presents to the initial package, which consisted of cotton textiles, clothes, spices and a number of eunuchs. He then sent some of his own eunuchs to accompany the embassy to Cairo, with money to trade for him during their voyage. When the Indian ship reached the coast of Jeddah, however, it sank. The Mamluk governor of the city sent divers to search for the drowned cargo and they eventually managed to rescue the textiles but the spices, ginger and myrobalan were damaged by the water and wasted. The governor reported the mishap to Barsbay, who ordered him to confiscate all the possessions of the Bengali embassy, including their own merchandise, and to ban them from travelling to Cairo.[95]

The Mamluks weighed their own gifts not only according to the recipient's status but also according to the actual circumstances. Some special occasions or particular reasons required gifts more valuable than the norm. The gifts that accompanied the entente negotiations with the Ilkhanid ruler Abu Sa'id in 1320 were worth the considerable amount of 40,000 *dinars*.[96]

The gift package sent in 1485 by Qaytbay to the Ottoman court of Bayazid II was worth 10,000 *dinars*, which was above the standard value, and was accompanied by a letter of investiture from the Abbasid caliph of Cairo. The reason for this generous gesture was to appease the Ottoman sultan, who had been infuriated by an incident that had occurred shortly before, for which the Mamluk sultan had to formally apologise.[97] Later, when al-Ghawri felt the heat of the Ottoman invasion coming closer, he sent a gift to Selim also worth 10,000 *dinars*.

Compared with the 'gifts' or *taqdima* offered to the sultan by the governors of Damascus, Aleppo or Jeddah, or other high dignitaries, which could amount to between 20,000 and 30,000 or more *dinars*, diplomatic gifts seem moderate.

The chronicles regularly mention that the Mamluk sultan shared the diplomatic gifts he received with his emirs. This seems to have been a custom and part of the emirs' remuneration. The emirs' expectations were particularly high regarding the opulent gifts from Yemen. The envoy of the Nasrid sultan of Granada, who came to Cairo in the 1450s to request support from Sultan Jaqmaq against the advancing Christians, reported that the sultan, after admiring and approving the Andalusian gifts, distributed them to his emirs and retinue.[98]

Reciprocated gifts to rulers of equal standing were normally sent with a specifically appointed envoy, who would accompany the returning foreign ambassador, rather than being handed to the foreign ambassador directly. Only personal gifts and robes of honour for himself and his retinue were given to the visiting ambassador. However, reciprocated gifts to vassals and sometimes to European states were given directly to their envoys. Reciprocated gifts to the doge of Venice are mentioned as having been given to his ambassador.[99]

Envoys to the Mamluk courts had to kiss the floor before the sultan. This rule seems to have also applied to kings of lower status, as we understand from the case of the king of Mali, who, not willing to do so, preferred to avoid an audience with the sultan altogether.[100] It happened that an Ottoman ambassador refused to kiss the floor before Khushqadam. The sultan, who was already displeased by the style of the letter brought by this envoy, which he found to be lacking respect, clearly demonstrated his displeasure to the envoy until the latter apologised and eventually kissed the floor. When Khushqadam tried to give the ambassador the reciprocated gifts for his master Sultan Mehmed II, he refused to take them, making the argument that protocol dictated that these should be delivered by a specifically appointed Mamluk envoy.[101]

Recycled, Used and Requested Gifts

Presents were often imported objects or recycled gifts, in particular when they had an exotic character or rare value. The *Book of Gifts and Rarities* provides on several occasions a long history documenting the illustrious owners through whose hands a precious object had passed, and for which it had become famous. Imported objects advertised the worldwide connections and, by the same token, the prestige of the donor. By travelling a long way, the object increased in value and acquired the flavour of the spice and silk roads.

The Ottomans sent European and Persian textiles to the Mamluk court alongside items of their own production. The Safavids sent silk from Bursa and Anatolian carpets.[102] It is not clear whether these had been purchased or were recycled gifts. A ceremonial silk tent and a painted wooden pavilion sent to Sultan al-Ghawri had been initially commissioned by the Aq Qoyunlu ruler Uzun Hasan, and then came into the possession of the Safavid Shah Isma'il (r. 1501–24), who eventually offered them to the Dhul Qadir 'Ala' al-Dawla, who in turn sent them to al-Ghawri.[103] The recycling of gifts was not exclusive to the Mamluks and their diplomatic partners, but it was common in other cultures as well.

The 'second-hand' nature of the gift was far from seen as a fault; rather it conveyed a pedigree and gave the object a historic patina.[104] In some cases a 'second-hand' object that had been used by the monarch who gave it was a sign of special appreciation. In the medieval culture of royal gifts there seems to have been a tradition that a ruler offered objects he had been using himself: the German emperor Friedrich II of Hohenstaufen sent the Ayyubid sultan al-Malik al-Kamil (r. 1210–38) his own horse along with complete luxurious trappings.[105] In 1267 the Rasulid ruler of Yemen requested from Sultan al-Zahir Baybars one of his own shirts as a token of *aman*, that is, protection and peace; the sultan responded by sending birds of prey at the same time, along with one of his own suits of armour with a message saying, 'We sent you objects of peace and war that were next to our body in the time of *jihad*.'[106] Similarly in 1281, the Rasulid al-Muzaffar Yusuf sent a request to Qalawun for an oath of *aman* to be written and sealed on one of his shirts.[107] When the Ilkhanid sultan Abu Sa'id took the initiative to end the hostilities with the Mamluks, he sent a message with gifts that included his own turban.[108] In 1427 the Ottoman sultan Murad II sent the clothes he had been wearing, including his turban, to Barsbay.[109] The custom of sending one's own clothes had been common at the Fatimid court as well,[110] and was also practised in other medieval cultures, for example in India, the Mongol Empire and Europe.[111]

Sometimes specific gifts were requested, such as when al-Nasir Muhammad asked the ruler of the Golden Horde to send him good-looking slave girls and Kipchak *mamluks*, or when Özbek Khan asked al-Nasir Muhammad for books on religious subjects,[112] and Shahrukh asked Barsbay to send him a copy of Ibn Hajar's commentary of Bukhari and Maqrizi's chronicle the *Suluk* for his library.[113]

Similarly, Jaqmaq, who was a bibliophile, requested Persian books from Shahrukh, and these were sent.[114] In 1393 the Ottoman sultan Bayazid I asked Sultan Barquq for a physician and medicine to treat his joints, and these were sent.[115] Sultan Murad II asked Barsbay for an elephant, which could not be sent immediately because it was winter, but was eventually dispatched by Sultan Jaqmaq after Barsbay had died.[116] A malicious request came from Sultan Selim to Sultan al-Ghawri while the latter was already in Aleppo in 1516 preparing himself for the battle that would terminate the Mamluk Sultanate: Selim asked for sugar and sweetmeats, a request with which al-Ghawri complied, being well aware, however, that this was nothing but a sham to appease him at this stage in order to take him by surprise later on.[117] Gift requests were not unusual between courts; the Venetians used to be exasperated by the repeated gift requests that came from members of the Ottoman court.[118] Francesco di Medici had no inhibitions in requesting gemstones from the New World from Philip II, in reciprocation for the gift he had sent him previously, a *piedra-dura* cabinet, disregarding not only etiquette but also his own lower rank.[119] Sometimes the requests implied a kind of swap or barter: 'I'll give you this and you give me that.'

PART TWO

GIFTS IN GEO-POLITICAL CONTEXTS

The patchy information provided by the available narrative sources on Mamluk diplomatic practice cannot evenly cover all aspects of the subject. The exchange of diplomatic visits and gifts, being rather a matter of routine at the Mamluk court, is mentioned and described in a selective manner. The chroniclers report special occasions and noteworthy events that correspond to the significance and prestige of the diplomatic partner, or to the importance of the diplomatic situation or the material value of the diplomatic gifts. For example, the material significance of the Yemeni gifts to the Mamluk court earned the regular and special attention of the historians, who provide some lengthy accounts on this subject. The following pages document the exchange of diplomatic gifts within these selective historical contexts, which are per se disparate. Although the result may be seen as an incomplete picture, it reveals an aspect of the Mamluks' perception of their diplomatic environment. Occasional non-Mamluk accounts, such as that of Pedro Mártir, can only confirm the subjective character of the picture.

Chapter 3

The Red Sea and Indian Ocean Connection

Yemen

The universal medieval conventions of diplomatic gift exchange did not preclude regional peculiarities and circumstantial considerations playing an important role in the shaping of gift packages. The spice trade was the source of Mamluk wealth and international status, and the gifts received from courts that were situated along the 'spice road' were associated with opulence and exotic splendour that enhanced the Mamluk image.

The gifts from Yemen in particular were among the most lavish and the best described in the Mamluk chronicles, and the Yemeni envoys who brought them entered Cairo in a great procession.[1] These were not mere gifts, but a kind of tribute imposed on the Rasulid sultans (1229–1454), whose status combined that of a major trade partner and vassal. The Yemeni gifts were expected to be of much higher value than the average diplomatic gift, because they were considered to be the Mamluks' entitled share of Yemen's benefits from the spice trade. The significance of Yemen as an intermediary in Far East trade is demonstrated by the message sent in 1283 from the ruler of Ceylon to Sultan al-Mansur Qalawun.

In this letter he offered his friendship to the Mamluk sultan and invited him to deal directly with him without the intermediary of Yemen, praising the goods he could provide such as elephants, *tuhaf*, a great deal of precious stones, textiles, spices, ships and all that the great overseas merchants (the Karimis) needed, and explaining that they were ready to be shipped directly to him.[2] The eventual history suggests that this scheme was not implemented. It is evident, however, that the Rasulid sultans were not easy and willing vassals of the Mamluks, but rather tried whenever they could to emancipate themselves from this bondage. Their ambition was based on their geographic advantage of being at the junction of the Red Sea and the Indian Ocean, and their proximity to the Hejaz with the holy cities of Mecca and Medina, claiming for themselves the right of their guardianship since the fall of the Abbasid Caliphate of Baghdad. They had already confronted the Ayyubids with this claim, prior to the Mamluks. According to Qalqashandi, although the Rasulids of Yemen were wealthy and well protected by the geography of their territory, they were obliged to gain the favour of the Mamluk sultans with valuable gifts because the latter were capable of attacking them from the Hejaz by land or by sea.[3]

The gift packages from Yemen had a customary and seasonal character, arriving on a regular basis every two or three years.[4] They included textiles, slaves and eunuchs, exotic animals, horses and luxury trappings, spices and scents, Chinese porcelain and a great deal of unspecified *tuhaf* or art objects from China, India and Africa.[5] Many of the imports and gifts from Yemen that were recycled as Mamluk gifts to other courts had already been imported by the Yemenis from the Far East and Africa. The Chinese brought porcelain, gold, silver, sandalwood, pepper and ambergris, precious stones, pearls, coral and rosewater to Yemen. The famous Chinese admiral Zheng He, on his visit to Aden, received lions, zebras, leopards, ostriches, white pigeons and a giraffe for the emperor from the Rasulid sultan, and as a personal gift was offered two bejewelled belts, two horns and other things.[6]

Al-Zahir Baybars and the Rasulid sultan al-Muzaffar Yusuf I (r. 1250–95) exchanged several embassies; in 1267 an embassy from Yemen brought 20 horses with complete trappings, elephants, a zebra, musk, ambergris, aloewood, Chinese silver, jade and porcelain. On this occasion Baybars was asked to send one of his shirts as token of protection.[7] Another Yemeni embassy during this sultan's rule included a black bear and an elephant.[8]

The arrival in 1281 of another embassy from the same Rasulid sultan with the usual assortment of gifts coincided with the triumphal return of Sultan Qalawun from Syria, where he had repelled a Mongol raid. On this occasion, the embassy was offered gifts of Mongol horses and chariots captured in this battle alongside textiles and *tuhaf*, including an emerald, and, following the specific request of the Yemeni sultan, a shirt belonging to the sultan and another one from his son and heir to the throne al-Salih.[9] Four years later, in 1285, another Yemeni embassy brought slaves, 13 eunuchs, 10 horses, an elephant, a rhinoceros, 8 sheep, 8 parrots, 3 large pieces of oudh/agarwood each carried by two men, lances, 70 camels loaded with spices, 100 crates of textiles and 100 metal plates filled with precious Yemeni *tuhaf*.[10] However, the envoys had to be reminded of the critical situation due to the Mongol threat in Syria and the Christian victories in Ethiopia against the Muslims, and were moreover told that under these circumstances this kind of gift was not acceptable to the Public Treasury, and that swords were more suitable than porcelain and *kalahi*.[11]

Whereas most available descriptions of Yemeni gifts are provided by Mamluk sources, a text in Yemeni chronicles describing a gift package sent in 1304 to the Mamluk court during the second interregnum of al-Nasir Muhammad, while the emirs Salar and Baybars al-Jashnakir were sharing power, mentions that the package was loaded on two ships. It included various types of silver ewer, trays, basins and incense burners, sticks of oudh/agarwood, sandalwood, large pieces of ambergris, along with vessels, plates and crates filled with musk, *shah sini* (a rampant plant for pharmaceutical use),[12] sappanwood or brazilwood (*baqam*), an East Asian type of wood used for pharmaceutical purposes and as red dye,[13] camphor, pepper, cloves, ginger and *lak*. There were also dishes and bowls of Chinese jade and porcelain of indescribable beauty, Indian bamboo, Chinese sofas (*maraqid*), Chinese gold brocade, fine muslin, as well as Ethiopian eunuchs, and animals clad with gold-brocaded silk textiles including an elephant, a zebra, a giraffe and Arab horses with their trappings. The chronicler adds that such gifts were sent to Cairo every two or three years.[14]

The arrival of the Yemeni cargos in Cairo was eagerly anticipated by the emirs, who received a customary share of the goods from the sultan, and would protest if their expectations were not met.[15]

Owing to the fact that the Yemenis were not always reliable vassals, or keen to send tributes to the Mamluks, controversies between the two sultanates are reported on more than one occasion. Following Qalawun's death, during the reign of Sultan al-Ashraf Khalil in 1294, al-Muzaffar Yusuf stopped sending the customary 'gift', which provoked the new sultan to send him a threatening message, reprimanding him for his frivolous lifestyle that kept him busy with amusements and women, adding 'other things that touched on his dignity' (*al-ashya' al-khariqa li-hurmatihi*).[16] Al-Muzaffar Yusuf complied, but his successor al-Mu'ayyad Dawud tried again in 1306 to withhold the tribute. As a reaction, al-Nasir Muhammad threatened military action to compel the Rasulid to deliver.[17] Instead of a military expedition, however, al-Nasir sent a letter to the Yemeni sultan reprimanding him, telling him to abide by his obligations and honour previous agreements.[18] An undated letter from al-Nasir Muhammad to an unnamed ruler of Yemen, which must have been compiled at that particular time, following his victory over the Ilkhanids in 1303 and his subsequent submission of Little Armenia, conveys a harsh message of admonishment, blaming the Yemeni sultans for accumulating wealth only to squander it on frivolities instead of assuming their share in the duty of the holy war by providing at least material assistance, while he (al-Nasir

Muhammad) was fighting and vanquishing Mongols and Christians to protect the realm of Islam.[19] In this letter al-Nasir writes menacingly that only because of his involvement in the holy war was he unable to send troops to force the Yemenis to do their duty.

Al-Nasir's letter may not have had an immediate effect; another letter sent in 1307 by the Abbasid caliph of Cairo orders the Yemeni sultan to pay his share to the Public Treasury (*bayt al-mal*) and comply with the rules of the Caliphate to which he owed his legitimacy to rule. The gifts of the Rasulid sultans were thus considered to be a fair contribution to the jihad led and the sacrifices made by the Mamluks for the cause of Islam. Indeed, part of the Yemeni remittance was spent on the double purpose of purchasing goods and supporting the Isma'ili strongholds of the Assassins, which al-Nasir maintained in order to disturb his Ilkhanid adversaries.[20] The other part was for the Mamluk sultan.[21]

In his description of the land of Yemen, Qalqashandi reiterates the image of the Rasulids as kings confined to their palaces, well-protected in their impregnable strategic location, spending their time with pleasures and frivolities, not being bound by any rules of government, not communicating with their officials about the situation in their realm or bothering to inspect their territory.[22] According to this account, Yemen's rulers accumulated the wealth of the Indian trade that was carried to their doors on Indian ships, having little to spend on budgets of military or public works. Their prosperous country attracted merchants from everywhere, and many craftsmen from Egypt and Syria were recruited to work for them. Obviously, the enviable situation of the Rasulids in their Arabia Felix irritated the Mamluks, in particular during this period of military conflict at the beginning of the fourteenth century. While in the early fourteenth century the Rasulid gift or tribute was fixed at 6,000 *dinars*, in the Fatimid period in 1050–1 a Yemeni gift was estimated at 10,000 *dinars*.[23]

Eventually, the regular flow of valuable goods from Yemen to Egypt resumed, and in 1312 an embassy arrived with 409 porters carrying crates filled with ivory, ebony, sandalwood, lances and other things; each crate was covered with a Yemeni *kurr*, which might be a kind of prayer rug.[24] The gifts also included a small elephant, 2 tigers, 4 leopards, 10 armoured horses, 10 good-looking eunuchs, *tuhaf* and cash.[25]

Two decades later, however, in 1330 al-Nasir Muhammad had reason once more to be furious at the Yemenis. The arrival of two Indian elephants sent by the Rasulid sultan al-Mujahid aroused his suspicion. Having previously been informed that the Tughluq sultan of Delhi had sent him gifts of unprecedented magnificence, worth a million *dinars* (*alf alf* according to 'Umari), that had never reached their destination because the envoy had been killed in Aden at the instigation of the Rasulid sultan and his vizir, he guessed that these two elephants were part of this gift and threw the Yemeni ambassador in prison.[26] During the following two decades no embassies were exchanged between the two sultanates.[27]

The text of a letter addressed to the Rasulid sultan al-Mujahid 'Ali ibn Dawud from an unnamed Mamluk sultan, who could have been al-Nasir Muhammad, but was most probably one of his nine sons who succeeded him in brief tenures during the period of al-Mujahid 'Ali's reign (r. 1321–63), expresses profuse thanks for the gifts received. The gifts included swords, horses of different colours, elephants, a giraffe, a zebra, a tiger, civet perfume, sandalwood, camphor and ambergris.[28]

Maqrizi reports that in 1353, during the reign of Sultan al-Salih Salih, another embassy of al-Mujahid 'Ali, which included his 11-year-old son al-Nasir ibn al-Mujahid, brought 60 slaves who survived the passage to Egypt from a total of 300 slaves, 22 pieces of muslin, 400 pieces of porcelain, 150 containers of musk, a container of civet perfume, garments, 150 *qintars*[29] of pepper, ginger, ambergris, spices and an elephant. These items were in addition to the presents dedicated to individual emirs. The envoys were hosted in the hippodrome and given a per diem of 500 *dirhams* as well as robes of honour; the costs of their maintenance from when they arrived at the port of 'Aydhab amounted to approximately 200,000 *dirhams* (10,000 *dinars*).[30] On his return four months later, the young prince was given lavish gifts that included not only many precious objects and curiosities, but also a number of skilled people, among them magicians and acrobats.[31] Egypt was renowned for its entertainers and performers and continued to be so in the following centuries, as is attested in the early eighteenth century by the illustrated Ottoman *Surname*, the manuscript describing the royal circumcision festival of Sultan Ahmed III's son. The document refers on several pages to Egyptian acrobats and magicians performing in Istanbul on this occasion.[32]

In 1361 Sultan Hasan received porcelain, luxury textile, slaves, eunuchs and a gorgeous tent in the shape of a reception hall (*qa'a*) with four *iwans*, which included a bath, and was decorated with appliqué patterns (*taqasis wa nuqush*). The sultan had it pitched outside Cairo during the spring and dwelt there for three months. People flocked in from remote towns and villages to look at it and the prominent poet Ibn Abi Hajla composed a poem in praise of its beauty.[33] Tents do not usually figure among the Yemeni gifts; this one might have come from India, as many other gifts obviously did. Among the exotic animals sent from Yemen in 1366 was a horse without genitals that urinated through a hole in its belly.[34]

A letter from the Rasulid sultan al-Ashraf Isma'il to Sultan Barquq, dated 1396, mentions falcons accompanied by their falconers, horses, 1,400 units (*qit'a*) of various spices and 7 pieces of silk as a gift to the Mamluk court.[35] It is interesting to note that the Egyptian merchant Burhan al-Din offered presents to the Rasulid sultan, probably to facilitate commercial deals, consisting of clothes, scents and edibles, horses and mules, hunting dogs, birds of prey, ceremonial saddles, textiles and other unspecified precious objects.[36] He belonged to the Karimi merchants, a kind of guild of wealthy Muslim merchants involved in the international, mainly spice, trade.

A later embassy in 1396 from al-Ashraf Isma'il to Sultan Barquq brought gifts that earned an exceptionally long description by the chroniclers, probably based on an official inventory,[37] indicating the quantity of each item on the detailed list. The gift package was composed of treasures from 'Yemen and India' worth 60,000 *dinars*. Its content of drugs, scents and spices documents the significance of the spice trade in the medieval world.[38]

The package included 20 slaves, 6 slave girls, 10 eunuchs, a sword with a gold overlaid hilt studded with carnelian, a bejewelled gold belt with carnelian mounted on silk, a chamfron[39] of silvered Indian mirror studded with carnelian of various colours, golden spurs with pearls, 200 lances, a chessboard of white and red carnelian, 4 fans adorned with gold, 700 *ratls* of raw silk, 5 pieces of coloured silk, 30 silk garments, 570 pieces of muslin of three different types,[40] 10 pieces of fabric from Zubayd, 5 house garments, 30 Indian velvet gowns, 20 ambergris scented towels, 4 Indian rugs, 5 gold-adorned leather rugs and 254 other leather rugs of various formats, 242 pieces of Chinese porcelain among them 51 of blue colour (*lazurdi*) and 102 of olive colour (probably celadon), 17 pieces of jade: 7 white and 10 blue. There were further spices, drugs and scents: 1,000 *mithqals* of musk and 1,000 of ambergris,[41] 70 *awqiya* of civet perfume, 100 flasks of *ghalia*, a cosmetic cream composed of several fragrant ingredients,[42] 4 containers of *shand/shanad*, a kind of resin used as incense,[43] 216 *ratls* of *qaqli*, a pharmaceutical plant,[44] 342 *ratls* of Goa gum, 2 logs weighing 364 *ratls* of *maqasiri* sandalwood, 216 *ratls* of oudh/agarwood, 424 *ratls* of pepper, 12 *ratls* of long pepper,[45] 53 *ratls* of nutmeg,[46] 213 *ratls* of cloves, 687 *ratls* of local ginger, 1,413 *ratls* of cinnamon and 51 *ratls* of cardamom. Some of these products had a pharmaceutical purpose, as was also the case with the following items: 200 stones of pissasphalt,[47] 2 *qintars* of *kabili* jam,[48] 70 boxes of ginger jam, 1,500 coconut shells,[49] 60 *ratls* of galingale,[50] 98 *ratls* of *bisbasa,* a plant,[51] 108 *ratls* of *lami,* a resin,[52] 290 *ratls* of *lak,* an Indian and Indo-Chinese resin for pharmaceutical use and an ingredient of lacquer,[53] a box with 48 *ratls* of zinc or zinc oxide from Kerman, India and China,[54] 275 *ratls* of spikenard,[55] a glass of elephant fat (?),[56] 5 large bottles of *kadi water*, a vegetal product,[57] and 50 containers of Indian indigo.[58]

An embassy to Sultan al-Mu'ayyad Shaykh in 1416 brought unusual artefacts and curiosities (*tuhaf ghariba*) that included three saddles studded with carnelian, silk textiles, Chinese porcelain, oudh/agarwood, gum, sandalwood, leather, sheep, live civet cats and rice, carried by 200 porters. The sultan ordered the sale of the gifts to finance the construction of his mosque, and they earned a very high price. His donation was more than compensated by the tax revenue he collected on the merchandise that came at the same time from Yemen with the merchants, which amounted to 90,000 *dinars*. The Yemeni envoy who brought the tribute spent a further 28,000 *dinars* on gifts for Mamluk high dignitaries.[59] When Sultan Jaqmaq married the daughter of a Dhul Qadir prince in 1440, most of the gifts worth 1,000 *dinars* he offered her, which included silk, musk, ambergris, rosewater and sugar, seem to have come from Yemen.[60]

We know less about Mamluk gifts to the Rasulids than the reverse. Besides the gifts mentioned above, one sent in 800/1397, and praised as impressive by the Yemeni chronicler al-Khazraji, consisted of 30 Turkish *mamluks*, 12 fine horses with their trappings, Anatolian (*rumi*) and Armenian female slaves and an experienced Jewish physician from Egypt, a large quantity of clothes, scents and edibles. The Yemeni sultan went to the port of Zabid with a large retinue to receive the embassy; 'it was a memorable day'.[61] Mamluk gifts to Yemen included on one occasion, in 1385, a coral tree and in the following year silk weavers were sent from Alexandria.[62] This gift is of particular interest: rather than offering silk textiles, weavers were sent instead. The question is whether they were sent as a loan or on a permanent basis. The dispatch of craftsmen seems to be a peculiar feature of Mamluk–Rasulid diplomacy. Qalqashandi, as mentioned earlier, referred to Mamluk craftsmen working for the Rasulid kings. This is confirmed by a number of fine objects made of silver inlaid metal and enamelled glass, in the style of al-Nasir Muhammad's reign, inscribed with the name of Rasulid rulers.[63]

India

Although Indian spices were the source of Mamluk prosperity, information about Indian embassies and gifts is relatively scarce. It usually refers to *tuhaf*, gems, spices, weapons, slaves and eunuchs, diverse textiles and exotic animals, notably elephants. The scarcity of information does not imply, however, that diplomatic gifts from India were not significant; a Tughluq sultan is reported by ʻUmari to have sent gifts to al-Nasir worth a million *dinars*.[64] When Indian rulers requested a diploma of investiture from the Abbasid caliph in Cairo, with the embassy they sent *tuhaf* and gems for the sultan and the caliph, as for example in 1343–4.[65] The Bahmanid ruler of Gulparga sent a gift for the sultan in 1427 and another for the caliph, along with cash to buy an estate for the foundation of a madrasa in Mecca; another envoy from Bengal likewise brought gifts for both the sultan and the caliph.[66] A Bahmanid gift in the following year, 1428, included 4 swords, 16 camels and textiles.[67] A gift from al-Muzaffar Ahmad of Bengal in 1436 included cotton textiles, clothes, spices and a number of eunuchs.[68]

In 1474 a big tent and a spectacular lion arrived from an unnamed monarch in India.[69] In 1512 an embassy from India marched in Cairo with two big elephants with beautiful trappings, attracting a huge cheering crowd. The elephants were displayed at the hippodrome where they performed a fight accompanied by drums and trumpets, to the sultan's great delight.[70] Such games are also mentioned by Clavijo in his description of Timur's elephants, which he had most likely brought along from his campaign in India.[71]

An interesting gift episode is documented in correspondence between the Khalji sultan of Malwa Mahmud Shah (r. 1436–69) and the Mamluk court. In a long letter dated 1467 and addressed to Sultan Qaytbay, Mahmud Shah complained bitterly and at length about the troubles and hardship, including robbery, expropriation and physical abuse, that his envoys had had to endure in Mecca during the reign of Qaytbay's predecessor, Khushqadam, at the hands of the Mamluk authorities and the population of the city. After having purchased land in the holy city to build a hospice for the poor, the governor of Jeddah, the Mamluk emir Janibak, confiscated the building and evicted its dwellers in order to use the estate for his own purposes. Moreover, cash donations dedicated to the holy sites were allegedly stolen and three shiploads of gifts for the sultan and the caliph were appropriated by the notables of the holy city, who also badly mistreated the members of the Indian embassy, beating them up and torturing them.

Mahmud Shah also complained in this letter about corruption and arbitrary taxation of foreign merchants in Mecca; a later embassy carrying an appeal to the Mamluk sultan and the Abbasid caliph with gifts and *tuhaf* worth 50,000 *dinar*s was of no more help than all the other attempts to obtain justice or compensation in this matter.[72] In this letter to Qaytbay, Mahmud Shah wrote that, out of fear that his emissary might be intercepted and robbed on the way, he had let him travel incognito with only a small package of gifts that was easy to conceal. It consisted of *bakzahr*, a stone extracted from animals for its medical faculties as an antidote, two rings with stones, which he describes as having the attributes of an antidote against various diseases,[73] and a necklace composed of nine pieces with diamond, ruby, pearls and peridot (*zabarjad*). The two apotropaic rings of Mahmud Shah might be the ones mentioned by Ibn Iyas years later, in 1515, when a plague broke out in Cairo and Sultan al-Ghawri took two ruby stones out of the treasury and had them set in gold rings; he used to wear them continuously as talismans even during his audiences, which Ibn Iyas commented on as being odd for a 'Turkish sultan'.[74]

Further in the same letter, Mahmud requested from Qaytbay to send him, as a sign of friendship, theriac, balsam oil and skink, which is a type of lizard the dried flesh of which was used as a medicine and aphrodisiac.[75] Qaytbay's response in 1468 addressed all aspects of Mahmud's complaints, assuring him that he had been informed about the previous abuses, for which he apologised, and that the situation had meanwhile changed. Qaytbay promised that Mahmud Shah would be compensated for Janibak's confiscation and for the demolition of the hospice he had sponsored, and that the abuses would be redressed. Appended to Qaytbay's letter is a list of his gifts to the Indian sultan. This list mentions a bejewelled sword, a ceremonial axe of steel and gold, an *azdaghani* mace, Alexandrian ceremonial textiles, garments and other things alongside the requested drugs, theriac, balsam and skink.[76] Mahmud Shah's account of Janibak's abuses in Jeddah is partly confirmed by Mamluk historians, who describe the emir as having become very powerful and of fabulous wealth after he assumed the governorship of Jeddah, which allowed him to expand his authority all over the Arab peninsula, and to correspond directly with the kings of India and Yemen, who offered him gifts of unprecedented lavishness. From his position in Jeddah, which involved him in the Indian Ocean trade, Janibak could also please the sultan by replenishing his treasury. He returned to Cairo as Great Secretary of Sultan Khushqadam with power only second to the sultan's. He was assassinated by the sultan's recruits, perhaps with their master's complicity, in 1463.[77]

CHAPTER 4

AFRICA

Ethiopia

Ethiopia, a Christian state the church of which was affiliated with the Coptic Patriarchate of Alexandria, was another link in the Red Sea trade connection, and, as Yemen, it was a trade partner and a territory where the Karimi merchants were active.[1]

The Ethiopians depended on the Mamluks for access to the Mediterranean and for their pilgrimage to the Holy Land, as well as for the safety of their churches and property in Jerusalem. The Coptic Patriarch of Alexandria invested the Ethiopian king, as the Abbasid caliph did with the Mamluk sultan, and he appointed the head or metropolitan of the Ethiopian church and the bishops from among the Coptic clergy in Egypt.[2] Making use of this authority, the Mamluks often employed the Coptic Patriarch as an intermediary in their contacts with Ethiopia.[3] The Ethiopian monarchs on their side regularly pressured the Mamluk authorities to show more tolerance towards their Coptic community. In the Ayyubid period in the early thirteenth century, during an exchange of embassies, King Lalibela sent al-Malik al-Kamil a magnificent crown of solid gold and exotic animals that included a giraffe, an elephant, a lion and an onager.[4] These lavish gifts, along with other gifts for the Coptic Patriarch, were explicitly meant to demonstrate gratitude to the Egyptian authorities, the sultan and the patriarch, for the dispatch of the metropolitan and the bishops and for the investiture of the king, and as reciprocation of these privileges, which were not always a matter of fact. Political crises between the two countries or the two churches could lead to long vacancies at the head of the Ethiopian church.[5] An amicable correspondence is documented in 1265 between Baybars and the *hitti*, as the Mamluks called the Ethiopian monarch.[6] But the tone was not always friendly between both states or even between both churches. In 1325 the Ethiopians threatened to let the Muslims in their country suffer the consequences of the persecution that the Copts were enduring under Mamluk rule, and furthermore to cut the flow of the Nile to Egypt.[7]

Beside the gift exchange, Ethiopia exported gums, scents, slaves and ivory and imported textiles from the Mamluks. Among the gifts al-Zahir Baybars once received from the 'king of Amhara' were lions 'black like the night!'.[8] In 1386 an Ethiopian gift package carried by 21 porters arrived in Cairo with gifts of textiles, exotica and curiosities (*tuhaf wa zara'if*), several jars filled with beads of pure gold the size of chickpeas, as well as gum, civet perfume, oudh/agarwood, slave girls, eunuchs and other precious items.[9]

Unlike other Christian states the Ethiopians do not seem to have had inhibitions about sending slaves, mostly eunuchs, to the Mamluks. It is not clear, however, where these were recruited; they might have originated in other African regions. Among the slaves sent from Ethiopia was Jawhar al-Qunuqba'i. Sayrafi and Maqrizi write that he occupied the function of *lala* meaning tutor for royal children. As a eunuch at the court of Barsbay, his career went far beyond, earning him the status of emir; he was highly esteemed, enjoyed great honours and acquired a large fortune.[10] His funerary madrasa abutting the Azhar mosque includes a stone mausoleum dome carved in a style that was a novelty at that time (Plate 2).

In 1443 an Ethiopian dignitary arrived in Cairo with a gift of 70 slave girls, many more having died on their way, a golden set of a basin with ewer, horse trappings of gold, a sword with gold overlaid decoration, a gold belt and other gold jewellery. He carried a long message from the Ethiopian king complaining about the situation of the Ethiopians in Jerusalem, who were not granted permission to build their sanctuaries, while Europeans and Georgians were allowed to have theirs. The letter referred to the past amicable relations with Sultan Barquq, compared the miserable condition of the Copts in Egypt with the better one of the Muslims in Ethiopia, and warning that the Ethiopians had the power to cut the Nile flood from Egypt.[11] The gift was generously reciprocated by Sultan Jaqmaq as indicated in a rare description of a gift package sent by a Mamluk sultan to the Negus of Ethiopia, which mentions 2 golden saddles, gold-brocaded textiles, wool and wool garments of two different types, 200 pieces of fabric, 2 bottles of fine oil (*al-zayt al-tayyib*), probably balsam, and interestingly, a rock crystal ewer carved in the shape of a cock in a gold setting (*muzayyak*) along with other things.[12] This is the only reference I found to a rock crystal vessel being offered by the Mamluks. It may well have been a recycled European gift or a Fatimid object, as no production of Mamluk rock crystal vessels has been documented so far.

Although the gifts of the Ethiopians were valuable, and expected to be so, their embassies were not frequent. Ibn Iyas writes that embassies from Ethiopia diminished in the fifteenth century, because due to the long distance and the declining situation of their country, the Ethiopians could no longer afford the costs of diplomacy.

The embassy that arrived in 1516 was the first to be seen in Cairo since 1481. Al-Ghawri received it in a low-profile audience, without ceremonial outfit (called *al-shash wa 'l-qumash*), as his predecessor Qaytbay had done four decades earlier.[13] The envoy, a prince whose father had been the envoy who came to Qaytbay's court, was accompanied by high dignitaries and pilgrims – a total of 600 people, who had been travelling for 11 months. Their procession from the city to the Citadel was accompanied by drummers on a camel, and attracted 'all the Christians of Misr'. The envoy wore a red velvet hat with golden leaves and precious stones and a big gem at its peak. The Coptic Patriarch was part of the procession, and he was dressed in a blue silk gown with golden embroidered bands. Only seven persons were admitted to the audience with the sultan, where they were forbidden from sitting on the iron chairs they had brought with them; a similar situation had occurred with the previous embassy when it had been received by Qaytbay. The Ethiopians were treated with honour and lodged in one of the hippodromes, the Maydan al-Mahara. In spite of his rank, this envoy, as mentioned earlier, was reprimanded for having brought gifts that did not stand up to Mamluk expectations.[14]

Nubia

Between Egypt and Ethiopia, Nubia had a role to play in the Red Sea trade. Moreover, Mamluks and Nubians had a common interest in fighting Bedouin raids on their respective territories.[15] However, Nubian embassies are not frequently mentioned in the chronicles. Mamluk relations with Nubia began with al-Zahir Baybars' military expedition to submit the Nubian king to the status of vassal, compelling him to respect Mamluk commercial interests. Nubia/Dongola became a Muslim state during the fourteenth century, and maintained a conditioned autonomous status under Mamluk supremacy. From the reign of Baybars through the fifteenth century, the Nubians were expected to present a tribute that consisted of 400 male and female slaves, camels, 2 elephants, 2 giraffes, as well as panthers and other animals.[16] This is very similar to what the Nubians sent in the Fatimid period, when slaves, monkeys, sheep, birds, a leopard and ivory were mentioned.[17] When a Nubian prince came to Cairo in 1304, he brought a gift of cattle, sheep, slaves, grinding stone and alum.[18]

The Maghrib

North Africa was a major source of horses,[19] black slaves and leather for the Mamluks. These were the main articles of export and the major diplomatic gifts sent to the Mamluk Sultanate and other parts of the world by the Merinids of Morocco and the Hafsids of Tunis, both successors of the Almohads. During the reign of Sultan Qalawun in the last quarter of the thirteenth century, an embassy from the Hafsid ruler of Tunis, who was lodged in the Residence of the Vizirs (*dar al-wizara*), brought a gift of 30 horses with golden trappings and 80 camels loaded with valuable gifts of all kinds.[20] In the year 1397–8 the Mamluk emir Qutlubugha al-Khalili, the Master of the Stables of Sultan Barquq, returned from the Maghrib, where he had been sent to buy horses for his master, accompanied by three envoys from the courts of Tunis, Fes and Tlemcen. They brought the sultan gifts of horses, different types of mules, all of which came with luxurious trappings, swords in gold and silver sheaths, gold and silver stirrups along with leather, silk and wool textiles.[21]

Ibn Khaldun (d. 1406), the great philosopher and historian of Tunisian origin who lived and worked in Egypt, invited and promoted by Sultan Barquq, was instrumental in boosting trade relations between Cairo and North Africa.[22] He was particularly interested in the subject of diplomatic gifts, and included in his world history a chapter on gift exchange between the Mamluk and the Hafsid and Merinid courts.

Ibn Khaldun reported that diplomatic relations with the western Muslim states were not particularly developed before he began playing a role in improving them. He advised the Hafsid sultan to contact Barquq, adding that horses were the best thing from North Africa that could delight the Mamluks, as they already had plenty 'of all the other items of luxury and *tuhaf* that the Maghrib had' (*wa amma siwa dhalika min anwa' al-taraf wa 'l-tuhaf bi 'l-Maghrib fa-kathirun ladayhim mithluhu*). Unfortunately, before reaching Alexandria the Tunisian ship with Ibn Khaldun's own family on board sank and with it the precious cargo of 'gorgeous horses of pure breed'. However, one of the envoys survived and diplomatic relations between Cairo and Tunis were eventually improved. Barquq reciprocated with a gift of priceless textiles from Iraq and Alexandria. The Hafsids then sent new valuable gifts with the next caravan to Mecca, which Barquq reciprocated with generosity towards the pilgrims and gifts of luxury textiles and weapons for the court in Tunis.

As Cairo was a stopping point on the pilgrimage route from Africa and the Maghrib to Mecca, the Mamluk sultans on more than one occasion had to host and honour monarchs or members of royal families from the west on their pilgrimages. On such occasions the royal pilgrims would present lavish gifts to the Mamluk host, in anticipation of his protection and hospitality, as did a Berber king who arrived in Cairo in 1396 and offered two white camels to Sultan Barquq.[23]

In 1303 the Merinid sultan Abu Ya'qub Yusuf sent a gift of 400 horses and a magnificent Qur'an manuscript with a golden cover studded with precious stones for the shrine of Mecca to al-Nasir Muhammad with a pilgrimage caravan on its way to Mecca. In return, the *sharif* of Mecca offered him garments made of the silk that had been used for the curtain of the Ka'ba (*kiswa*). In the following year another Merinid embassy brought similar lavish gifts to Cairo; al-Nasir honoured the envoys and reciprocated with luxury textiles and animals that included a giraffe and an elephant, which were sent with a special Mamluk embassy to their destination.[24] Maqrizi's version mentions 20 Tartar horses and 20 Mongol prisoners in their full military equipment including their drums and bows.[25]

The Mamluk embassy on its journey to Morocco had to endure great difficulties at the hands of the Abdalwadid ruler of Tlemcen, who was on hostile terms with the Merinids. To make things worse, the embassy was harassed by Bedouin bandits on the roads. Annoyed by these incidents, al-Nasir Muhammad sent a message to the Abdalwadid ruler Abu Hamu Musa blaming him for the treatment of his envoys. The gift that accompanied the message, 2 containers of balsam oil and 5 Turkish Mamluk lancers, was received with scorn, being found to be too shabby in comparison with the gifts the Merinid rivals had received. In his reply to al-Nasir Muhammad, Abu Hamu wrote 'As for the balsam, we are Bedouins who know only [usual] oil, and as for the Mamluk lancers, we have conquered Seville with [such lancers], and we are sending them back to you so that you may reconquer Baghdad!'[26]

It is no wonder that diplomatic relations between the Mamluks and Morocco were frozen for the next three decades, until a Merinid princess of Sultan Abu 'l-Hasan 'Ali's family planned to go on pilgrimage in 1338, and stopped in Cairo on her way.[27] There, she was welcomed by the *mihmandar* with great honours on the Nile shore at Giza and accompanied to the southern cemetery on the eastern shore. According to a tradition that a princess who went on pilgrimage would travel in a sumptuous cortège, lavishing with gifts and alms on her way, the Merinid princess brought gifts of legendary opulence to al-Nasir Muhammad from Sultan Abu 'l-Hasan. Al-Nasir duly lodged the pilgrims in a hippodrome on the Nile shore and gave them sheep, bread, sugar and other food for their maintenance and, of course, robes of honour. For their transport to Mecca, camels were hired costing the treasury (*bayt al-mal*) 60,000 *dirhams* (*c.*3,000 *dinars*), in addition to travel expenses worth 75,000 *dirhams* (*c.*3,700 *dinars*).

Mamluk authors report that the gifts brought by the Merinid princess were 'unheard of in East and West' and, according to Maqrizi, they were worth 100,000 *dinars*. His description is rather brief: 118 horses and mules beautifully caparisoned, 32 falcons, a bejewelled belt studded with precious stones, a bejewelled sword, 10 swords, 2 golden saddles studded with precious stones, 38 silver inlaid saddles, 50 mule loads of the most luxurious textiles, pearls and gemstones of the finest kind and many other things. The princess also brought a splendid Qur'an manuscript for the shrine of Mecca penned by Sultan Abu 'l-Hasan himself on fine velum and illuminated with gold, with its dedicated box of ebony, ivory and sandalwood covered with gold sheet and studded with rubies and other gems and wrapped in silk brocade. Ibn Khaldun's enumeration of this gift package refers to 500 horses with trappings, textiles of silk, wool and linen, leather objects, gemstones such as rubies and pearls, ceramics and other Moroccan artefacts including garments and weapons.[28] These gifts, he adds, 'remained in people's memories for a long time'. They were displayed in a solemn ceremony at the Mamluk court. Sultan al-Nasir Muhammad kept the gems for himself and distributed the rest to his emirs, as was customary.

The Merinid gifts to the Mamluk sultan must have been an outstanding episode in Merinid history, for two other contemporary North African authors, Ibn Marzuq and Ibn al-Khatib, describe them in much greater detail than Maqrizi and Ibn Khaldun. Both accounts, which show only a slight variation between them, list the number of items. This suggests that their information was based on inventory data.[29] The gifts included gems: 225 large and fine hyacinths, 128 emeralds of finest colour (*dhubabi*),[30] 28 beryls and 364 fine pearls of large size. There were also a variety of gold embroidered fabrics and garments of silk and wool, and various types of linen.[31] The package also contained furnishing objects: 200 pillows, 20 gold embroidered bed covers, 2 wall hangings of silk, 119 rugs of silk and wool, and a leather bed adorned with gold and silver. There were weapons and horse trappings: 10 bejewelled scabbards with pearls, 10 saddles with stirrups and spurs made of pure gold, 3 pairs of silver stirrups and 6 others of gilded silver with enamel, 2 bejewelled belts, a bejewelled headgear, 10 silver embroidered saddles and 10 silver bridles, 10 gold embroidered standards, 10 gold embroidered banners, 10 gold embroidered saddle cloths, 30 striped caparisons, and 200 leather shields, 2 of which had a golden button and 18 of which had a silver button. The package also included 4,000 lamb hides, 2 ceremonial tents – one with 4 doors, the other made of silk and with masts of ivory and ebony – and animals: 34 falcons, 335 horses, 120 mules and 700 camels that carried the gifts. The tents were pitched and the gifts placed within while the animals remained outside.

The magnificence of the Merinid gifts is also echoed in the letter sent by al-Nasir to Abu 'l-Hasan, thanking him for the gifts that were so plentiful that 'they could not be carried by the sea; how could they be carried by animals?' and continuing at length in this mode.

The letter also informed the Moroccan monarch that the princess had been duly taken care of.[32] Abu 'l-Hasan's gifts were reciprocated with a separate embassy;[33] according to Ibn Khaldun, the Mamluk gifts were worth 50,000 *dinars* and included Alexandrian and other silk textiles, 10 fine horses with gold and silver trappings studded with precious stones, accompanied by grooms.

What the Mamluk sources do not report, although Ibn Khaldun does, are a pavilion and two tents, one of which, he describes in detail as made in Damascus of silk and linen of monumental dimensions. It was composed of several residential structures and ceremonial *iwans*, a kitchen and a number of towers, one of them for the sultan to sit and watch parades and the others for the guards. The tent also included a mosque on columns with a mihrab and a minaret.[34] The second tent, to which it was connected, was circular with a conical roof, and functioned as a courtyard providing space for more than 500 horsemen. The tent complex was accompanied by specialised craftsmen in charge of pitching it. On its way from Egypt to Morocco the gifts passed through Tunis, where they were displayed in front of the Hafsid sultan. Ibn Khaldun adds that 'they remained for long time a subject of wonder on all lips' (*wa baqiya al-ta'ajjub minha dahran 'ala 'l-alsina*).[35]

A century later, in 1446, the wife of the Merinid sultan Abu Faris arrived in Cairo on her way to Mecca, carrying precious gifts for the Mamluk sultan: 30 horses with ceremonial trappings and 10 others with gold trappings and 20 crates with Moroccan silk textiles. Sultan Jaqmaq granted her and her retinue befitting hospitality, and hosted her in the hippodrome complex.[36] Although the chronicler Ibn Taghribirdi also performed his pilgrimage that same year, he does not comment on the princess' visit.

West Africa (Mali and Borno)

Perhaps the most spectacular and anecdotal account of princely pilgrims passing through Cairo was that of the legendary King of Mali (Takrur) Mansa Musa, who arrived in Cairo in 1324 with a huge retinue that allegedly included 12,000 female pages dressed in silk gowns. He was heavily loaded with gold – 100 loads (*himl*) – which he spent in Cairo so lavishly that during his visit the value of the gold *dinar* went down to 6 *dirhams* (from a minimum of 25). Mansa Musa presented one load of gold to Sultan al-Nasir Muhammad, apart from what he distributed to the emirs and officials. When it came to meeting the Mamluk sultan, however, Musa showed great reluctance as he did not want to kiss the floor before him, as was the custom. His excuse was that he came only for pilgrimage, and would not bend before anyone but God. His wish was respected and, moreover, Sultan al-Nasir Muhammad treated him with great respect and bestowed on him most lavish robes of honour with the usual golden belt with gems, a bejewelled sword and two horses with trappings. He also granted him generous hospitality, providing camels and fodder for his caravan, and ordering the Emir of the Hajj to give him special treatment in the Mamluk pilgrimage caravan. On his way back, Mansa Musa gave another present to the sultan, who again responded with *tuhaf*, beautiful things and luxury textiles. During this visit the African king also received a robe of honour and a diploma of investiture from the Abbasid caliph of Cairo, and pledged that the Friday sermon (*khutba*) and the coinage of his country would be in the name of the Mamluk sultan.

The less glamorous aspect of this episode was that Mansa Musa and his retinue spent yet more gold than they had carried along with them on shopping in the markets of Cairo, so that at the end of his journey the king had to borrow cash from Egyptian merchants, who charged him a usury interest rate of more than 200 per cent (700 *dinars* on each 300). The loans were apparently never repaid, but, according to al-Dawadari, the loans would not have sufficed anyway to cover the Africans' cash deficit, so they were ultimately obliged to sell much of what they had bought in Cairo at half the purchase price. The Egyptians had good reason to be content with such a lucrative business. Mansa Musa told people in Cairo that gold in his country used to grow like a plant to be harvested.[37] Had the Spaniards been aware of the Eldorado of Takrur, Mansa Musa might have met the same fate as the Inca Atahualpa.

A rather extraordinary gift arrived one day at the court of the Mamluk sultan al-Zahir Barquq from the African ruler of Borno, a Muslim country south-east of Mali in today's Nigeria,[38] the ruler of which at that time was 'Uthman ibn Idris, who claimed to be of Yemeni descent. His gift to the Mamluk sultan was mercury and other unspecified things, which Qalqashandi praised as a *hadiyya saliha*, meaning a 'good present', a rather unusual description for a diplomatic gift.[39] This attribute may have referred to the healing purpose of the mercury, which was used in medicine and in the processing of gold and silver. The sixteenth-century physician Dawud ibn 'Umar al-Antaki wrote about the pharmaceutical external use of mercury in ointments against skin disease that were produced at the hospital of Qalawun.[40] Another curious feature of this gift from Borno is the fact that this metal was not extracted in Borno or any other place in that region, which suggests that the king of Borno must have received it from elsewhere. Having no use for it, since his country did not process gold, and, knowing the importance of the hospital of Qalawun, he forwarded it to Cairo. Mercury was also used in alchemy. In 1330, when a Syrian alchemist arrived in Cairo with the promise that he would fill the sultan's treasury with gold and silver, he required mercury, which proved difficult to provide, and had to be ordered everywhere in Cairo and Alexandria. When the fraud became evident, however, the alchemist was jailed and tortured to death.[41]

In the message that accompanied the mercury, 'Uthman complained to Barquq about the Arab tribe of Judham on the borders of his country, who had captured some of his relatives to sell them on the slave market. The letter requested information on these people from the Mamluk sultan, and his intercession to prevent their sale in Egypt or Syria. Barquq's reply is unknown and no reciprocated gift is mentioned.

CHAPTER 5

THE BLACK SEA, ANATOLIA, IRAN AND CENTRAL ASIA

The Golden Horde at the Black Sea

After having conquered Central Asia and Iran, the Mongols led by Hulagu took Baghdad in 1258, terminating the Abbasid Caliphate, and aiming further at Syria and Anatolia. Their advance in Syria, however, was brought to a halt two years later at the Battle of 'Ayn Jalut, where for the first time they had to accept a defeat by a Muslim army, led by the Mamluk sultan of Egypt, Qutuz, and his general, al-Zahir Baybars. Qutuz was not intimidated by the aggressive message sent by Hulagu demanding his submission; rather he executed the envoy and ordered that his head be displayed at the southern gate of Cairo, Bab Zuwayla. The triumph at 'Ayn Jalut showed the Mamluks to be the only power capable of challenging the Mongols so far. However, the Battle of 'Ayn Jalut did not bring about the end to hostilities between the two powers. The ghost of Jenghiz Khan continued to haunt the Mamluk Sultanate through his successors, the Ilkhanid dynasty of Iran, who after converting to Islam and adopting Iranian culture as their identity, continued to challenge Mamluk supremacy both on territorial and religious grounds.

The Mamluks were not alone in standing up to the Ilkhanids.

They found an ally in the Golden Horde, a tribe of the house of Jenghiz Khan that had settled in the Kipchak steppe north of the Black Sea. Berke Khan, who was their first ruler to convert to Islam, challenged the scheme of Ilkhanid hegemony in the Muslim world. An alliance between Berke and Baybars was celebrated by a special Mamluk gift package sent with an embassy to the Golden Horde in 1263.[1] This gift earned one of the most detailed accounts in Mamluk chronicles, being repeated by a number of authors with slight variations. Its heterogeneous composition remained singular in Mamluk gift tradition.

The pièce de résistance of the gift package was a Qur'an manuscript penned by the caliph ʻUthman ibn ʻAffan, wrapped in red gold-brocaded textile within a leather case lined with silk and included in a box (*kursi*) made of ivory and ebony inlaid with silver and equipped with a silver lock and latch. There was also a large number of Venetian gowns, prayer rugs and other rugs of various colours, drapes, leather and leather furnishings, Frankish helmets with silver brims, gilded lamps with gilded silver chains, many candlesticks some of which silver-inlaid, pairs of ceremonial inlaid lanterns with their stands,[2] silver lamps, some of which had Venetian shades,[3] large gilded metal lamps, *manjaniqat li 'l-shamʻ madhuna bi aghshiyya* (?): painted and wrapped *manjaniqat* (?) (for candles/wax ?),[4] *qaljuri* swords with silver hilts,[5] painted silver *kawalij* (?), ornamented saddle elements (*athfar*), gilded iron maces, bows and crossbows including ceremonial bows with silk strings from Damascus, long lances of the *qana* type with Arabian iron tips,[6] *saruqat* (?) for the lances, magnificent arrows in leather boxes, arbalests,[7] painted shields, Khawarizmian saddles with upholstery,[8] felt horse covers (to be used underneath the saddles),[9] bridles with silver inlay work and other gold and silver inlaid horse trappings, silver ornamented Bulgarian leather bags, mats, jewellery, female slave cooks, black eunuchs, Arabian race horses, rare Nubian camels, fast animals of burden, Egyptian donkeys, an elephant, a giraffe, zebras and monkeys, all animals with their fine textiles and trappings, Alexandrian textiles, *tiraz* gowns and other garments, jewellery, porcelain,[10] mats, earthenware cooking pots (*qudur biram*), and raw and white sugar.

Ibn 'Abd al-Zahir adds that the gifts included 'other curious things, strange *tuhaf* and art objects the like of which cannot be found [even] in a great king's treasury' (*ashya' mustatrafa wa tuhaf mustaghraba wa lata'if la yujad mithluha fi khizanat malik kabir*). The cooking pots were not a casual gift as one may think. According to Qalqashandi, cooking pots belonged to the paraphernalia of royalty that monarchs were proud of possessing in large quantity, to display opulence and hospitality. In this context he refers to King Solomon, whose pots were produced by the djinns.[11] The fact that the embassy with this gift package did not arrive safely and in a timely manner at its destination, having been held in Constantinople for a long time, not surprisingly caused tension between the Mamluk and the Byzantine courts.[12]

There is a difference between the composition of the gifts sent by the Mamluks to the Golden Horde and those received. The latter's assortment, which consisted mostly of animals, including falcons and other birds, fur, leather, *mamluks*, and slave girls, is more limited, albeit not necessarily less valuable.[13] *Mamluks* and slave girls were items that the Mamluks themselves imported for the army and the harem respectively.

In 1282 Sultan Qalawun sent an embassy to Möngke with armour, bows, *tuhaf* and 16 loads (*ta'bi'a*) of luxury textiles and garments; the package also included gifts for emirs and prominent ladies of the Golden Horde court. By the time the embassy arrived Möngke was dead, but his successor Töde Möngke was delighted with the gifts.[14] The inclusion of gifts for the ladies here is remarkable and recalls that Qalawun was married to the daughter of a Mongol refugee who had fled from the Ilkhanid court of Abaka, and that the Mamluks were familiar with Mongol customs.[15] He was thus familiar with the affinities and customs of the Mongol court, where women were visible members.

Another gift sent by Qalawun to the Golden Horde in 1287 is of particular interest because it reveals the significance of Mamluk textiles and their hierarchical function.[16] The gift consisted of 200 embroidered white gowns from Dar al-Tiraz, half of which were embroidered with gold epigraphic bands 'in the name of the sultan', and the other half embroidered with silk epigraphic bands containing honorific titles; 150 gowns belonged to another type of Alexandrian textile embroidered with epigraphic bands of gold and silk;[17] 150 gowns of Damietta textile were adorned with epigraphic bands of gold and silk with the 'usual titles' (*bi-alqab al-'ada*) and 100 other gowns had silk and gold unspecified epigraphic bands. The package also contained white and candy sugar and the 'usual drugs'. There were also goods worth 2,000 *dinars* for the mosque being built in the city of Saray, and Mamluk masons to carve the name and titles of Sultan Qalawun on this mosque with their equipment of necessary material and paint.[18]

This gift package was quite different from that of Baybars a quarter of a century earlier. The 600 gowns inscribed in hierarchical categories with the name of Qalawun and other Mamluk titles, along with the masons in charge of carving the monumental inscriptions of a mosque, emphasise the Qalawunid passion for honorific inscriptions and convey a clear message of Mamluk self-representation. The significance of *tiraz* textiles is clearly demonstrated here as an emblem of the Mamluk donor. The sheer number of 600 inscribed gowns would have widely advertised the Mamluk presence at the court of the Golden Horde. Ibn al-Furat, who describes this gift package, does not indicate the occasion or circumstances in which this gift was sent.

When in 1304 the Khan Toqta asked for the support of the Mamluks against his Ilkhanid rivals, he sent with his message 200 slave girls, 400 *mamluks*, most of whom, however, died during the journey at sea. A decade later, in 1313, Toqta's gift consisted of 80 *mamluks* and 20 slave girls beautiful like the 'rising moon', bear skins, skinks and *sayram* (?). To his request for military support, al-Nasir responded by sending Toqta 1,000 suits of armour with helmets and 1,000 pieces of horse armour, along with textiles of the Dar al-Tiraz, golden ceremonial belts and brocaded headgear.[19] This gift is characteristic of the diplomatic gift style established by his father Qalawun.

When in 1316 al-Nasir Muhammad asked for the hand of Muhammad Özbek's daughter so that he might be related to Jenghiz Khan's lineage, he sent him presents that can be described as insignia of royalty: 200 complete armour sets including horse armour, gold brocaded ceremonial gowns and coats, horses with bejewelled trappings, a parasol and a bejewelled sword and golden belts, brocaded headgear and muslin.[20] In return, Muhammad Özbek sent an embassy to al-Nasir Muhammad with 6 *mamluks*, 3 falcons, a suit of armour, a helmet and a sword. The envoys returned home with Mamluk presents worth as much as 10,000 *dinars*.[21] Perhaps encouraged by al-Nasir's largesse, Muhammad Özbek responded to the request for the princess' hand by demanding an extravagant bride price, which led al-Nasir to withdraw his request. However, after tough bargaining between the two courts, the marriage was finally concluded three years later in 1320, and Princess Tulunbay arrived in Cairo, where she was received with great pomp. The alliance was not successful, however; a disenchanted al-Nasir Muhammad doubted the princess' authenticity and eventually divorced her and married her to one of his courtiers. Diplomatic exchanges went on with the Golden Horde on a lower key, and were gradually overshadowed by the Mamluk–Ilkhanid entente.[22]

The Ilkhanids and the Jalayirids in Iran and Iraq

After the tensions between the Mamluks and the Mongols in the wake of the Battle of 'Ayn Jalut and preceding Ghazan's raids on Syria, Baybars' diplomatic correspondence with his Ilkhanid counterpart Abaqa was unfriendly. A symbolic gift sent by Baybars in 1271–2 to Abaqa, consisting of a mail shirt with a helmet, and a bow and a quiver with arrows, did not contribute to improving relations between them.[23] Although the Mamluks did regularly offer weapons to Muslim rulers, in this case the choice may have had a hostile connotation, or at least it has given reason for such an interpretation.

Even after his conversion to Islam, the Ilkhanid ruler Ghazan (r. 1295–1304), now bearing the title 'sultan', did not abandon his predecessors' goal to subdue the Mamluks, annex their territory and supplant them as representatives of the Abbasid Caliphate and guardians of the Muslim holy cities.[24] Following a series of episodes of Mamluk support to Mongol dissidents and vice versa, Ghazan attacked Syria in 1299, causing significant devastation, but failing to hold any territory there. A second military expedition in 1300 ended without a battle, and a third one in 1303 ended with the victory of al-Nasir Muhammad. During these confrontations the young Ghazan continued to entertain a correspondence with the equally young Mamluk sultan, in which he kept boasting of his lineage to Jenghiz Khan and his divine right to the throne, while emphasising at the same time his Islamic virtues and qualification for religious patronage in contrast to the Mamluks' lack of royal blood and kingship pedigree. His successor Öljaytu (r. 1304–16) invaded Syria but had to retreat without achieving his goal. Intermittent hostilities continued for a while until Abu Sa'id came on the Ilkhanid throne (r. 1316–35), introducing a period of truce followed by negotiations for an entente with the Mamluks, which began in 1320 and led to the signature of a treaty two years later.

At the outset of these negotiations, in 1320, an embassy that included the wife of an Ilkhanid high dignitary, accompanied by her two sisters and retinue arrived in Cairo, where they were welcomed with due hospitality.[25] A couple of months later another embassy arrived with gifts for al-Nasir Muhammad consisting of a Qur'an manuscript in 60 volumes, a magnificent tent, *tuhaf* and precious objects as well as Abu Sa'id's own turban to accompany the offer of peace and Abu Sa'id's request to marry al-Nasir's niece, the daughter of his predecessor al-Malik al-Ashraf Khalil.[26] Abu 'l-Fida, who gives a different description of the gift that came that year from

Abu Sa'id, mentions *tuhaf*, *mamluks* and slave girls, and indicates its total value as 50 *tumans*, which would be equivalent to around 25,000 *dinars*.[27] To this gambit, al-Nasir Muhammad responded with a gift package that included a zebra, 20 priceless horses from the sultan's personal stable with their full trappings, Mamluk pages, 50 camels, bejewelled belts among which one was worth 257,000 *dirhams* (*c.*12,850 *dinars*), 2 items of brocaded headgear and textiles brocaded with gold and silver.[28] Maqrizi's brief description of this gift mentions only a brocaded ceremonial gown, and some other gowns – some of which were 'Tartar style' (*qiba' tatari*) – along with other unspecified items; the whole package was worth 40,000 *dinars*.[29] Abu Sa'id's envoys received privileged treatment like no other embassy to al-Nasir Muhammad's court had ever seen. They were lodged in the quarters of the sultan's deputy at the Citadel, the royal residence.[30]

The Mamluk embassy that went to Tabriz to negotiate the terms of the entente and other ensuing matters, and brought back the signed agreement, was led by Emir Aytamish, a high-ranking educated courtier of Mongol origin at al-Nasir's court, who travelled three times to Abu Sa'id's court, where he enjoyed high prestige.[31]

On these occasions, he and his retinue were equipped with the most magnificent outfit that did not fail to impress their Ilkhanid hosts.[32] According to Maqrizi and 'Ayni, Aytamish returned from the first mission with gifts worth 200,000 *dirhams* (*c.*10,000 *dinars*). During his journey, the emir had purchased pearls for 40,000 *dirhams* that were in fact worth 100,000 *dirhams* (*c.*5,000 *dinars*), which he presented as a gift to al-Nasir Muhammad, refraining from keeping anything for himself. The sultan accepted all the gifts and gave Aytamish a bonus of 100,000 *dirhams* (*c.*5,000 *dinars*).[33] Al-'Ayni's version mentions that the gifts Aytamish brought back included four bejewelled ceremonial belts, one of them double the usual size, that were worth 200,000 *dirhams*, and textiles, and he adds that the purchase of large and fine pearls for 40,000 *dirhams* was from Aytamish's own purse as his personal gift to his master, which al-Nasir reciprocated with the bonus. In the following period an intense exchange of embassies, two per year, took place, during which both sides did their best to impress one another with ceremonies, hospitality and gifts.

In 1324 Abu Sa'id sent a gift of 3 Tartar horses (*akadish*)[34] with golden saddles studded with gemstones, 3 bejewelled golden belts, a sword in a golden sheath studded with gemstones, gold embroidered brocades and 11 caparisoned Bactrian camels loaded with chests filled with 700 pieces of fabric of local production adorned with the sultan's name. Dawadari gives a diverging description, mentioning horses with bejewelled trappings, Bactrian camels with their trappings carrying chests loaded with leather, commenting that this gift was 'unlike what the Mongols usually offer', meaning that it was lavish.[35]

On his third mission to the Ilkhanid capital, Tabriz, in 1326, Aytamish had at his disposal a large budget that amounted to 200,000 *dirhams* (*c.*10,000 *dinars*) in addition to a gift of luxury weapons (*asliha muftakhara*), Alexandrian gowns embroidered with the names and titles of Sultan Abu Sa'id and his regent Choban, and many other things.[36]

In 1329 the Ilkhanid sultan sent 14 Tartar horses with ornate trappings, 10 birds, 7 *mamluks* and *tuhaf* that were not displayed; this embassy brought Abu Sa'id's request for the hand of a daughter of al-Nasir Muhammad. The Mamluk sultan replied that she was still too young, and that the matter should be delayed until the time came; he also requested the province of Diyar Bakr as the bride price. On this occasion, the Ilkhanid envoy offered the amount of 60,000 *dirhams* (*c.*3,000 *dinars*) to spend on a banquet for the emirs.[37] It should be recalled that nine years earlier Abu Sa'id had asked for the hand of al-Nasir's niece; it is not reported what happened with this initiative.

In 1331 Abu Sa'id sent 8 *qitars* (pairs?)[38] of Bactrian camels, 10 horses, 10 *mamluks*, 2 singer slave girls, 4 maces (*dababis*), textiles and a golden bird,[39] and a year later, his gift consisted of 6 Tartar horses, 8 *mamluks*, 2 *qitars* of Bactrian camels, 3 leopards, arrows and local textiles.[40]

The rise of the Mongols and the Mamluks began around the same time. However, the zenith of Ilkhanid rule in Iran was in the first quarter of the fourteenth century, slightly preceding the Mamluk golden age of al-Nasir Muhammad, which took place in the decades that followed the entente. This explains the Mamluk fascination with their rivals, and the Ilkhanid impact on Mamluk arts and other aspects of their culture. As Donald Little has pointed out on the basis of al-'Ayni's account, Aytamish's diplomatic mission had an impact on Mamluk architecture, as is evident from the report that he brought back to Cairo the builder, or one of the builders, of the mosque of Vizir 'Alishah in Tabriz, who introduced a new style of minaret architecture and decoration there.[41] Aytamish built a mosque, which has now vanished, in a village that belonged to his estate in the Delta. It had a minaret that displayed a 'spiral' pattern, which was probably a feature of its tile decoration, as can be seen on examples of that time in Iran. In the following period, an Ilkhanid style of tile decoration was adopted on various Mamluk buildings in Cairo, suggesting that ceramic craftsmen must also have come to Cairo at that time.

Ilkhanid influence is also perceived on the pottery of that period. The Mamluk art of the book and costume fashion also came under Mongol influence during the fourteenth century.[42] The intensive exchange of embassies and gifts are likely to have contributed to this influence. The Ilkhanid Qur'an manuscript of 60 volumes mentioned here is not known; the famous Qur'an manuscript in Cairo in the name of Öljaytü consists of only 30 volumes.[43]

The Jalayirids, who were Mongols, governed Iraq under Ilkhanid rule and eventually succeeded the Ilkhanids as rulers of Iraq and Azerbaijan until Timur raided Baghdad, compelling Sultan Ahmad ibn Uways to seek refuge in 1394 at the court of Sultan Barquq in Cairo. There, the Mamluk sultan welcomed him with ceremonial pomp, lavish hospitality and friendliness, crowning his largesse by marrying Ahmad's niece Tandi.[44] Barquq helped Ahmad to return to Baghdad, but shortly afterwards, in 1401, Timur attacked the city for a second time and Ahmad fled again, this time to Syria. During the war between Timur and the Ottoman sultan Bayazid I, Ahmad returned to Baghdad, but was forced yet again to flee to Syria, where he stayed until Timur's death in 1405.

The welcome ceremony upon his arrival in Cairo, which has been vividly described in Mamluk chronicles, was meant to, and did, annoy Timur. On this occasion Ahmad was offered the traditional emblematic gifts of a purple robe of honour lined with ermine and embroidered with a large golden *tiraz* band, choice horses among them one with a gold saddle, a gold chain and a gold-brocaded caparison. In another ceremony Ahmad received 200 pieces of Alexandrian silk brocade, 20 choice *mamluks* with their horses and textiles and 20 slave girls each with her trousseau and cash to the value of 200,000 silver *dirhams* (*c.*10,000 *dinars*).[45]

We know little about Jalayirid gifts to the Mamluks; some years earlier, in 1383, while he was still on the throne, Ahmad ibn Uways offered Sultan Barquq, probably on the occasion of his accession to the throne, a remarkable leopard, eagles and falcons, four bundles of luxury textiles and other things.[46]

The Timurids in Iran and Central Asia

Like the Ilkhanids before him, Timur boasted that he was of Jenghiz Khan's lineage and entitled to rule the entire Muslim world including, of course, the territory of the Mamluks. The diplomatic correspondence between the two courts was accordingly hostile. When in March 1393 a gift from Timur arrived at Barquq's court with 9 slave girls and 9 *mamluks* along with velvet, wool and fur, the sultan and his entourage were dismayed to discover that the 9 *mamluks* were not real *mamluks*, who should have been non-Muslims, but, with one exception, were all Muslim high dignitaries enslaved by Timur during his conquest of Baghdad, one of them being the son of the city's chief judge. This was of course a blatant breach of Islamic law and ethics. Barquq set them free and bestowed on the judge's son the ceremonial outfit of scholars.[47] With this gift Timur had clearly undermined his own claims to the leadership of the Muslim world. Later that same year another embassy of Timur brought an aggressive message of 'thunder and lightning' to Barquq accompanied by a symbolic gift of a quiver and a sword, which are not mentioned by the chroniclers, but in a letter from Barquq to Timur dated April 1394. The response to the threat symbolised by the gift and explicitly expressed in the letter included the following poem commenting on the gift:

We taught warfare to the sword, the lance and the arrow.
Ask them and they will tell.
When we meet in battle they will prove.
Beware, God's sentence will strike you.
God honoured us to serve the Haramayn [i.e. the Holy
Cities],
He gave us lands to rule
And awarded us favour and sweet victories.
Go and read History to find the evidence.
The prophets are our strong support,
Their greatness has ruined our enemies.
What can be feared by those who have the support of
God the Victory-giver?
These words should be enough![48]

In 1400–1, Timur ravaged Syria with great brutality. After his raid of Aleppo, he advanced towards Damascus, where Sultan Faraj ibn Barquq moved to confront him. Faraj, at that time only 13 years old, asked the historian and philosopher Ibn Khaldun, who was then the chief judge in Cairo, to accompany him and act as his emissary to Timur.

Faraj, however, did not stay to fight his adversary, but, with the pretext of averting a rebellion of emirs, he left Syria to its fate and returned to Egypt. Ibn Khaldun, who narrates these events in his autobiography, remained in Syria and was given multiple audiences by Timur in his encampment, during which they had long conversations on historical, religious and intellectual subjects, shortly before Timur devastated the country.[49]

Apparently it was Timur who took the initiative and inquired about Ibn Khaldun. When Ibn Khaldun went to meet him, he took a gift with him, having been advised to take some kind of personal symbolic objects that would touch and make a good impression on Timur. The historian went to the book market of Damascus and chose a magnificent Qur'an manuscript, to which he added a copy of Busiri's famous mystic poem *al-Burda* in praise of the Prophet, a fine prayer rug and Egyptian sweetmeats.[50] When Timur saw the gifts, he raised the Qur'an manuscript above his head in a sign of devotion, kissed the rug, shared the sweets with his retinue, and inquired about the significance of the *Burda*, which Ibn Khaldun explained to him. During their last meeting, Timur asked the historian whether he had a mule, and whether he would sell it to him. When Ibn Khaldun replied 'God bless you! Someone like me does not sell to someone like you. I would offer it and yet more things to you if it belonged to me.' Timur replied that his intention with this request was rather to have the opportunity to reward the historian with reciprocated generosity. Ibn Khaldun responded that he had already been more than generously rewarded with the honour of being admitted to Timur's audience and enjoying his kind hospitality, for which God in turn may reward him. These were the last words exchanged between the philosopher and the conqueror, followed by a silence. However, Timur did take the mule![51] After his return to Egypt, Ibn Khaldun received the price of the mule from a Mamluk official. After he made an attempt to decline it, he was told by Sultan Faraj that he had the authorisation to accept it. He did so, noticing that the amount was insufficient to cover the price of the mule, for which the emissary apologised, saying that it was all he had been given.[52]

Timur's war on Syria dealt a severe blow to the Mamluk economy and to the image and status of Faraj, who in Timur's eyes had now become his vassal. After Timur's triumph against the Ottoman sultan Bayazid in 1402, Faraj sent gold coins, gemstones, luxury garments and Alexandrian textiles, valuable horses, swords and other rare and precious things to Timur.[53] The cash and gold suggest that the gift was a tribute.

In 1403 Timur sent Faraj an elephant carrying a palanquin with a man waving green banners, along with a leopard, two eagles and textiles. In Ibn Iyas's version, the palanquin carried musicians playing cymbals. Perhaps it carried the man with the flags as well as musicians.[54] Elephants with palanquins that could carry several passengers were described in detail by the Spanish envoy Clavijo when he visited Timur's court in September 1404. The animals were clad with silk and carried yellow and green banners, and had room for five or six men, while a man straddling the elephant's neck would coach the animal and conduct its performance.[55] The Khalili collection has a ceramic sculpture from twelfth-century Syria in the shape of an elephant with a palanquin carrying musicians, showing that the parades of musicians on an elephant had a long tradition (Plate 3). Faraj responded the following year with a gift package of 15 loaded camels and 20 horses, ostriches,[56] and a giraffe that received a detailed description from Clavijo.[57]

The Persian historian Sharaf al-Din Ali Yazdi, writing some 20 years after Clavijo, records in his *Zafarnameh* or *Book of Victories*, a laudatory biography of Timur dedicated to his grandson Ibrahim Sultan, the embassy and the gifts. He writes that the Mamluk ambassador Mankalibugha presented nine ostriches to Timur (Clavijo mentions six) and a giraffe, among other gifts that included *tuhaf*, cash, precious stones and lavish textiles.[58] The cash might have been a remittance imposed by Timur on Faraj, who had been a short-term vassal. In spite of the hostility between the Mamluk and the Timurid courts, the Mamluk envoy, Emir Mankalibugha, was highly praised by the Persian historian as a cultivated man who knew the entire Qur'an by heart.[59] The giraffe sent to Timur was commemorated in a double-folio composition in an illustrated manuscript of Yazdi's *Book of Victories*, executed in Shiraz in 1436 (Plates 4a and 4b). The presence of this image in a book dedicated to celebrating Timur's achievements attests to the significance of diplomatic gifts in enhancing a monarch's image. Indeed, Yazdi's text constantly refers to the gifts and rarities that arrived at Timur's court from across the whole world.

The horses the Timurids offered to the Mamluk court are described as *akdish* (pl. *akadish*), a Tartar breed described as slow.[60] Unlike the Timurid gifts to China, which are reported to have included a large variety of local and imported items, the Mamluk sources mention only a small selection of gift items: horses, turquoise, jade, fur and camels.[61] Yazdi in his laudatory biography of Timur refers to textiles, horses, animals and *tuhaf* as the universal gifts exchanged between him and other courts. Robes of honour with headgear and bejewelled belts were Timur's gifts to foreign envoys.

Timur's son Shahrukh corresponded with Sultan Barsbay. His goal was no longer to conquer Mamluk territory, but to have a presence in the holy cities of Mecca and Medina, which were under the jealous guardianship of the Mamluk sultans. Repeated embassies carrying Shahrukh's request to sponsor the curtain (*kiswa*) of the Ka'ba in Mecca were met with the consistent and adamant refusal of Barsbay. Shahrukh's gifts to Barsbay were often accompanied by messages that displeased the Mamluk sultan.[62] His gift in 1434, which consisted of 80 pieces of silk brocade and 1,000 pieces of turquoise, was worth altogether 'a maximum of 3,000 *dinars*'.[63] The ambassador was hosted at the Dar al-Diyafa and granted appropriate maintenance. Shortly afterwards, in 1436, the Timurid message and gift were openly offensive: the letter asked Barsbay to let the *khutba* be dedicated to Shahrukh and coinage struck in his name. The accompanying gift was that of a monarch to his vassal: a crown and a robe of honour. The envoy was beaten up and subjected to waterboarding.[64]

Shahrukh was not the first monarch who aspired to donating the *kiswa*; the Ilkhanid Abu Sa'id had made an attempt in this direction in 1319.[65] The Rasulid rulers of Yemen also considered themselves to be the legitimate guardians of the holy cities. Seeing an opportunity immediately after the death of Sultan al-Nasir Muhammad in 1342, the Rasulid al-Malik al-Mujahid sent a *kiswa* to Mecca, with lavish presents and gold for the *sharif*, who governed the holy city. He rejected the gifts with the argument that the authorisation had to come from Cairo, where, as was to be expected, it was not granted. This was not the first initiative in this direction to be made by the Rasulids, who since their accession to power had tried to bring the Hejaz under their hegemony.[66] Neither had a similar attempt by the Aq Qoyunlu ruler Uzun Hasan had any success. However, when Jaqmaq succeeded Barsbay, he was willing to soften the diplomatic style between the two courts, and show more leniency towards Timurid aspirations.

When an embassy from Shahrukh arrived in Cairo in 1440 to congratulate Jaqmaq on his accession to the throne, offering him a plate with 200 pieces of turquoise, silk and other textiles, a large quantity of fur and 30 Bactrian camels and musk, the total package worth 5,000 *dinars*,[67] it was greeted with an exceptional reception staged by Jaqmaq. Cairo was decorated and candles were lit everywhere; musical performances took place while a crowd flocked in to watch the embassy cortège, which was accompanied by a Mamluk military procession from its residence to the Citadel, where a banquet was given in its honour. The envoys attended the ceremonial audience known as *khidma*, presented their gifts and were given robes of honour and horses. Jaqmaq reciprocated with a gift package worth 7,000 *dinars* consisting of a horse with a golden saddle and horse textiles worth 1,000 *dinars*, horse trappings, silk velvet, *tiraz* textiles embroidered with gold threads worth 500 *mithqals*, other Alexandrian silk textiles, swords adorned with gold and other precious things. With the additional sum of 15,000 *dinars* spent on hospitality, this embassy, which cost the sultan a total of 22,000 *dinars*, introduced a new friendly tone into Mamluk–Timurid relations.[68]

A few years later, in 1444, Shahrukh tried again to acquire the permission to donate the curtain of the Ka'ba from Jaqmaq; he sent a curtain with an embassy of 100 members, among whom was Timur's widow, who generously distributed gifts and alms on her way. They came with a caravan of Bactrian camels loaded with gifts. Unlike his predecessor Barsbay, Jaqmaq received the embassy with great honours and gave his permission for an exceptional donation of the Timurid *kiswa* that year, on the condition that it would be hung within and not outside the sanctuary, where the Egyptian curtain would be displayed as usual. On this occasion, Jaqmaq threw a great reception with a military parade at the Citadel, which was attended by all the sultan's *mamluks*. This gesture did not, however, find the approval of Jaqmaq's entourage or that of the populace. It rather triggered violent demonstations against the members of the Timurid embassy. On their return from the Citadel to their lodgings a wild mob joined by Mamluk soldiers waited for them and met them with a barrage of stones, beat them and robbed them of their horses and all the valuables they had with them. Only thanks to the interference of an emir, who happened to dwell nearby, could the Iranians be rescued. The sultan reacted promptly with a raid against the suspects from the mob, who were brought before him and beaten up. Ibn Taghribirdi writes that some of the Mamluk soldiers were punished, but according to al-Sayrafi, the soldiers were spared any kind of punishment. The sultan paid compensation to the victims and ordered his emirs to offer them lavish hospitality that cost 200 *dinars* in addition to horses and robes of honour.[69]

The Turkmens

Diplomatic exchange between the Mamluk court and the Turkmen principalities of Anatolia and Mesopotamia was not on an equal basis, but the matter of a vassal and suzerain relationship, as was the case with Yemen. However, the Mamluks did not expect gifts from these vassals of the kind that they received from Yemen, being content instead with a reliable territorial stability between their land on one side and the Ottomans and Timurids on the other. The reports of embassies from the Turkmen rulers arriving in Cairo are more numerous than the mentions of gifts exchanged. The reason is not difficult to guess: the gifts sent by these principalities were usually repetitive and a matter of routine, as were, for the most part, the Mamluk gifts that were intended less to impress with *tuhaf* than to consolidate alliances with emblematic gifts.

The Qara Qoyunlus

The Qara Qoyunlus (Black Sheep), who traced their ancestry back to Jenghiz Khan and controlled East Anatolia, Iraq and western Iran, were vassals of the Timurids and rivals of the Aq Qoyunlus (White Sheep). However, they repeatedly took initiatives to liberate themselves from this vassalage. For a while, during the reign of Qara Muhammad (r. 1380–90), the *khutba* in Tabriz was held and coins struck in the name of the sultan Barquq.[70] His son Qara Yusuf (r. 1390–1420) called off Timurid suzerainty, which led to a renewed rapprochement with the Mamluks.

A letter from Sultan al-Mu'ayyad Shaykh to Qara Yusuf mentions gowns from Dar al-Tiraz, tigers, horses, gorgeous saddles, birds of prey, bows and Chinese porcelain as his gift to the Qara Qoyunlu ruler.[71] In 1435 Qara Yusuf's son, Iskandar (r. 1420–38), sent the Mamluk court the severed heads of the Aq Qoyunlu ruler Qara Yoluq 'Uthman and two of his sons and other heads of dignitaries. Cairo was decorated for the parade of the heads carried on the tips of lances before they were displayed for three days at the gate Bab Zuwayla.[72] Barsbay responded by sending Iskandar 10,000 *dinars* in cash to support him against Shahrukh.[73]

Another son and successor of Qara Yusuf, Jahan Shah (r. 1439–67), offered Sultan Jaqmaq his friendship by sending an embassy that included his own nephew offered as a '*mamluk*'. The embassy also brought Bactrian camels and armour.[74] Jaqmaq offered the envoy 2,000 *dinars* to cover travel expenses along with gifts of Alexandrian textiles and silk worth 15,000 *dinars*.[75] A year later, in 1452, Jahan Shah's brother, Hasan 'Ali, conquered the city of Diyarbakr/Amid from the Aq Qoyunlus and sent its keys to Sultan Jaqmaq;[76] in 1457 he sent weapons captured from his brother, and the sultan was delighted.[77] Two years later, in 1459, the Mamluk sultan Inal received the keys to a Georgian fortress.[78]

Jahan Shah's son, Pir Budaq, acting on behalf of his father, sent Sultan Jaqmaq a mule, weapons and silk in 1452; the sultan gave the mule to one of his bureaucrats.[79] Pir Budaq continued, on his father's behalf, the correspondence with Jaqmaq's successor Sultan Inal, by sending him a letter in 1455 in which he offered his friendship and announced his plan to attack Timurid territory in Sistan and Khurasan, to which Inal responded with a letter of appreciation and good wishes, mentioning that the envoy was treated with honours and offered hospitality and a robe. A subsequent letter from Budaq announcing victory against the Timurid suzerains was answered by Inal in 1457 with congratulations and thanks for the gifts he sent. A list of the reciprocated gifts, appended to this letter, mentions an elaborate piece of horse armour, a golden saddle, a gold overlaid steel axe, a gold overlaid mace, a velvet robe and a velvet gown and five containers of candy sugar from Hama.[80]

Jahan Shah's ambitions did not stop at shaking off Timurid suzerainty but drove him further to attack the Aq Qoyunlus of Iraq and Azerbaijan, eventually leading to his death at the hands of Uzun Hasan (r. 1457–78), who sent his head to Cairo.[81]

The Aq Qoyunlus (Plates 7a and 7b)

During the reign of Barsbay, diplomatic correspondence between Mamluks and Aq Qoyunlus confirmed Mamluk suzerainty and the alliance between the two courts in the face of Ottoman expansion. Barsbay sent a gift to Hamza ibn Qara Yoluq that included a horse with golden trappings, Alexandrian textiles, weapons and a copy of the Qur'an on which Hamza was to swear his allegiance to the Mamluk sultan.[82]

In 1462 Uzun Hasan emerged on the Mamluk diplomatic scene. His first gift to be mentioned was sent to Sultan Khushqadam and included a falcon, a *mamluk* and a horse.[83] In 1466 he sent an unusual emissary to Cairo: she was no less than his own mother, the Lady Sara, who brought with her the keys of her son's recently conquered city of Kharput for Sultan Khushqadam, and requested him to bestow his favour on her son. The sultan received her with honour, hosted her at the Citadel, and offered her 1,500 *dinars*, Alexandrian textiles and robes of honour for herself and her retinue. She stayed for only a few days.[84]

Two years later, in 1468, following his victory over Jahan Shah, Uzun Hasan confirmed his allegiance to Sultan Qaytbay by sending him his rival's head and describing himself humbly as his *mamluk*. Gradually, however, the series of embassies carrying keys of fortresses conquered allegedly in the name of Qaytbay and the Aq Qoyunlu ruler's growing zeal for expansion created uneasiness at the Mamluk court. When in 1469 the head of the Timurid sultan Abu Sa'id arrived in Cairo, Qaytbay, astonished and disturbed, refused to display it as was the custom, but instead ordered its burial without publicity. Qaytbay did not rejoice, not only because of his doubts regarding the authenticity of the head, but also out of a certain reverence (*ijlalan*) towards the Timurid monarch.[85] He did bestow a robe of honour on the ambassador though. At this stage, the head of the Timurid sultan was likely to have been perceived as a sign of menace rather than reverence from the increasingly ambitious Uzun Hasan. The relations between Uzun Hasan and the Mamluk court eventually deteriorated. While advertising his exploits, Uzun Hasan was gradually advancing towards Mamluk territory. After his siege of Ruha/Edessa in 1472, which was under Mamluk rule, he was forced to retreat the following year by a military expedition led by Emir Yashbak. Likewise, his attempt in 1472 to impose his name on the *khutba* in the holy city of Medina and donate the curtain of the Ka'ba was unsuccessful.[86]

Apart from severed heads and keys of conquered Qara Qoyunlu fortresses in Azerbaijan, Uzun Hasan offered some other gifts to Qaytbay. In 1468 he sent five Bactrian camels, two Circassian *mamluks* and a suit of armour; Qaytbay responded with the usual emblematic gift of textiles, horses, weapons and 1,500 *dinars*.[87] In 1470 Uzun Hasan sent Qaytbay a spinel (*balakhsh*) and a cat's eye,[88] and in 1472 he sent a suit of armour, a helmet, sable and squirrel hides and carpets from Aqsara'i.[89]

However, even when they were welcomed by the sultans, the gifts of the Aq Qoyunlus were not highly regarded by the chroniclers, who mention them only occasionally and laconically. A gift from the Aq Qoyunlu ruler, Qara Yoluq 'Uthman, of nine Tartar horses and coins struck in the name of Sultan Barsbay was scorned by the chronicler Ibn Taghribirdi.[90] Al-Sayrafi described a gift sent by Uzun Hasan as 'mean (*hayyina*), as is customary among the Turkmen princes',[91] and similarly, Ibn Taghribirdi refers to the mean presents of Uzun Hasan, 'as is usual with the Turkmens'.[92]

The Dhul Qadirs

Although the Dhul Qadir dynasty, which ruled in Ilbistin in Little Armenia, accepted Mamluk suzerainty, the episode of Shah Suwar shows that the Mamluks could not fully rely on their allegiance. Towards the end of Khushqadam's reign, after sending his brother Budaq (r. 1465–6, 1472–9), a reliable ally of the Mamluks, into exile, the Dhul Qadir ruler Suwar (r. 1466–72) rebelled against his suzerains. Shortly after his accession to the throne, Sultan Qaytbay found himself compelled to deal with Suwar's capture of the Mamluk city of 'Ayntab and his threats to Syria. A successful expedition in 1472 led by the great secretary and general Yashbak min Mahdi ended with the capture of Suwar, who was dragged to Cairo and hanged at the gate Bab Zuwayla.

The gifts of the Dhul Qadirs usually consisted of *mamluks* and animals. In 1455 the gift consisted of 100 Tartar horses, 50 mules and 50 Bactrian camels.[93] During his short reign Suwar sent, in 1470, Bactrian camels, *mamluks* and slave girls to Cairo.[94] The Mamluk bureaucrat Ibn Shihna describes the gifts presented by Shah Budaq to Qaytbay on the occasion of their meeting in Aleppo in 1477 as including horses, camels, mules, sheep, wild animals and falcons, silverware and slaves. Among the gifts were also two of Shah Budaq's sons, who were offered as 'cook assistants' for the Qaytbay's kitchen. This offer must have been rather a humble diplomatic gesture of understatement in the hope that the sons might join Qaytbay's Mamluk aristocracy. Qaytbay reciprocated with a robe of honour for Budaq and ceremonial garments for his sons, and a mare with ceremonial trappings.[95]

An outstanding gift from the Dhul Qadir court was the last one offered by this principality to a Mamluk sultan. It was sent by 'Ala' al-Dawla to Sultan al-Ghawri in 1512 and was described in detail and with enthusiasm by the historian Ibn Iyas. The package included, besides horses and Bactrian camels, a large silk tent decorated with representations of trees and birds along with a wooden circular pavilion painted with gold and lapis and other marvellous colours, depicting wild animals attacking their prey. The pavilion was covered with blue felt joined with ropes and eyelets of red silk; it had a wooden door with a bolt and its floor was covered with a round carpet of strange and unique craftsmanship. The sultan was so impressed by their beauty that he ordered their display in the Citadel to be publicly admired.[96]

Three years later, it was 'Ala' al-Dawla's own head that arrived at al-Ghawri's court, as a gift from the Ottoman sultan Selim to announce his conquest of Dhul Qadir territory, thus announcing that the march towards Mamluk land had begun.

The Safavids

Although the main danger for the Mamluk Sultanate had been perceived already by Ibn Khaldun as being the Ottomans, the Safavids were another challenge. They emerged in history in the last two decades of the Mamluk Sultanate. The short relationship between the two courts was not a friendly one. The raids of Shah Isma'il (r. 1501–24) in south-eastern Anatolia in 1503 obliged the Ottomans and Mamluks to share concerns and seek collaboration. A second episode was the incursion in 1507 of Isma'il's troups inside Mamluk territory close to Malatya, leading al-Ghawri to mobilise his army for a massive expedition. Shah Isma'il, however, withdrew his troops and presented the excuse to al-Ghawri that this action had not been authorised by him.[97] The ambassador who brought the message was received with pomp at the Citadel, although his and his companions' demeanour was perceived as 'very insolent'. Ibn Iyas adds that with their red bonnets they lacked the glamour of the Ottomans![98]

The following episodes were yet more alarming. In 1511 al-Ghawri was informed that Shah Isma'il was trying to concoct an alliance with European powers to attack Egypt.[99] After being informed that Isma'il had raided Bukhara and killed the Özbek khan, Muhammad Shaybani (r. 1500–10), al-Ghawri was seriously concerned. Shortly afterwards a Safavid envoy of Isma'il arrived in Cairo with a gift of a Qur'an manuscript, a prayer rug, a ceremonial bow and a box that was opened before the sultan to uncover the severed head of the Özbek Muhammad Shaybani.[100] The envoy transmitted at the same time an oral message, which was a poem in Persian that was translated into Arabic:

The sword and the dagger are our basil[101]
We sneer at the narcissus and myrtle[102]
Our wine is our enemies' blood,
Our cups are their skulls.

This inflammatory poem not only enraged the Mamluk court, but also provoked a barrage of Mamluk counter-poetry composed by prominent poets, to which Ibn Iyas dedicates several pages.[103] They said, amongst other things, 'If your sword is basil, your wine is blood and your cups are skulls, we sneer at you, scum of all people', 'drinking blood is not our custom', 'the narcissus does not stink but the skull does', 'our basil is the Qur'an and our drink is its recitation'. This embassy ended up as a diplomatic disaster. Al-Ghawri, already seriously perturbed by the Safavid expansion, rightly interpreted the severed head and other statements made by the envoy as insulting and menacing. He broke the bow after the ambassador left the audience and ordered that the khan's head be buried.

The following year, a new Safavid raid on Mamluk territory in East Anatolia was repelled by the governor of Sis in Little Armenia, who sent 10 severed heads wearing red bonnets to al-Ghawri. The red bonnets were the Safavid traditional red headgear worn under the turban and protruding above it.[104] The heads were pitched on lances and paraded in Cairo before they were displayed at the southern gate of the city, Bab Zuwayla. Shortly afterwards, in 1512, a Mamluk envoy to the Safavid court, who had been ill-treated and kept waiting in Tabriz for two years, returned to Cairo, accompanied by a Safavid envoy with a retinue of a hundred men, who were given a cool reception with a low-profile yet martial ceremony at the Citadel, with a military parade and the display of weapons and banners raised at the gate of the arsenal.[105] In spite of the tension, the Safavid gifts on this occasion were impressive: 40 porters carried silver and golden vessels, complete suits of armour, coloured velvet gowns and horse textiles, ceremonial bows, Bursa silk brocade, *baalbaki* fabric,[106] Anatolian (*rumi*) carpets, 9 leopards,

2 of which died during the journey, and many other things. Pagani, the secretary of the Venetian envoy, who was in Cairo at that same time, saw the Safavid embassy and described the gifts it brought as 36 crates filled with silk, fine carpets, horse trappings, bows and 8 leopards.[107]

The Ottomans

In spite of the friendly tone, the gorgeous gifts, the lavish receptions, the positive chroniclers' accounts and the contrast with the diplomatic relations with the Safavids,[108] the Mamluks and Ottomans perceived themselves as rivals. Already Ibn Khaldun, more than a century prior to the Ottoman conquest of Egypt and Syria, warned that the true danger for the Mamluks was not Timur: 'There is nothing I fear more for Egypt than the Ottomans.'[109] The Mamluks needed therefore the vassalage of the Turkmen rulers of South and East Anatolia to keep a buffer zone between themselves and the Ottomans. Throughout the fifteenth century the Ottomans were busy conquering Christian lands in the west, which enormously boosted their prestige in the Muslim world, including the Mamluk Sultanate. Having realised the old Muslim dream of conquering Constantinople, the Ottomans needed then to crown their triumphs and earn the ultimate legitimacy as the new guardians of Islam by ruling the Arab heart of the Muslim world, Iraq, Syria and Egypt, and, most importantly, the holy cities of Mecca and Medina. In the meantime, however, they needed the alliance of the Mamluks against Timur, and later on against the Safavids of Iran. When al-Ghawri began to feel the Portuguese threat to Mamluk interests in the Red Sea and the Indian Ocean, Bayazid II and Selim I gave him material support.[110] In 1511 Selim sent al-Ghawri material and labour for the construction of ships. Anticipating that he would soon control Mamluk territory, Selim was acting only in his own interest.

Diplomatic correspondence between Mamluks and Ottomans is regularly documented from the reign of Bayazid I. The earliest reference dates to 1388, when an Ottoman embassy arrived in Cairo with an unspecified gift.[111] A few years later, in 1393, Bayazid requested a physician to treat his joints. On this occasion he sent a white falcon to Sultan Barquq.[112] The following year he sent the amount of 200,000 *dirhams* (*c.*10,000 *dinars*) to assist Barquq in his confrontation with Timur.[113] In 1402 he himself fell into Timur's hands and was executed.

In the course of their glorious series of conquests, the Ottomans continued to proudly send captured Christians to the Mamluk court. Ottoman embassies were usually met in Cairo with great pomp and their gifts were praised by the historians. Although it is difficult to confirm, it is likely that the Ottomans, who in the early fifteenth century were still newcomers in the Muslim diplomatic world and eager to establish themselves as major players by advertising their conquests in Christian territory, would have sent more embassies with presents to the Mamluk sultans than they received.[114]

In 1396, after his conquest of Nicopolis (in today's Bulgaria) from King Sigismund of Hungary, Bayazid I sent 200 prisoners from different nations, including French and Italians, to the Mamluk sultan. The Venetian merchant Piloti, who dwelt in Cairo at that time, saw them and spoke with them; he reports that they were converted to Islam and integrated into the military establishment: 'They were young, handsome and choice [*mamluks*].'[115] In 1401 Bayazid I sent Sultan Faraj 10 *mamluks*, 10 horses, 10 pieces of felt, several silver vessels as well as gifts for the emirs.[116] Thanks to the Ottoman conquests and the resulting booty, European *mamluks* were numerous at the Mamluk court in the later period. In Cairo, Fabri met a Hungarian prisoner sent by Bayazid II, probably after his conquest of Croatia in 1480, to Sultan Qaytbay. This gift was a way for the Ottomans to get rid of the man. Having not managed to convert him to Islam, not even under threat of death, they converted him into a diplomatic gift. As a *mamluk* in Cairo, he was allowed to openly keep his Christian faith.[117]

Coming back to the early fifteenth century, an anonymous

Mamluk letter during the reign of Faraj ibn Barquq addressed to Bayazid I's son, Sulayman Çelebi, ruler of Rumeli between 1403 and 1411, expresses thanks for a gift package that included fur (ermine, sable, squirrel, fox, lynx), mats, silver vessels and birds of prey.[118]

In 1415 Bayazid I's successor, Mehmed I, sent 5 sets (of 9 pieces each) of Anatolian textiles,[119] 3 sets (9 pieces) of European textiles and 2 bundles of Persian textiles, which al-Mu'ayyad Shaykh reciprocated with 2 horses, 2 golden saddles, Egyptian textiles from Alexandria along with Indian textiles,[120] and in 1420 he sent 30 *mamluks*, birds of prey and silk garments.[121]

In 1427 Murad II added a new dimension to the existing norm of Ottoman–Mamluk diplomatic gifts by sending Barsbay the clothes he had himself been wearing, including his silk turban with a cap of pure gold.[122] We do not know how Barsbay reciprocated. Slightly later, Murad's gift of 50 Anatolian slaves, a eunuch, birds and wild animals, an assortment of various types of fur and European velvet garments were reciprocated by Barsbay with slaves and textiles.[123] Murad II's gift package to Barsbay's successor Jaqmaq in 1440 included 30 *mamluks*, silk garments and fur, and was estimated in Cairo to be worth 5,000 *dinars*.[124] In that same year, Jaqmaq added to the usual pattern of Mamluk diplomatic gifts to the Ottoman court by offering the Ottoman sultan a particularly lavish gift package.[125] It included 26 items among which was a Qur'an manuscript penned by the caliph 'Uthman, 2 gold and silver inlaid *qaljuri* swords and other inlaid arms,[126] a helmet of steel and silver and 2 brigandines (*qarqal*) with gold,[127] which is a kind of ceremonial armour or metal padded vest of velvet textile reinforced with metal, a golden saddle with its brocaded textile (*'arqa*) made of 600 *mithqals* of gold,[128] 15 other saddles, a choice piece of horse armour made by Muhammad Filfili, 4 steel axes, a gold ornamented '*ajanat* (?), a silver inlaid *durkash* (?),[129] a golden billhook, bows made by Ibrahim ibn 'Abd Allah, textiles of various types including turban muslin, 100 pieces of Alexandrian *kamkha* silk fabric,[130] 7 silk garments, kerchiefs, camphor-scented document wraps, 4 pieces of gold brocade (*nakhkh mudhahhab*),[131] 3 elephants, and balsam oil mixed with camphor. The Qur'an penned by 'Uthman is noteworthy. The brigandines are very likely to have looked like the unique extant specimen at the Bargello Museum in Florence, which bears the name of Jaqmaq. It bears few traces of the red velvet surface and is embroidered with nails (*mismar*) (Plate 6).

It is also interesting to note that this gift package, registered in Ottoman archives, is not described in any Mamluk source known so far, although it seems to exceed in opulence even what Jaqmaq's successor, Inal, sent Mehmed II following the conquest of Constantinople.[132]

One of the three elephants sent to Murad by Jaqmaq is likely to have appeared nine years later in the celebration of the wedding of Mehmed II, while still a prince, to a Dhul Qadir princess in Edirne. Scott Redford has drawn attention to a Byzantine manuscript of *Ptolemy's Geography* from the early fifteenth century, perhaps a diplomatic gift, that depicts, in its double frontispiece, on one side the princess sitting on an elephant in a finely draped palanquin and on the other side her brother, the future Dhul Qadir ruler Arslan, with Islamic regalia and textiles.[133]

In 1445 Murad II sent Jaqmaq 16 Christian high dignitaries as prisoners, probably captured in the battle of Varna, riding their horses with full steel armours. Their parade in Cairo attracted the entire city, including women and children, and was 'more magnificent than the Mahmal procession'. Sakhawi describes with pride and delight the bravery of the Ottoman soldiers during this battle. The chroniclers, who emphasise the triumphal message of this gift, add that the Ottoman sultan boasted about similar gifts to Shahrukh and the Qara Qoyunlu ruler of Tabriz.[134] Sultan Jaqmaq kept some of these prisoners for his household and distributed the others to his emirs. The captives were converted to Islam, but after a while they began to gradually sneak away to their home countries![135] Besides the captured soldiers, Murad II also sent 50 beautiful *mamluks*, 5 slave girls, who may also have been captured during the same campaign, as well as silk and other luxury textiles.

In 1446 Murad II sent an embassy to announce his abdication in favour of his son Mehmed II with a gift of 25 crates divided into 5 groups filled respectively with silver vessels that included cups and sugar pots, wool textiles, velvet, gold-brocaded velvet, silk fabric with flower patterns and Anatolian slave girls.[136]

Following his conquest of Constantinople, in 1453 Mehmed II sent an embassy to announce his triumph; the envoys were greeted with a solemn reception at the Citadel and cheered by the masses in the streets of Cairo, which were decorated for several days and filled with the sound of ceremonial music. The envoy brought with him 2 captured Byzantine high dignitaries, 30 *mamluks* and 9 crates of each of the following items: hides of ermine, sable and squirrel, gold-brocaded velvet, coloured plain velvet and silk.[137] Inal's gifts on this occasion were a gold overlaid sword,[138] *buzdughani* maces and steel axes,[139] 2 laminated suits of armour with red velvet and golden nails (*mismar*), a golden saddle with a choice brocaded horse cover (*'araqa*), a piece of horse armour with embroidered velvet with nails, a red embroidered tapestry with gold coins, 31 garments and 100 pieces of Alexandrian silk fabric (*kamkha*), silk brocade (*nakhkh*),[140] gold ducats, a choice mare and 2 choice stallions, 2 elephants, a zebra and balsam oil.[141]

In 1456 Inal received, again from Mehmed II, a letter announcing his latest conquests and a gift package of 30 *mamluks*, and 9 crates each of sable, lynx, wool and silk. Mehmed's letter mentions briefly *mamluks*, prisoners and textiles.[142] Inal's response to Mehmed II includes praise for his conquests, thanks for the gifts received and congratulations on the circumcision of his two sons; a list of the reciprocated gifts is appended to the letter:[143] there was a gold overlaid sword, a gold overlaid short sword or sabre *nimjah*,[144] a red velvet brigandine (*qarqal*) with nails (*mismar*), 5 *buzdughani* maces, 100 Alexandrian fabrics, 3 choice horses, a choice piece of horse armour, a golden saddle with a brocaded blanket or cover (*'arqa*),[145] an elephant, 22 pieces of silk fabric (*kamkha*), 3 *sarihs*

(?),[146] 526 Venetian gold sequins (*bunduqi*), 3 gowns, 10 silk wraps for documents,[147] and 4 large containers of candy sugar. The list also includes gifts for Mehmed's two sons whose circumcision is mentioned in the letter: for each there is a gold overlaid sword, a brocaded brigandine (*qarqal*), a golden saddle, a *buzdughani* mace and 46 horses.

In 1464 Mehmed II sent an embassy to announce the abdication of his father, Murad II, in his favour, with a gift of 30 *mamluk*s, sable, lynx, ermine, grey squirrel hides and various types of luxury textiles, each item filling 9 crates.[148] On this occasion the envoy brought a letter that annoyed the sultan; he considered that the address formula, which did not mention his due titles, showed a lack of reverence. His displeasure increased when the envoy refused to kiss the floor before him and he dismissed the envoy without offering him the traditional robe of honour. Only in the following audience, after the envoy's apology and his kissing the floor, could the damage be partly repaired. However, the sultan refrained from appointing a Mamluk official with a gift to Mehmed to accompany the envoy on his return, as was the custom.[149]

The intensive diplomacy and exchange of precious gifts did not imply a wholeheartedly amicable relationship between the two courts. The first serious cracks on the friendly façade of Ottoman–Mamluk relations appeared soon afterwards, in 1468, with Mehmed II's incursion into the south-eastern Anatolian territory ruled by the Ramazanoghlus, who were vassals of the Mamluks. Although the incursion ended with an Ottoman debacle, it triggered serious alarm in Cairo.

Ottoman intrusion into the Mamluk sphere of interest continued under Mehmed's successor Bayazid II, who began in 1484 to pressure another Mamluk vassal, the Dhul Qadir ruler 'Ala' al-Dawla, into submission, thus undermining Mamluk supremacy. In the course of these events a diplomatic controversy about a gift further troubled the relations between the two courts. Ibn Iyas reports that a gift package sent by the Bahmanid ruler in India to Bayazid II had been intercepted and confiscated on its way by the Mamluk governor of Jeddah and sent to Qaytbay, who decided to keep it for himself. Among the items included in this gift package was a dagger with a hilt studded with precious stones. Bayazid, who was informed about the incident, did not conceal his displeasure, and Ibn Iyas viewed this episode as the provocation that led to Bayazid's initiative in Dhul Qadir territory. Qaytbay eventually returned the bejewelled dagger along with all the other Indian gifts and with his apology. Ibn Iyas's poem on this occasion does not flatter the Mamluk sultan:

> *An open offence publicly spread is by a secret apology*
> *only confirmed,*
> *Whoever thinks public shame is effaced by hidden*
> *excuses is utterly mistaken.*[150]

When subsequently, in 1485, an envoy of Qaytbay travelled to Bayazid II, he offered him gifts worth 10,000 *dinar*s and a letter of investiture from the Abbasid caliph of Cairo. According to Ibn Iyas, this gift was intended to appease the angry Ottoman sultan. This could not prevent, however, Ottoman troops from marching on Mamluk territory in East Anatolia and launching a long series of skirmishes that lasted until 1489, when Qaytbay could finally celebrate victory. Soon afterwards, on Bayazid's initiative, diplomacy and gift exchange resumed. In 1492 Bayazid's embassy of reconciliation brought Qaytbay *mamluks*, slave girls, camels, gowns, silk textiles, gold and other things.[151] Qaytbay reciprocated in 1494 with slaves, precious metals, gemstones and weapons,[152] and in 1496 he sent him a lion, a giraffe and a red parrot, along with textiles.[153]

In 1502 Bayazid II sent an embassy to Sultan al-Ghawri to congratulate him on his accession to the Mamluk throne and to offer him a gift of 50 *mamluks*, 30 crates of silverware, sable and lynx. The envoy spent 70 days in Cairo where he received particularly pleasant treatment.[154] In 1510 al-Ghawri sent Bayazid II a beautifully crafted tent, 2 black eunuchs, 6 horses with lavish trappings and textiles, one of them with a golden saddle, one with a plate caparison and the four others with silk caparisons, ceremonial gilded plate armour and 4 silver inlaid shields, 2 shoulder bags (*bisachi*), iron lance tips, 3 gold ornamented scimitars, *gambelli tre coradori* (?) perhaps camel wool, a beautiful braisier (?) (*ciminier*), silk textiles some of which were scented, and 10 large porcelain trays.[155]

After having congratulated the new Ottoman sultan, Selim I, on his accession to the throne, the following year, in 1513, al-Ghawri sent him an ambassador whose appearance particularly struck Ibn Iyas, who described his outfit as being of unprecedented and astonishing lavishness. The purpose of this visit may have been to request assistance against the Portuguese.[156] The following year the sultan rode to Suez with great pomp to inspect the shipyard set up with the help of the Ottoman navy.[157] A year later, an Ottoman embassy from Selim arrived with 25 porters (*hammal*) carrying velvet gowns from Bursa, coloured Samarqand fabrics, 25 young good-looking *mamluks*, silverware and fur (sable, ermine and lynx). Ibn Iyas praised the appearance of the envoy, his outfit and retinue.[158]

While Ottoman–Mamluk relations remained uneasy, an Ottoman envoy being robbed could only add to the tension and cause embarrassment and even panic at the Mamluk court. While passing by the town of Salihiyya on his way to Cairo in 1514, the envoy was robbed of a bundle that contained all his belongings and a letter from Selim to al-Ghawri. Upon hearing the news, the Mamluk sultan tore his beard out of anger and ordered the chase of the Bedouins in the area, holding their chieftain responsible and threatening to let him pay with his life for this loss. The chieftain eventually managed to catch the thief and return the stolen goods. While reporting this incident, Ibn Iyas recalled the previous similarly embarrassing robbery of Shahrukh's embassy by the Cairene mob and how at that time 'Cairo was almost ruined [...] and no one suffered as much as the people of Egypt!'[159]

The robbery of the Ottoman envoy could not, however, have

been the motivation for the menacing gift that Selim sent al-Ghawri soon afterwards, in 1515, which was the severed head of his Mamluk vassal, the Dhul Qadir ruler 'Ala' al-Dawla (called 'Ali Dawlat in Mamluk sources) along with the heads of his son and his vizir. Al-Ghawri was dismayed but may not have grasped that the message of this gift implied: 'You are next', for he wondered: 'Why is he sending me these heads as if they were the heads of defeated Frankish kings?' He then ordered the heads to be buried in the northern cemetery, where previously the Dhul Qadir Shah Suwar had been buried, after he was captured in a military campaign and executed for having betrayed his alliance with Mamluks to side with the Ottomans.[160] While reporting this episode, Ibn Iyas was aware that with the termination of Dhul Qadir rule by Selim I the end of the Mamluk Sultanate was in sight. However, the exchange of gifts continued to take place between Selim and al-Ghawri during the following year, until only one month before the Mamluk sultan fell in the battlefield while fighting the Ottomans.

Selim preferred to keep al-Ghawri in the dark as long as possible about his scheme to invade Egypt and Syria, continuing to send him lavish gifts and trying to make him believe that his army was marching against Safavid not Mamluk territory. Shortly before marching on Syria, in 1516, he offered al-Ghawri 40 *mamluks*, fur, velvet, wool and silk gowns, and he sent separate gifts to the Abbasid caliph and other dignitaries.[161] The presents to the caliphs and other dignitaries may have been meant to pave the way for his taking control of the Mamluk state with its apparatus and the transfer of the Abbasid caliph to Istanbul. Indeed, Selim was interested in maintaining a certain administrative continuity after the conquest of Egypt and Syria, where he appointed a Mamluk emir as the first Ottoman governor. This was indeed the most ironic gift exchange of Mamluk history. Al-Ghawri, still hoping to avoid a military confrontation, reciprocated with an unspecified gift package worth 10,000 *dinars* and a message offering peace.[162] This was the last Mamluk embassy to an Ottoman sultan, while al-Ghawri was already near Aleppo. The emir who brought the gifts and the message was arrested by Selim, and paraded on a mule, wearing a filthy gown and a bonnet, and carrying on his head a basket with the droppings of his horse.[163] A few days later, in September 1516, al-Ghawri fell in the battlefield of Marj Dabiq near Aleppo.

The first governor of Egypt instated by Selim after his conquest was Khayrbak, a former governor of Aleppo who had collaborated with the Ottoman conquerors. In 1520 he sent his new master in Istanbul a lavish gift of 50 choice horses, a mule worth 500 *dinars*, a large quantity of silk fabric and garments of Alexandrian production and fine muslin, some pieces of which were 120 cubits long, 500 *qintars* of sugar cooked with musk, a large variety of jams and drinks, Chinese porcelain of the blue (*lazurd*) and transparent types and 'many of the strange *tuhafs* that are offered to kings'.[164] *Lazurd*, which means blue, may refer to the blue-and-white commonly imported porcelain.

Apart from the repeated gifts of captured Christians, the typical Ottoman gift package to the Mamluk sultans consisted of textiles, the product of a major industry in Bursa, silver vessels, which probably came from the important production of the Balkans, *mamluks*, female slaves and eunuchs, who must have been provided by the conquered territories, as well as animals, birds of prey and fur that the Ottomans acquired in large quantities in Russia.[165] Ottoman gift packages were often composed of sets of nine pieces, called *tuquzat* from *toquz* meaning nine of each kind, following 'an oriental tradition' (*'ala qa'ida muluk al-sharq*), as Ibn Taghribirdi observes. Indeed, Clavijo refers to this custom at the court of Timur.[166] Timur is even reported to have been offended by an Ottoman gift package that was not composed according to this pattern.[167] It is interesting that Sultan al-Mu'ayyad reciprocated a gift of *tuquzats* from Mehmed I likewise, with Egyptian *tuquzats* of textiles.[168] However, this tradition seems to come to end with the reign of Bayazid, whose gifts, as those of his successor Selim I, no longer show this pattern.

The Mamluk gifts to the Ottomans consisted mainly of textiles of various types that also included imports, arms and horses with their trappings and exotic animals. While the Ottomans included European and Persian goods in their gifts, the Mamluks included Indian and the Far Eastern goods in theirs.

CHAPTER 6

EUROPE

Castile and Aragon

Trade, access to the Christian holy sites and the exchange of prisoners were the driving forces behind the diplomatic exchange between Europe and the Mamluk state and the exchange of gifts contributed to ease negotiations. Ransoms paid to free prisoners or prisoners exchanged during the Crusades and afterwards, when piracy supplanted conventional warfare, were an aspect of diplomatic gifts.

One of the earliest references to a European gift for a Mamluk sultan is the one accompanying a message from Charles of Anjou to al-Zahir Baybars offering friendship; the gifts included a number of grey falcons.[1] In 1284 Rudolph of Hapsburg sent Sultan Qalawun 32 camel loads (*sic*), 14 of which carried sable and squirrel hides, 5 with *s.q.l.a.t* (?) and 13 with Venetian silk brocade.[2] An embassy from Genoa that came at the same time brought 2 loads of *sarsina* (?), 6 falcons and a striped (*ablaq*) dog 'bigger than a lion' and another from Byzantium brought a load of silk and 4 loads of carpets.[3]

Sultan al-Zahir Baybars, who can be considered the founder of Mamluk diplomacy, entertained multiple and intensive diplomatic relations with Latin Europe and Byzantium. The giraffe seems to have been one of his favourite gifts to European courts. Spanish sources record the arrival in Seville in 1261 of an embassy from him to Alfonso X of Castile (r. 1252–84), carrying lavish gifts that consisted of a large variety of textiles, various animals including an elephant, a zebra and a giraffe.[4] The exotic and awesome appearance of the envoys entering Seville with their long beards and wearing gorgeous outfits, accompanied by the exotic beasts, attracted a large crowd in the city.[5] The purpose of this diplomatic exchange seems to have been the promotion of trade between the two states. Seville was a major exporter of olive oil in the Mediterranean. We do not know what presents Baybars received from Seville, but later on, in 1282–3, Qalawun received a gift of 15 horses and mules from Alfonso.[6]

Al-Nasir Muhammad continued to cultivate diplomatic and commercial relations with Castile. A letter from the early period of his reign, dated 1300, to Ferdinand IV, addressed wrongly to Alfonso, mentions a gift[7] of five coloured garments and five coloured Venetian garments,[8] three mail shirts or shields,[9] two containers of balsam oil, two pieces of oudh/agarwood, ginger and three caskets.[10]

The report mentioned earlier by ʻUmari and repeated by Qalqashandi, of an offensive gift sent by Alfonso XI to al-Nasir Muhammad that included a sword, a Venetian gown and a coffin-like object, which the Mamluk sultan reciprocated with a similarly offensive gift of a black rope and a stone, does not provide any information about the date or the historical circumstances that led to this exchange of insults.[11]

Although Aragon was a major player in Mediterranean trade and one of the main partners of the Mamluks, the activity of the Catalan pirates against Mamluk ships and coastal cities strained the relationship between both powers, which remained mostly unstable, alternating between agreements and hostilities.[12] This did not prevent a friendly diplomatic correspondence from taking place between the Mamluk and the Aragonese court, which began with a peace treaty between Sultan al-Mansur Qalawun and James II and continued under his successors al-Ashraf Khalil and al-Nasir Muhammad. In the course of these contacts Khalil received a gift of 70 Muslims, who had been in captivity for a long time.[13] Al-Nasir's correspondence with James II dealt with trade and pilgrims' access to the Holy Land, the release of prisoners, and the situation of the Copts and their churches, the latter being a matter of particular concern to Aragon.[14]

The following episode took place in 1303 during the period of this correspondence. In that year an Aragonese embassy arrived in Cairo carrying gifts more valuable than normal, with the usual message of intercession for the Copts, and a request to the sultan to reopen their churches that had been closed in Palestine.

The particularly high value of the gifts, which included *tuhaf*, luxury items, jewellery, crystal and gold for the sultan and the emirs, was not accidental. The envoy came with an agenda that was different from the official one; it was concerned with what turned into a tragi-comic episode in a family matter caught in the web of Mamluk–Crusader conflicts. During his audience with al-Nasir Muhammad, the Catalan ambassador presented him with a request to free a man, who was a relative of his and who happened to be among the Christian prisoners of war held in Cairo. The sultan responded to the envoy's request and set this man free and the embassy departed from Cairo, with the freed prisoner, to embark from Alexandria.

In the meantime, one of the companions of the freed prisoner, who had been captured along with him and was probably resentful at having been left behind, informed the Egyptian authorities that the man they had just set free was a prince in his home country, whose ransom was worth 'a shipload of gold'; he was very wealthy, owned a large commercial business in Tripoli, which he used to visit on a regular basis and several warehouses on the island of Arwad,[15] where he happened to be when he was captured by the Mamluks during their reconquest of the island from Crusaders in 1302.

When this prisoner's sister was informed that he was alive and held in a prison in Cairo, she spared no effort in motivating the king of Aragon, James II, to intercede on his behalf, and gave him presents worth 40,000 *dinars* for the Mamluk sultan to persuade him to free her brother. This was indeed the main reason of this embassy, and not just the intercession for the Christians and their churches in Mamluk territory. Upon hearing this, the sultan immediately sent orders to Alexandria to halt the departure of the envoy and return the prisoner.

Fortunately for the Egyptians, bad weather had delayed the departure of the ship, allowing them to get the prisoner back. Eventually the ship sailed from Alexandria with the envoy on board in the embarrassing situation of having to face the anger of his companions, who had just realised that they had been lured onto the mission without knowing its true purpose. Following a row during which they even considered killing him, his companions agreed to deprive the envoy of all his possessions and put him in a boat to row back to Alexandria with nothing but the clothes he was wearing. From there the Mamluk authorities sent him to Cairo, where tears and lament about the huge debts he had been obliged to take and the loss of his fortune in this undertaking did not impress the emir in charge, Salar, who replied 'We deal with envoys not with merchants'.

Eventually, the envoy was sent back to the prefect of Alexandria, who was ordered to arrest all Catalan merchants and keep the sultan informed about any new arrival from Aragon.[16]

A brief mention in the same year refers to a ship with European (*faranj*) merchants arriving in Alexandria with a substantial cargo of merchandise that would yield a profit of 40,000 *dinars* to the sultan.[17] This was probably related to the episode of the Catalan envoy and the prisoner, being meant to appease the sultan and let him release the envoy. Aragonese sources indicate that diplomatic contacts between al-Nasir and James II went on undisturbed by this incident.[18] It also seems that the Aragonese ambassador was eventually rehabilitated, since Mamluk accounts refer to another embassy arriving at the sultan's court in 1305 with the same ambassador, called Eymerich Dusay, carrying a message requesting safe passage for merchants and pilgrims and the release of Christians held in Mamluk captivity. Mamluk sources report that on his way back from Cairo to Alexandria, the ambassador was accompanied by Fakhr al-Din 'Uthman al-Aframi, the Mamluk official and ambassador, who had been in charge of the Aragonese envoys during their visits. While Fakhr al-Din was, according to protocol, bidding Dusay farewell on his ship, a row broke out between them, which led the Aragonese envoy to dismiss Fakhr al-Din and put him with his companions on a boat after having stripped them of their possessions, letting them return home in dishonour.[19]

Catalan sources report that Fakhr al-Din eventually travelled to Barcelona carrying diplomatic gifts,[20] while the Aragonese ambassador had to escape to Ferdinand II of Aragon in Sicily, where he surrendered his ship before returning in disgrace to Barcelona.[21]

A letter from al-Nasir Muhammad in early 1306 contains a list of gifts 'from the royal treasury' sent to James II. They consisted of 20 pieces of fabric and garments of various use, materials and colours, including Venetian (or Venetian style) items and products of the Dar al-Tiraz, 10 bows, and 5 crossbows, a glass container filled with balsam oil mixed with oudh/agarwood weighing 120 *mithqals* (*c.*0.5 kilo).[22] The letter, which also acknowledges the gifts previously received, confirms the sultan's approval of the release of the Christian prisoners in his captivity. Later correspondence refers to the gifts exchanged between James II and al-Nasir Muhammad: jewels from James were reciprocated with one big gem from India that al-Nasir possessed and James wished to have.[23] During this correspondence, James II made an unusual request to the sultan, asking him for the relics of Santa Barbara from her church in Old Cairo. The sultan replied in elusive terms; no mention has ever been made of a surrender of these relics.[24]

A letter sent nine years later, in 1315, by al-Nasir Muhammad to James II, contains an appendix with a list of gifts more varied and plentiful than the previous one,[25] consisting of 6 pieces of velvet fabric, 3 pieces of *kanji* fabric, a gown with silver-embroidered *tiraz* bands, 6 gowns made at Dar al-Tiraz,[26] 3 embroidered white garments, 2 pieces of red silk muslin, 3 *mudamma* (?),[27] 1 embroidered (word missing in the text), 5 embroidered gowns (*mufraja*), a rug,[28] 3 large blocks of rock crystal (*billawr*), 15 bows,[29] 15 mail shirts or shields (?),[30] 1 sword, 12 (word missing) of balsam, oudh/agarwood for incense, *zaynat al-fumm* (?),[31] ginger jam in 5 caskets, 2 *kinar* (unidentifiable), 3 honey (*sic*).

The letter that accompanied these gifts is formulated in a warm amicable tone, thanking the king for the gifts he had previously sent and speaking of goodwill, friendship and even affection (*mahabba*) between the two monarchs, for the sake of which the sultan agreed to James's request to free some Christian prisoners, although these had been captured while supporting the enemies of Islam. Some years earlier, in 1312, a letter from James II to al-Nasir confirming the friendship between the two kings, includes a list of his gifts, which consisted of 5 falcons, 1 piece of vermilion red fabric ? (*preset vermeyl*) from Douai, 1 piece of fabric from Festris, fabrics from Jalon, 1 piece of fabric from Ypres, 6 pieces of fabric of Reims, 1 clear blue (?) (*blau clar*) fabric and 8 squirrel tails.[32]

Diplomatic correspondence and the exchange of gifts continued between al-Nasir Muhammad and James's successor on the throne of Aragon Alfonso IV; in a letter dated 1330, al-Nasir expresses his gratitude for the marvellous falcons Alfonso sent him.[33]

Little is reported about exchange of diplomatic gifts with the Nasrid court although embassies were exchanged and a correspondence took place, in which the Nasrids requested the support of the Mamluk court in their fight for survival. In a poem composed in praise of Muhammad VII, the Andalusian poet Ibn Zamrak (d. 1390s) refers to the diplomatic gifts he received from the sultan of Egypt, at that time al-Zahir Barquq, as books and poems.[34] A Nasrid embassy to the court of Sultan Jaqmaq in the 1450s brought silk and pottery from Malaga and Granada.[35]

The last episode of Iberian–Mamluk diplomacy was the famous

embassy of Pedro Mártir in 1501–2, sent from the Catholic kings Ferdinand of Aragon and Isabel of Castile to the court of al-Ghawri, and was noteworthy for its lack of gifts. The envoy, who was an Italian from Milan, was sent to Cairo to dissuade al-Ghawri from implementing the reprisals he was planning against Christian interests. With the deplorable situation of the Muslims of Spain, whose complaints of persecution and compulsory conversion were forwarded to al-Ghawri by the Maghribi states, pressuring him to take action against the Christians, coinciding with raids by the Knights Hospitallers on vessels carrying Mamluk merchandise in the Mediterranean inflicting disastrous damage, the sultan's vexation towards Europe could but escalate. Pedro Mártir arrived not only without any gifts but also without the usual large retinue that was expected to accompany ambassadors at that time. Although Pedro had to face the outrage of the sultan's officials at these shortcomings, his pronounced self-confidence does not seem to have been in any way shaken. To excuse himself he replied that it was not the custom at the court of his masters for ambassadors to offer gifts to other kings; what seemed to be in this country a sign of honour would be viewed at the Spanish court rather as an offence. However, he added, had he been aware that this old custom existed at the Mamluk court he would surely have complied with the rule.[36] This reply may have been clever but it is quite surprising considering the long tradition of gift exchange between the monarchs of Aragon and Castile and the Mamluk sultans. Moreover, Pedro sailed to Alexandria from Venice, where he had spent some time. At least there he would have been informed about the custom of gift exchange in diplomacy with the Mamluks. The lack of gifts and the absence of a retinue in connection with this embassy are indeed difficult to explain, unless they were meant to be offensive.

Pedro Mártir was nevertheless admitted to see Sultan al-Ghawri and given the customary hospitality that included tours to the Pyramids of Giza and to the Virgin's Tree at Matariyya, to which he dedicated long descriptions. He also received the customary robe of honour adorned with ermine and gold-threaded embroidered inscriptions.[37] According to his own self-righteous account, his mission was successful. He spoke to the sultan with assertiveness, emphasising the power of his masters as the rulers of a large part of the world, and putting the blame of the misunderstanding on the intrigues of the evicted Spanish Jews and Muslims and their North African spokesmen, whose envoys were at that time lobbying at the Mamluk court for reprisals. The Maghribi envoys apparently found support among the Mamluk establishment and the local population for their pressuring the Sultan to take harsh measures against the Europeans.[38] Under these circumstances the dispatch of an empty-handed ambassador to handle such a delicate matter was rather bold. Pedro Mártir's mission may not have been that successful after all; shortly afterwards, al-Ghawri sent a monk from among his Christian subjects, called Peter Mauro, to Pope Alexander VI with a message of protest about the persecution of the Muslims in Spain and the Portuguese attacks on Mamluk commercial interests in the Indian Ocean, threatening reprisals against Christian merchants and pilgrims and their churches in the Holy Land. The Pope referred both matters to the Spanish and Portuguese courts respectively.[39]

The Cyprus Connection

When in March 1366 an unspecified European (*faranj*) embassy arrived in Cairo with lavish gifts, the circumstances of the visit and the reason for the gifts were not business as usual.

A few months earlier, in October 1365, the Alexandrian Crusade had been carried out by a European alliance led by Pierre of Lusignan, the king of Cyprus. It was a catastrophe from which Alexandria, a wealthy commercial and industrial centre, would not recover until the early ninteenth century, when Muhammad 'Ali Pasha took the initiative to turn it into a modern Mediterranean city. For several days the Cypriots and their allies led a massacre and took prisoners among the population, who, expecting Venetian commercial ships, were totally taken by surprise. Lusignan and his allies plundered the city and its markets, which had been the showcase of the spice trade, and burnt them down. Although the governor of Alexandria managed to capture 50 European merchants among the local residents, and to drive them out of the city as his hostages, the disaster was a traumatic event in Mamluk history; it was neither forgiven nor forgotten, although commercial exchanges with Europe had to resume in the interest of both sides.

This crusade was the first heavy blow to the Mamluk Sultanate, which was at that time under the rule of the 11-year-old al-Ashraf Sha'ban. The leadership had underestimated the Cypriots with the consequence that the image of the Mamluks as warriors and heroes of Islam was severely damaged. From the European perspective, the triumph was ephemeral, however. A march on Cairo could not take place as envisaged, and the Mamluks cut their commercial relations with European states for some years and closed the Church of the Holy Sepulchre.

The embassy mentioned here was one of repeated attempts to resume trade relations with the Mamluks, offering to return the Egyptian prisoners taken to Cyprus in exchange for the reopening of the Church of the Holy Sepulchre in Jerusalem. However, fearing retribution from the Alexandrian population at the sight of Europeans disembarking on their shore, the envoys asked Sultan Sha'ban to send them some of his men to be held as pawns on board their ship during their visit until the envoys returned safely. The sultan and his advisors agreed to the deal, but, not quite trusting the *faranj* and expecting that the men would be executed, they sent them a group of convicts dressed up as rich Alexandrian merchants. To refine the picture, they staged a scene of women and children pretending to be the family of the alleged merchants, wailing and lamenting after them in fear that they might not return! The *faranj*, satisfied with their hostages, disembarked. On their arrival in Cairo they were received in a lavish tent on a hunting ground on the outskirts of the capital, where an elderly man with a long white beard, who looked highly dignified, was sitting in state on a golden throne surrounded by his retinue. This was not the sultan himself, who at that time was an adolescent, and might not have impressed the envoys, but Yalbugha, the chief of the army, acting on his behalf. The Mamluks eventually rejected the embassy's request, and the latter departed without achieving its goal, but the sultan accepted the gift package, which is not described, except that Yalbugha selected for himself a crystal ewer mounted with gold and a box of unknown content and distributed the remaining gifts to his entourage (Plate 5).[40]

In the following decades political instability, which led to the rise of the Circassian Mamluks as the rulers of the following century, and Timur's raid on Syria, the second heavy blow to the sultanate with yet more devastating consequences than the sack of Alexandria, a declining economy and a suffering image did not allow immediate retaliation against the Lusignans and their allies. It was not until 1427 that the conquest of Cyprus by al-Ashraf Barsbay achieved the long-awaited revenge of Alexandria. From that date until the fall of their sultanate, the island remained tributary to the Mamluks. Tribute rather than gifts was expected from the kings of Cyprus, and it was to be delivered in cash or in kind. However, gifts are also mentioned occasionally. In 1427 the king of Cyprus sent seven of his dignitaries to serve the sultan as his soldiers, two of whom converted to Islam.[41]

As suzerain of Cyprus, the Mamluk sultan happened on more than one occasion to be involved in issues of succession to the throne of the island, and to offer hospitality to Europeans involved in this matter. Mamluk sources relate that following the death of John II of Cyprus, his illegitimate son James arrived in 1459 at the court of Sultan Inal, where he spent more than a year campaigning for the sultan's support against the claim of his half-sister Charlotte to the throne.[42] The sultan, who initially favoured James, sent an embassy to Cyprus to communicate his choice. The Mamluk ambassador returned, accompanied by a number of Cypriot high dignitaries, who managed to change the sultan's mind in favour of Charlotte. The sultan received these dignitaries with great honour and bestowed them with robes in a festive ceremony. James, who was present among the audience of this ceremony, could not bear the spectacle and burst into tears, protesting that he was the rightful heir to the throne. Opinion about this issue among the Cypriot community in Cairo, as among the Mamluk establishment, was extremely divided, which put the sultan in an embarrassing situation, not knowing exactly how to handle the matter. The dispute became so passionate that following the ceremony, a terrible fight broke out between the two parties, who were joined by some young Mamluk partisans of James, who attacked the Cypriot delegation, tearing down the robes of honour they were wearing. Finally, the sultan found himself compelled to withdraw his support for Charlotte and endorse James instead, who eventually returned to Cyprus accompanied by a large Mamluk garrison, to be invested as the new king, James III.

While he was the sultan's guest for almost a year and a half, James was invited to attend the celebration of the Prophet's birthday beside religious dignitaries; this invitation was considered to be an extraordinary gesture from a Mamluk sultan towards a Christian. Ibn Taghribirdi, who reports that this incident shocked some people at the court (*'azuma 'ala 'l-nas*), adds conciliatorily that the sultan must have meant to impress his guest with the 'glory of Islam and humiliation of the unbelievers'.[43] Whether or not the chronicler was aware that James was the archbishop of Nicosia is not told.

This was not the last instance of Mamluk involvement in matters of Cypriot succession. After James's premature death, his Venetian widow Caterina Cornaro succeeded him to the throne of Cyprus, but with the loss of her newborn son and her legitimacy being questioned, the fight for the throne went to another round. Ferdinand of Aragon, the king of Naples (r. 1458–94), who hoped to see his illegitimate son Alfonso (born *c.*1462) on this throne, strove to gain Qaytbay's support for his cause. In 1476 Alfonso sailed with two vessels and 500 soldiers towards Cyprus, but having failed to achieve his goal, he navigated instead towards Egypt, where he found refuge at the court of Qaytbay.[44]

Little is mentioned about Mamluk gifts to the court of Cyprus, and we do not know the circumstances that led Sultan Qaytbay that same year to send his vassal Caterina Cornaro a silk gown with ermine along other silk textiles, a golden saddle, 14 pieces of Chinese porcelain, aloewood, benzoic resin,[45] theriac and a flask of balsam oil.[46] This package was unlike the ones normally sent to Muslim vassals as it lacked armour and weapons, but it did include a golden saddle. The gift might have been related to Alfonso's presence in Cairo, and intended perhaps to dissipate worries on the side of the Venetian queen. Some years later, in 1483, Alfonso was seen by the travellers Félix Fabri and Joos Van Ghistele during their visit to Cairo. Fabri reported that Alfonso dwelt in a palace where he had a remarkable menagerie, and that he used to attend Mamluk ceremonials at the court, dressed in his European outfit.[47]

Van Ghistele noted that two embassies from Cyprus and Naples were simultaneously negotiating issues of succession in Cairo, and that the king of Naples had sent Qaytbay a very unusual gift that consisted of a ship loaded with military equipment, which delighted the sultan and shocked the Europeans who witnessed its arrival at court. The cargo contained a large number of complete sets of armour of various kinds including mail armour, helmets, brassards, armour gloves and other items, various types of lances including pertuisanes, halberds, axes, maces, swords, daggers, javelins, bows, arbalests, catapults, lead projectiles, many culverins and other firearms and artillery equipment as well as a large quantity of gunpowder.[48] This gift, demonstrating a blatant disregard for the Pope's ban of strategic goods to Muslim countries, could not be a mere reciprocation of Qaytbay's gifts, which included textiles and a giraffe, sent in 1480 to Ferdinand.[49]

Armour and weapons from a Christian king were indeed exceptional at this period but these were supposed to serve Ferdinand's ambitions in Cyprus, which did not materialise nonetheless. After spending more than a decade in Cairo, Alfonso returned to Naples in 1487, where he was reported to have made a triumphal entrance, dressed in a Mamluk outfit![50] He was eventually appointed bishop.

However, Europeans at the Mamluk court were not an unusual sight in the late fifteenth century. Some of the prisoners taken in the war of Cyprus were adopted by the Mamluk establishment, and they made brilliant careers as emirs. One of them, the emir Bardabak al-Ashrafi (d. 1464), also nicknamed *al-faranji* (the European), was brought to Sultan Inal, who favoured him, married him to his daughter, and appointed him second secretary with special authority in foreign affairs. He was involved in the dispute regarding the competition between James of Lusignan and his sister for the Cyprus throne, and was accused by the Mamluk supporters of James of defending foreign interests.[51] Sultan Qaytbay himself had family connections with Cyprus. His brother arrived in Cairo in 1495 with two sons, coming from Cyprus where he had lived for 30 years. The three of them were circumcised, converted to Islam and appointed emirs in distinguished posts at the Mamluk court.[52]

Venice

Whereas Mamluk chroniclers are not very talkative about the gift exchange with European courts, Italian accounts and archival sources of the fifteenth century contribute to filling some of these gaps. When it comes to the sultans' gifts to Italian courts, in particular, all the information available is based on foreign accounts.

Owing to their mutual interests in the spice trade, and their respective leading roles in its distribution worldwide, the gift exchange of the Mamluks with Venice was among the most significant in their diplomacy with Europe. The reported Mamluk gifts to Venice, which are mainly from the fifteenth century, appear to have had a standard composition, consisting basically of porcelain, spices, scents and textiles, items that to a great extent represented the Mamluk monopoly on Far East trade. Sultan Jaqmaq's gift to Doge Foscari in 1442 consisted of 30 pieces of porcelain, theriac and a flask of balsam oil.[53] In 1461 the Mamluk sultan, either al-Mu'ayyad Ahmad or Khushqadam,[54] sent a similar package of 20 pieces of Chinese porcelain, 30 *ratls* of benzoic resin, 20 *ratls* of aloewood, balsam, civet perfume, 2 pairs of carpets, and raw and candy sugar.[55] It is interesting to note the absence of the customary textiles in these two gift packages, apart from carpets in the latter; they reappear, however, in Qaytbay's gifts. In 1473 Qaytbay offered Doge Nicolò Tron, as enumerated in a list appended to a letter, 20 porcelain vessels, 5 pieces of muslin, 2 containers of sugar, 15 *ratls* of aloewood, 30 *ratls* of benzoic resin, 1 container or flask (*zucha*) of balsam, 10 containers (*bossoli*) of theriac, a horn of civet perfume, 2 *qintars* of sugar and 2 containers (*gentòle*) of candy.[56] The only textile in this gift is muslin; the usual Alexandrian textiles are not mentioned. However, although the gift to Doge Agostino Barbarigo in 1490 had a similar composition, it included 13 pieces of various types of luxury textiles along with a flask of balsam oil, 2 horns of civet perfume, 25 containers (*bossoli*) of theriac, 35 *ratls* of aloewood, 35 *ratls* of benzoic resin, 33 pieces of Chinese porcelain and 100 containers (*panni*) of sugar and candy.[57]

The gift sent in 1499 by Sultan al-Zahir Qansuh, who ruled for less than two years, included a silver gilded saddle, another saddle of crimson velvet with silver elements along with horse textiles – a blanket (*coverta de cuerpo*) and a silk gold-embroidered caparison (*ta di gropa de cavalo*),[58] a silk coloured gown lined with ermine, an assortment of textiles that included 4 pieces of silk camlet, 4 pieces of muslin, 14 vessels of Chinese porcelain, medical powder for the eyes, theriac, 15 *ratls* of benzoic resin, 10 *ratls* of aloewood and 1 horn of civet perfume.[59] The absence of balsam oil here and henceforth confirms the reports about the destruction of the plantation in 1497.

A very similar gift package was sent by al-Ghawri in 1503 to the Venetian governor of Cyprus. It also included a saddle of gilded silver, a horse blanket made of gold and velvet along with a silk gown with ermine and other textiles, 10 vessels of Chinese porcelain, 1 horn of civet perfume, aloewood and benzoic resin and 10 boxes with containers (*bussoli*) of theriac.[60] The same year the Venetians sent 40 blocks of cheese, fur, luxury garments and textiles of various types to Cairo.[61]

Information about the exchange of diplomatic gifts with Venice becomes more substantial in the late fifteenth century, when political and military conflict between Europe and the Mamluk Sultanate began to escalate to the extent of seriously threatening the established commercial exchange. The news of Vasco da Gama's achievement in 1497 of sailing around the Cape of Good Hope heading towards Calicut came as a shock to the Mamluk court. Soon afterwards, in 1502, the Portuguese attacked seven commercial ships in the Indian Ocean carrying Mamluk merchants and goods, and they began establishing strongholds along the coasts of Malabar, forcing the Mamluks to change their itinerary and buy their spices from Ceylon, Malakka and Sumatra instead. This was bad news for the Venetians as well. The emergence of the Portuguese in the Indian Ocean and the Red Sea and their attacks on Mamluk ships were as much a threat to the Venetians' vital interests as to the Mamluks'. It was Portuguese interference in the spice trade, and not just Sultan al-Ghawri's threats of reprisals against the Europeans, that caused the Venetians to worry about the future of their role and predominance in Europe's international trade.[62]

Under these circumstances, they were compelled to intensify their diplomatic contact with the Mamluk court, competing with the French, who were trying on their side to repair the damage caused by the St John Knights' naval attacks on the Mamluks. The Venetian ambassador Domenico Trevisan arrived at the same time as the French embassy in 1512, a year that was most successful for Portuguese advances in the Indian Ocean and the worst moment in the history of the Mamluks; it was five years before their sultanate was overthrown. Al-Ghawri, with Ottoman support, was engaged in warfare against the Portuguese, not only in the Indian Ocean but also in Yemen, where he had to deploy troops to fight the Portuguese advance in the Red Sea, while at the same time, his Ottoman allies were already treading on Mamluk territory in Anatolia, and heading towards Syria.

Both parties endeavoured to present themselves with the

greatest glamour while bestowing the highest honours on the other. Trevisan's embassy, which included 50 men, is famous and well described on both sides by Zaccaria Pagani and Ibn Iyas. They arrived in beautiful outfits in the Egyptian capital, escorted by no less glamorous Mamluk officials and pages in ceremonial attire.[63] At the Citadel, they were greeted with salute shots. Ibn Iyas described Trevisan's gifts to the sultan as including crystal vessels mounted with gold, luxury textiles of velvet, brocades and silk, as well as pure gold. Pagani lists a total of 150 gowns of different materials and colours – 8 with gold threads, 14 of various colours of velvet, 26 of various colours of satin, 2 of different brocade types, 50 of silk and gold, 50 of wool – 120 hides of sable, 4,500 hides of squirrel, 400 hides of ermine and 50 cheese blocks. There was also a special gift package of gowns for the wife of the sultan: 1 of crimson velvet, 6 of different colours of satin, and 3 pieces of Reims fabric. The Great Secretary (*dawadar*) received 6 gowns of velvet, satin and 6 blocks of cheese and other officials were also given textiles and cheese.[64] Pagani's account does not refer either to the rock crystal or the gold reported by Ibn Iyas. Cheese, which is mentioned only in Italian accounts and not in Mamluk sources, was a common diplomatic gift.[65]

The reciprocated Mamluk gift to the doge, handed to Trevisan, is odd. Unless there is a misunderstanding somewhere in Sanudo's account or its interpretation, the components of this gift package are very similar to those of the gifts the sultan had just received through Trevisan. Instead of the usual porcelain, spices or scents, al-Ghawri offered 100 luxurious gowns of various style and weave, including 8 items woven with gold and, surprisingly, 120 hides of sable, 400 of ermine, 4,500 of squirrel and rabbit, and 50 blocks of cheese.[66] Whereas the textiles and cheese may be of a different kind from the ones just received from the Venetians, the sable, ermine and other animal hides are the same items and in the same quantities that Trevisan had brought to the sultan!

There were probably many other gifts that were not reported in the diplomatic context, as it appears, for example, from the episode of the scholar who saw that Qaytbay owned eyeglasses that were sent to him as a gift from an unnamed European ruler. He asked the sultan to give him a pair, but the sultan rejected his request.[67] It is not reported who the ruler was who sent this gift. Although no such gift is recorded elsewhere, Pero Tafur, who wrote in the first half of the fifteenth century, saw crocodile skins in the palace of the doge, and he described them as gifts from Mamluk sultans.[68]

Crystal, which is mentioned by the Mamluk chroniclers but not in European accounts, was a major and highly valued gift item from Venice. The Mamluk chroniclers call it *billawr*, which is also the term for rock crystal. It is not clear whether *cristallo*, a particularly fine type of glass with the clarity of rock crystal, believed to have been invented in the mid-fifteenth century by Angelo Barovier in Murano, was introduced at some stage in these gifts.[69] Crystal objects were mounted with silver, gold and enamel work. Carved rock crystal had been a highly esteemed Fatimid export to Europe, but in the thirteenth and fourteenth centuries it was supplanted by Ayyubid and Mamluk enamelled and gilded glass;[70] that, however, ceased to be produced in the fifteenth century. It might be that gifts of crystal glass were meant to advertise European production to the Mamluk market, where it was indeed appreciated and probably also needed in the absence of a local supply. However, already in 1310, when Mamluk glass production was at its peak, crystal was one of the diplomatic gifts sent to Cairo. A set of a basin with a ewer made of *billawr* mounted in gold and studded with precious stones was sent by the king of Armenia to al-Nasir Muhammad to congratulate him on his return to the throne.[71]

Fur must have delighted the Mamluks, in particular from the early fifteenth century when it became an obligatory element of their costume. To what extent the gifts of fur covered the considerable needs of the Mamluks cannot be assessed here.

If we compare the gifts sent by Venice in 1415, which consisted of goblets of crystal with enamel, four basins, four ewers, dishes, goblets and bowls of enamelled silver, glass vessels, a silver spoon with a coral arm, silk velvet, wool fabrics and sweets,[72] with the gifts brought by Trevisan a century later, which were mainly textiles and fur, there seems to have been a change over time in favour of textiles. This may have been intended to promote export.

On the Mamluk side, the addition of the golden saddle to later Mamluk gifts to Venice raises the question of whether this item implied a promotion of the Venetian status in Mamluk diplomacy.

The Venetian gift selection to the Mamluks seems to have been different from what they sent to the Ottoman court in the late sixteenth century, when bejewelled objects predominated, following very specific requests from the recipients.[73]

Florence

Florence appeared rather late on the Mamluk diplomatic scene and reports about this relationship are rather meagre. Following the decline of Pisa's presence in the commercial network of the Mamluks during the fourteenth century, Florence, its rival and conqueror, took over its position. A Florentine commercial community, which exported wool textiles, is reported to have been settled in late fourteenth-century Alexandria. In 1422 a commercial treaty was concluded between the Florentine Republic and Barsbay. Two decades later, in 1444, Florence took the initiative to send trade ships to Alexandria on a regular basis,[74] and at the same time requested that the same commercial privileges be granted to other Europeans, notably of Venice and previously of Pisa. This included having a *fondaco* in the port city. Moreover, Florence wanted its florin (Arabic *ifrinti*) to have the same status in Mamluk lands as the Venetian sequin, which in the fifteenth century became widespread as the standard gold currency. Shortly afterwards, a Florentine consul was settled in Alexandria, although there is no evidence for the existence of a Florentine *fondaco* there.[75]

It took some time, however, for Florence to acquire the full privileges it had asked for. In the late 1470s or early 1480s, during the rule of Lorenzo di Medici, a Florentine embassy was sent to Qaytbay's court to negotiate a commercial treaty based on the pattern applied with Venice, but with additional items. The negotiations dragged on for some years until Qaytbay sent a special emissary to Lorenzo. The emissary arrived in November 1487 to grant Florence the commercial privileges that Lorenzo eventually approved. While Lorenzo was eager to increase his role in the global commercial scene, Qaytbay, who was getting increasingly nervous about the rising power of the Ottomans, was keen to intensify diplomacy with Europe. In 1496 a commercial treaty was signed between Cairo and Florence, and three years later another more comprehensive one followed.[76]

The famous gift package that accompanied the embassy of Qaytbay to Lorenzo in 1487 is not recorded in Mamluk narrative sources, although it made a great impact at the Medici court and in Florence in general, where it was echoed in Florentine art of the time. Qaytbay's gift became a memorable event not only because of its assortment of Chinese porcelain, the like of which had not been seen before – fine cotton textiles including muslin of the kind used for turbans, a tent, a large flask of balsam oil and other drugs and scents including civet perfume and aloewood, large jars of sweets,[77] a horse, goats and sheep with long ears and big tails hanging to the ground and a lion – but most of all for the famous giraffe, whose arrival in Florence caused a sensation.[78] Lorenzo the Magnificent, surrounded by the city's high dignitaries, received the ambassador Ibn Mahfuz al-Maghribi in the loggia of the Signoria, which was decorated for the ceremony with hangings and carpets, while a large crowd gathered in the piazza to watch the event. Poems and eulogies were composed in praise of the giraffe, and a poem praised Qaytbay himself for having sent the spectacular creature. According to Giovio (d. 1552), 'It was for a long time a wonderful sight, not only in Tuscany but throughout Italy'.[79] Having heard about the wonderful beast, the regent of

France Anne de Baujeau wrote to Lorenzo, begging him to send her the animal and promising him to generously reciprocate the favour, but when her message arrived in 1489 the giraffe was already dead.[80]

Qaytbay's giraffe, better known in Europe as the 'Medici giraffe', has been commemorated in several Renaissance paintings. The arrival of such an exotic creature would have given the opportunity to draftsmen to depict it for pattern books used subsequently by many artists.[81] Qaytbay's giraffe must have been the model for the giraffes depicted shortly afterwards in the 1490s by the Florentine artist Piero di Cosimo in his painting of Vulcan and Aeolus (Plate 15). The author of a history of Siena, Sigismondo Tizio, wrote an account of Qaytbay's embassy, which he illustrated with a giraffe led by a turbaned groom, also indicating its height[82] (Plate 16). At about the same time, Domenico Ghirlandaio included a giraffe in his fresco of the *Adoration of the Magi* in the apse of the church of St Maria Novella in Florence.[83] Bernardino Luini (1480–1532) also included a giraffe arriving with an oriental caravan in his *Adoration of the Magi* at the church of Santa Maria dei Miracoli at Saronno (Plate 17), and another in a painting on the same subject at the cathedral of Como (Plate 18).

Giorgio Vasari's better known depiction of Qaytbay's embassy in the apartment of Cosimo di Medici in the Palazzo Vecchio dates from 1550, almost seven decades later; its giraffe must have been based on previous drawings (Plate 19). The painting showing horses, lions and a giraffe accompanied by Middle Eastern-looking persons surrounding Lorenzo commemorates Qaytbay's gifts. Qaytbay's embassy and the Pope's eagerly awaited appointment of Lorenzo's son Giovanni as cardinal are thus represented as two major events of the reign of Lorenzo. The significance of the embassy is emphasised not only through its conjunction with the Pope's blessing, but through the prominent position of Vasari's painting, being in the centre of the ceiling of the room designed to commemorate Lorenzo's reign. For the viewer of that time, the giraffe might also have bestowed an aura of power on Lorenzo because it created a parallel with Julius Caesar's famous procession in Rome on his return from Egypt, which was reported to have included this animal.[84] The offering of a giraffe, however, was a less extraordinary homage from Qaytbay than has been suggested,[85] being rather a common gift in Mamluk diplomacy.

The sight of an oriental cortège bringing exotic spices and animals had inevitably to evoke the image of the Magi venerating Christ. The mural depiction of the cavalcade of the Magi in the chapel of the Medici's palace in Florence by Benozzo Gozzoli in the 1470s shows an oriental cortège with loaded camels and mules. Although it precedes Qaytbay's famous embassy, it is likely to have been inspired by the arrival of similar embassies.

Qaytbay's embassy was reciprocated by Lorenzo in 1489, when an envoy arrived in Cairo. He was warmly welcomed, and offered Qaytbay gifts of gold brocaded silks and velvet along with a bed inlaid with ivory – which allegedly pleased Qaybtay as much as if they had been made of gold – a blanket chest and a mirror also inlaid with ivory. The governor of Alexandria and the Great Secretary were each offered a table and a chest inlaid with bone, along with textiles. The gifts must have been lavish not only as reciprocation of Qaytbay's previous gifts, but also because Florentine merchants were complaining that they were not as well treated by the Mamluks as other nationals who brought valuable gifts.[86]

After Qaytbay's death in 1496 relations went on undisturbed between the Mamluks and Florence.

France

France did not occupy a great role in the Mamluk diplomatic scene because it was not a major player in world trade of that time, being rather dependent on Venice, Genoa, Florence and Aragon for its overseas commerce. The few diplomatic relations with France in the fourteenth century were confined to matters related to the Crusades.

The situation changed, however, in the mid-fifteenth century during the reign of Charles VII (r. 1422–61), which successfully terminated the Hundred Years' War, unified France and established a new order, where security, a zeal for innovation and a growing appetite for consumption favoured a commercial opening into the Mediterranean.

The new trends were embodied in the person of the illustrious Jacques Cœur, an overseas merchant, innovative entrepreneur, treasurer and supplier of the king, and the wealthiest man in France, before his dramatic fall from grace and his trial in 1453.[87] As he had travelled to Damascus in his earlier career, one of his main goals eventually became to secure a place for France on the international scene and the Orient market alongside Venice, Florence, Genoa and Aragon. He founded a commercial fleet as a vehicle to trade directly in the Mediterranean Sea. His agents had access to Sultan Jaqmaq, who granted them significant privileges. Among the goods sold by Cœur was coral from Provence and silver, which he traded for spices and silk.[88] His influence and prestige allowed him to negotiate with other monarchs on behalf of Charles VII; he was successful in arranging, through his agent, a treaty between the Knights St John in Rhodes and Jaqmaq, and obtaining the release of Christian prisoners from Mamluk captivity. This mission followed the initiative of Charles VII, who was concerned with French commercial interests, which were threatened by a boycott imposed by Jaqmaq on the Catalans. Following one raid by the Catalans, who were allies of the Knights, on Mamluk ships in 1442, the sultan ordered not only the confiscation of all goods stored in the Catalan *funduq* in Alexandria, inflicting heavy losses on them, but also broke off all commercial relations with them, which in turn harmed French foreign trade.

In the course of the following amicable relations with the Mamluks, Jacques Cœur assumed through his agents a diplomatic role, and managed the exchange of gifts with Sultan Jaqmaq on behalf of the king of France. His agent and the king's ambassador, Jean de Villages, offered Jaqmaq a mail shirt, six glaives, six axes and a steel crossbow with a quiver containing six arrows. French sources also mention lavish horse trappings. This gift, along with the sale of silver and arms (and the dispatch of craftsmen to produce them), provided arguments in the trial against Jacques Cœur on charges of anti-Christian behaviour. Regarding the gift of armour and harnesses, he defended himself vehemently with the argument that this was only an adequate token of gratitude to the sultan for the significant privileges he granted to French merchants, adding that it had been offered in the name of the king.[89] The gifts reciprocated by Jaqmaq are mentioned in his translated letter to Charles VII. The following items are listed:[90] balsam, a beautiful leopard, 9 vessels of Chinese porcelain of various shapes and functions, a container of ginger and another of green pepper, almonds and almond kernels, 50 pounds of a fine variety of musks,[91] and fine sugar. We notice here that textiles are missing while almonds and almond kernels are unusual gift items.

After the episode of Jacques Cœur, which ultimately did not have a great impact on the commercial landscape of the Mediterranean, the French presence in the Mamluk diplomatic world receeded. Decades later, however, in 1512, an embassy of King Louis XII arrived at the court of Sultan al-Ghawri, at the same time as the Venetian envoy Trevisan, to soften the sultan's anger over recent raids of the St John Knights on Mamluk ships. It brought gifts worth 2,000 ducats consisting of silver vessels, silk and wool textiles and hides.[92]

This was one of the many embassies that the court of al-Ghawri hosted that year, for which full diplomatic glamour was deployed, before the lights went off on the Citadel of Cairo.

PART THREE

THE GIFTS

CHAPTER 7

TRADITION AND LEGACY

Traditional Diplomatic Gifts in the Middle East and the Muslim World

The Mamluk sultans selected the diplomatic gifts they sent to other courts according to a composite pattern. This followed some basic conventions valid worldwide at the time combined with the ancient Middle Eastern legacy that was amply documented in Arabic literature, and local traditions inherited from their immediate predecessors, to which they introduced their own specific variations and predilections.

The descriptions of diplomatic gifts in the *Book of Gifts and Rarities*,[1] compiled in the eleventh century, show that the basic elements of diplomatic gift packages changed little over time. Although the text belongs to a literary genre aimed at entertaining and fascinating the reader with descriptions of rarities and precious things from pre-Islamic time to the present, many of its accounts are confirmed in the chronicles, indicating that they do have a documentary value for the diplomatic gift exchange of the earlier and classical age of Islamic history.[2] Moreover, some descriptions of gifts included in this text seem to have been based on palace inventories and other official registers of diplomatic and other gifts. *Tuhaf* and bejewelled objects, textiles, slaves, horses with lavish trappings, exotic animals, rock crystal, spices and scents had been common diplomatic gifts between the Mediterranean and the Indian Ocean since antiquity, as were the customs of recycling gifts or offering imported items or requesting specific gifts.[3] The tradition of offering spices goes back to ancient times; the Sasanian kings liked to receive musk and ambergris.[4] The Queen of Sheba brought King Solomon spices and the Gospel of St Matthew describes the gifts offered by the Magi to Jesus, who they viewed as a king. These gifts were gold, frankincense and myrrh, the kind of items that continued to be offered throughout the entire premodern age. The gifts reported to have been offered to the Prophet Muhammad by the Byzantine governor of Egypt included the basic features of the universal medieval diplomatic gift: slaves, animals, gold and linen.[5] As in the Muslim world, textiles, horses, bejewelled objects, exotic animals and Chinese porcelain were also cherished as gifts in medieval and Renaissance Europe.

The multiple European accounts and references regarding the gifts exchanged between Harun al-Rashid and Charlemagne at the turn of the ninth century are famous in European tradition, and often embellished and stylised into legends, although they are not mentioned in Arabic sources. This has been plausibly explained by the lesser significance of Charlemagne for the Abbasid court. Carolingian sources refer to wool textiles from Flanders and hunting dogs offered by the emperor to the caliph, both items being common gifts from medieval European courts. Harun al-Rashid's most remarkable gifts consisted of an Asian albino or white elephant named Abu 'l-'Abbas, a silk tent and other valuable textiles.[6] The annals of the period also refer in the year 807 to an elaborate waterclock with 12 figures rotating to mark the hours. Whereas the elephant and the textiles continued to be a regular diplomatic gift, the clock is unusual in the Islamic tradition and rather unlikely at that early date, suggesting rather that it might have been a recycled Byzantine gift.

The following description of a North African diplomatic gift provides an example of the universality of diplomatic gift traditions around the world at the time of the Mamluks. At the end of the fifteenth century, an embassy from the ruler of Tanzita, a region in the Atlas Mountains of North Africa with abundant gold ore, brought gifts to the Merinid sultan of Fes. These have been described by an eyewitness, himself a notable of Fes, Hasan ibn Muhammad al-Wazzan, better known as Leo Africanus because of his career at the court of Pope Leo X, who baptised him as Giovanni Leoni. Commissioned by the Pope, he wrote a description of the countries of Africa that also included North Africa and Egypt, which is the first compilation of its kind and contains many accurate and lucid observations. Hasan or Leo describes the gifts carried by the embassy of Tanzita as including: 50 male black slaves worth 10 *mithqals* each, 50 female black slaves worth 15 *mithqals* each, 10 eunuchs worth 40 *mithqals* each, 12 camels worth 50 *mithqals* each, 1 giraffe, 16 civets worth 200 *mithqals* each, a pound (*ratl*) of civet musk and a pound of ambergris worth 60 *mithqals* each, 600 hides of deer for the production of light shields worth 8 *mithqals* each, horses with luxury trappings, silk gowns, a beautiful tent and many other things, such as dates and spices from Ethiopia.[7]

This description is interesting not only because it indicates the individual and relative value of the gifts, showing, for example, that a pound of ambergris was worth six slave girls, and a slave girl was worth less than two deer hides, but also because it confirms yet again the significance of monetary value in the exchange of diplomatic gifts. The exact amounts indicated in this list have an inventory character and must have been recorded in some official document. Another interesting feature of this gift package is its universal character. Although it was a matter of inner African diplomacy, sent from an African provincial court to a North African monarch, its composition included, with the exception of precious metals and stones, the same categories of presents that were exchanged between any other medieval Islamic monarchs.

Five centuries earlier the gifts offered by Sultan Mahmud of Ghazna to the Qara-Khanid ruler of Eastern Turkestan Qadir Khan (r. 1026–32) likewise included animals and spices as well as imported textiles of various origins. There were gold and silver goblets, precious stones, mules with gold trappings, female asses, valuable horses with gold bridles, 10 female elephants with gold bridles, hunting dogs, hunting falcons and eagles, tiger skins, litters or palanquins with embroidered textiles, bejewelled sticks and goads, Armenian and other valuable carpets, printed fabrics from Tabaristan, rarities from Baghdad, luxury weapons including Indian swords, aloe, *maqasiri* sandalwood and ambergris. These gifts were reciprocated by Qadir Khan with horses with gold trappings, falcons, Chinese fabrics, objects of valuable leather, various types of fur, tusks of *khutuw* (may be walrus), and Turkish slaves with gold belts and quivers.[8] A previous Qara-Khanid gift to Mahmud consisted of minerals, musk, horses, camels, male and female slaves, falcons, fur, tusks of *khutuw*, nephritus and precious things from China.[9]

However, if the basic components of a diplomatic gift package appear to vary little over time and space, the proportions of the components and the emphasis within their composition varied according to regional and political peculiarities. The iconography of the gift packages along with the mise en scène of the gift exchange followed cultural realities.

In the medieval world, textiles were the major item of gift and all other kinds of social recognition. The textiles sent as diplomatic gifts could be of diverse kinds. There was prominently silk, velvet and brocade, but there were also varieties of cotton and wool, either in the form of fabric or ceremonial robes or garments fashioned in the style of the donor, carpets, furnishings, horse textiles and tents.[10] Ceremonial tents seem to have always been highly appreciated as gifts, and it would be wrong to associate them exclusively with nomadic culture.

Ibn Khaldun in his Prolegomena (*Muqaddima*) dedicates a chapter to tents, which he considered as an insignia of royalty in sedentary courts.[11] His interest in tents is also evident in the detailed descriptions of them included in his world history (*'Ibar*). Tents belonged to the material culture of medieval Europe as well, where some courts had an itinerant character, functioning as 'mobile forts', and designed with the features of feudal palace architecture, to serve as alternatives to palaces during military campaigns and hunting seasons and to fulfil ceremonial functions. Byzantine and Oriental tents were highly valued by medieval Europeans.[12] Following the negotiation of a truce with Nur al-Din Zanji of Aleppo, in 1159 the Byzantine emperor sent him, along with other textiles, horses, gems and a magnificent silk tent.[13] A German medieval source refers to a beautiful tent offered by an Ayyubid sultan, perhaps al-Malik al-Kamil, to the emperor Friedrich II in 1232. Its ceiling was decorated with celestial images showing the sun with the moon and planets, a decorative programme that recalls the zodiac imagery in contemporary Islamic metalwork. Friedrich kept this tent in the royal treasury.[14] In 1361 Sultan Hasan received a tent from Yemen that earned a poem by the court poet Ibn Hajla. Sultan al-Nasir Muhammad sent a monumental tent complex to the Merinid ruler of Morocco, and it was said to have remained for a long time in people's memory.[15] Qaytbay included a ceremonial tent among his gifts to Lorenzo di Medici, and al-Ghawri sent tents to Bayazid II and to the doge of Venice, but we do not know where they were produced.

Horses were a universal diplomatic gift from antiquity to premodern time.[16] They figure as diplomatic gifts, disregarding whether or not they originated in the country from where they were sent. Berber horses with lavish trappings were the main diplomatic gift of the Hafsids of Tunis and the Merinids of Morocco to the Mamluk and European courts. The Ottoman sultan Bayazid gave a shipload of horses to the duke of Mantua, who reciprocated with a shipload of cheese,[17] which was a specific Italian diplomatic gift.

Imported goods enhanced the value of the gift at the same time as they advertised the donor's worldwide political and commercial network. Exotic animals of all kinds had been standard gift items in almost all cultures of the world since the beginning of history, and they continued to fulfil this function for a long time. Following the medieval Japanese and Koreans practice of offering exotic animals as diplomatic gifts, the Portuguese and Dutch likewise adopted this practice, and gave wild beasts, horses, birds of prey and dogs to Far Eastern courts to support their commercial interests.[18] Although the Chinese are reported not to have much enjoyed animals as gifts, today China has become a leading donor of diplomatic animals, having created the notion of 'panda diplomacy' by offering these animals first to the United States and later to other Western countries to break the ice of the Cold War.

Owing to their ubiquity as diplomatic gifts, it appears sometimes as if courts would swap animals as collectors do to complement their series. Since antiquity menageries had belonged to the paraphernalia of royalty, being associated with the hunt, the traditional royal sport, and fulfilling at the same time the purpose of the later *wunderkammer* in European palaces.

In Renaissance Florence, as in Mamluk Cairo, fights of exotic animals were staged to entertain the rulers and their prominent guests.[19] Once the Portuguese and Spaniards found their own access to the overseas sources of spices and exotic animals, they took over the role of the Mamluks by sending spices and exotic animals as diplomatic gifts to other European courts. In 1515 King Manuel I of Portugal sent Pope Leo X an elephant and a rhinoceros, which became famous through Dürer's inexact depiction based on a previous picture.[20] The rhinoceros reached Lisbon on a ship loaded with spices (cinnamon, pepper, myrrh, sandalwood, aloewood, indigo, incense, rhubarb, cloves and ginger). The rhinoceros was a diplomatic gift from the sultan of Gujarat to the governor of Portuguese India, Albuquerque, who passed it to Manuel, who then offered it to the Pope. Although the precious cargo drowned before reaching Rome, the exotic beast, which had been depicted upon its arrival in Portugal, had a tremendous impact on European arts and crafts, as is beautifully narrated by Clarke.[21] The arrival of this rhinoceros in Lisbon in 1515 can be seen as marking the end of the Mamluk monopoly over the Far East access to the sources of spices and exotic animals. Henceforth elephants and other exotic animals were transported to Europe on a regular basis. At the courts of the Renaissance and in the age of discoveries, the collection of wild animals became a symbol of power and rule over the continents.[22]

Like exotic animals, strange and rare objects including jewellery and bejewelled objects of all sorts belonged to the traditional gift culture of princely courts. Mamluk as well as Iranian and Turkish texts consistently mention *tuhaf* in connection with diplomatic gifts. The Mamluk chroniclers do not always specify what these items were, probably because they were not shown publicly; in one case they are mentioned to be kept secret.[23] Chinese artefacts and undefined objects sent from Yemen and Ethiopia were often described as *tuhaf*.

One of the diplomatic *tuhaf* was the clock that arrived from Byzantium in 1375 that displayed musicians coming out with a melody to signal every hour.[24] The fascination with clocks and other automata has a long tradition in Islamic culture, based on Greek sciences and further nurtured by Byzantine diplomatic gifts that also included organs.[25] With the European technical progress in the following period, the Ottomans in particular, but also the Safavids, were delighted to receive clocks and automata from English, French, Hapsburg and German monarchs.[26] The fascination with clocks and other automata, beautifully documented in the famous illustrated manuscript of al-Jazari in the mid-thirteenth century, had a long tradition in Islamic culture, inspired from the ancient Greeks and further nurtured by Byzantine diplomatic gifts.

The Fatimid and Ayyubid Legacies

As well as the broader context of Middle Eastern ancient and medieval traditions, it is also interesting to look at the practice of diplomatic gift exchange that might have had a direct impact on Mamluk diplomacy, that is, the legacy of the Fatimids and Ayyubids whose last sultan had been the master of the first Mamluks. It is known that many aspects of Mamluk court ceremonial were influenced by the Ayyubids and their Abbasid lords in Baghdad.

The information available about the diplomatic gifts of the Fatimids reveals a degree of opulence and extravagance that is not matched by their successors. The gifts exchanged between Byzantium and the Fatimid court were as much a competition in splendour as was the Byzantine exchange with the Abbasid court of Baghdad. For example, in 1045–6, Byzantium sent gifts worth 30 *qintars* of gold, meaning a total of 210,600 *dinars*, which seems excessive and far beyond anything known from the Mamluk period. This package included horses of the most valuable and finest ever breed, each one clad with embroidered silk textiles, 50 mules carrying 100 containers lined with silver filled with gold and silver vessels, including 100 enamelled objects, alongside various types of silks and textiles. The reciprocated Fatimid gifts of gems, musk, oudh/agarwood and *tiraz* textiles from Damietta and Tinnis are reported to have been of yet higher value than those received.[27]

In 1076–7 the Fatimid vizir Badr al-Jamali sent the Byzantine emperor a gift of 60 pearls each one weighing 1 *mithqal*, a ruby weighing 17 *mithqals* and many other *tuhaf*.[28]

The number of horses sent by the caliph al-Hakim in 1001 to an unnamed Maghribi monarch, amounting to 300 with their trappings, along with 40 mules, gold, silver, weapons and clothes, exceeds Mamluk parallels.[29] The gifts received by the Fatimids were no less impressive. In 1060 an Andalusian ruler sent Caliph al-Mustansir gifts of gemstones and silk worth 100,000 *dinars*.[30]

In 1028–9 the Zirid ruler of Qayrawan in Tunisia al-Mu'izz ibn Badis sent the Fatimid caliph al-Zahir 20 beautiful slave girls wearing silver lockets, 3 horses – one of them black wearing a saddle made of Maghribi goldsmith's work weighing one *qintar* of gold, another white and wearing a saddle studded with pearls, and the third black, wearing a saddle of white silver that weighed 100 *qintars* – along with 3,000 *manns* of saffron,[31] 20 black eunuchs, 12 Slavic slaves, a large quantity of lances, 50 ceremonial leather shields wrapped in silk, 1,000 *qintars* of wax (or candles: *sham'*), 1,500 pieces of silk and other textiles, garments from Sousse and Sicily and several thousand turbans.[32] The Fatimid caliph reciprocated with exotica from India, China and Khurasan and a large quantity of scents and gemstones, ceremonial banners, a giraffe with textiles and apparel, several Bactrian camels with various types of palanquins including some made of ivory, ebony, sandalwood, silver and gold, surmounted by a gold crescent, upholstered with luxury textiles and containing beautiful finely dressed female musicians and dancers; the package also included many eunuchs, fine Arab horses with gold and silver saddles studded with precious stones and stuffed with ambergris and camphor, ceremonial suits of armour and weapons.[33] Female musicians seem to be a Fatimid specialty; in 1024 al-Zahir included two female musicians in his gift package to the Muslim ruler of Sicily Abu Ja'far Ahmad.[34]

Some more modest gifts, however, were also reported in this period. When Caliph al-Hakim sent the document of investiture to his Zirid vassal in Qayrawan, it was accompanied by a robe of honour, banners and three horses with ceremonial trappings.[35] A gift from Mahmud of Ghazna, the ruler of Khurasan, to Caliph al-Zahir consisted of silk, camels, birds and parrots. The camels were loaded among other things with leaves of the *talh* (a type of acacia) and black myrobalan or chebulic myrobalan (*ihlaylij*) trees.[36] The chebulic myrobalan is mentioned as a medical drug, which may be also the case with the *talh*.[37]

The sheer quantities involved in Fatimid gifts and the importance of gemstones and precious metals are not paralleled in Mamluk diplomatic gifts. It is rather likely that gemstones were integrated in the ceremonial weapons and horse trappings that occupied a central place in the Mamluk gift selection. The Byzantine gifts to the Mamluks are also more moderate than those sent earlier to the Fatimid court. In 1312 the emperor sent 42 loads of wool and brocade along with falcons, eagles and *tuhaf*.[38] Although one may wonder whether the discrepancy in gift exchange between the Fatimid and the Mamluk periods should be attributed to the specific narrative tropes of the respective periods or to changing realities, the evidence of the lists of gifts appended to diplomatic letters confirms the scarcity of gemstones in the official Mamluk gift exchange.

Coming to the Ayyubid predecessors of the Mamluks, a gift package sent by Salah al-Din in 1173, after he was enthroned as sultan of Egypt, to Nur al-Din Zangi, the ruler of Syria, is described in contemporary sources in relative detail. This gift had special significance, considering that Nur al-Din was Salah al-Din's master, who had sent him with a Syrian army led by Shiriku, Salah al-Din's uncle, to help the last Fatimids fight Amaury's crusade in Egypt. After having accomplished this mission, and following his uncle's sudden death, Salah al-Din overthrew the Shi'i Fatimid Caliphate in 1171, thus bringing Egypt back to the Sunni Abbasid Caliphate of Baghdad and putting himself on its throne. The gifts consisted of five Qur'an manuscripts, one of them in 30 volumes (*juz'*) penned by the calligrapher Yanis and wrapped in blue silk brocade, one in 14 volumes penned by Rashid and wrapped in pistachio-green silk, one penned by the famous calligrapher Ibn al-Bawwab, one penned by Muhalhil, and another by al-Hakim al-Baghdadi. The package also included three large spinets, weighing respectively 22, 12 and 10.5 *mithqals*, six emeralds, one of them weighing 13.75 *mithqals*, a ruby of seven *mithqals* and a blue stone of six *mithqals* as well as 100 gemstone necklaces weighing 800 *mithqals*, 50 flasks of balsam, 20 pieces of rock crystal, 14 ewers and a basin of jade, an enamelled golden ewer, Chinese porcelain dishes, bowls and sugar bowls, a large quantity of oudh/agarwood, 100 silk brocaded gowns, 24 golden turbans, and other textiles worth 20,000 *dinars*, horses, male and female slaves and a large quantity of weapons.[39]

Another source adds that the gift included a zebra and an elephant and that Nur al-Din forwarded some of the gifts to his nephew, the ruler of Mosul, who forwarded them to the caliph in Baghdad. Nur al-Din commented that it was not gold he needed but military support against the Crusaders.[40] The fact that diplomatic gifts were interchangeable with military support in time of jihad confirms that the principle that they were the property of the Public Treasury and not the personal property of the sultan, although a distinction in this matter is very problematic.

The gifts of Salah al-Din to Nur al-Din were obviously taken from Fatimid treasuries confiscated by Salah al-Din and offered as the booty of the successful Egyptian campaign; their content conforms to Fatimid tradition. Such patterns of continuity are also revealed in the Ayyubid paraphernalia of investiture, which remained faithful to the tradition of the Abbasid court of Baghdad that was also partly shared by the Fatimid court. A robe, a turban, a sword and a necklace were the insignia sent from the caliph in Baghdad to the Ayyubid ruler of Egypt al-Malik al-'Adil.[41] The turban, which was also an insignia of the Fatimids, is no longer mentioned in the Mamluk period, neither is the necklace, which the Mamluks replaced with a belt. It thus seems that the Ayyubids maintained only for a short while the custom of the Abbasid and Fatimid courts to include an important share of gems and jewellery in their diplomatic gifts.

Later gifts sent by the Ayyubid al-Malik al-Kamil to Friedrich II of Hohenstaufen, the German emperor and king of Italy, included, according to a European source, elephants, bears and monkeys.[42] According to Maqrizi, al-Kamil reciprocated the gift of the emperor that consisted of horses, including his personal mount with its golden saddle studded with precious stones and other unusual things (*tuhaf ghariba*), with *tuhaf* from Yemen, India, Irak, Syria, Iran and Egypt alongside a golden saddle studded with precious stones worth several thousand *dinar*s, this whole package exceeding the value of the received items.[43] A few years later, in 1233–4, al-Kamil received from the emperor a white peacock along with a 'white bear with hair like that of a lion, which can dip in the water to feed itself with fish', a description that points to an arctic bear.[44] The diminishing significance of gemstones and the increasing significance of exotic animals and horse trappings seems to have set the new trend that would be followed in Mamluk diplomacy.

CHAPTER 8

GIFTS FOR AND FROM THE MAMLUKS

Gifts for the Mamluks

Fur was mentioned regularly as being among the diplomatic gifts sent from various courts to the Mamluks. The Byzantine emperors, whose commercial relations with the Mamluks mainly involved the transit of Kipchak men from north of the Black Sea as well as horses and fur, used to include fur among their diplomatc gifts.[1] In the fifteenth century, when the Russians replaced the Bulgars in the domination of the fur trade, they regularly distributed fur as a diplomatic gift to other courts in Europe and elsewhere.[2] From the early sixteenth century, the Ottomans imported fur from Russia on a large scale, which, like the Circassian Mamluks, they used in their ceremonial outfit.[3] They also regularly included fur in their diplomatic gifts to the Mamluk sultans. Also within the Mamluk establishment, the governors of Syria used to bring fur to the sultan as part of remittance that was expected from them.[4]

Human beings were a valuable diplomatic gift. They were usually sent as male or female slaves, eunuchs and as *mamluks*. The *mamluks*, by being adopted into the recipient's establishment, and the slave girls, who might acquire a high status in a sultan's harem, introduced a special human link that could consolidate relations between states. Among the eunuchs and slaves regularly brought as diplomatic gifts from Ethiopia to Cairo, Jawhar al-Qunuqba'i became a prominent figure of the Mamluk establishment. Another noteworthy gift of this kind was the emir Arghun Shah al-Nasiri (d. 1349),[5] who was sent to al-Nasir Muhammad by the Ilkhanid sultan Abu Sa'id, who himself had received him from China. Arghun became one of the most prominent emirs of al-Nasir Muhammad's reign, having served as the governor of Damascus and major-domo of Sultan al-Kamil Sha'ban. Human beings were not included in the gift exchange between Christian and Muslim rulers.

In times of warfare, captured enemy soldiers were offered alongside weapons and other items of booty. During the Crusades freed prisoners of war were exchanged as diplomatic gifts from both sides. As a gesture of goodwill after signing a truce with the Crusader king Hugh of Jerusalem, Baybars sent him 20 Christians who had been in his captivity.[6] The Ottoman sultans Bayazid I, Murad II and Mehmed II boasted their series of conquests of Christian lands by sending prisoners to their fellow Muslim rulers, as al-Nasir Muhammad had done earlier by sending Mongol captives to the Merinid sultan to advertise his military victory.[7]

A special type of human gift is described as *mamluks*, and they figure on almost every list of gifts received from and sent to other Muslim rulers. These were young men of the kind purchased by the Mamluk establishment, and like themselves were eligible to serve in the army and the government. Such gifts were, of course, very valuable.

Human beings could also have a value as gifts when they were dead, as revealed in the macabre use of severed heads as diplomatic gifts. The meanings of such presents were multiple: they could boast about a triumph by displaying the trophy, deliver irrefutable evidence of a victory, or threaten the recipient that he might be next. Such gifts to the Mamluks are recorded from Muslim courts, notably the Turkmens, Iranians and Ottomans.

In 1419 the Turkmen ruler of the East Anatolian Dhul Qadir principality, Nasir al-Din Muhammad, sent the head of the son of his Qaramanid neighbour in south Anatolia to Sultan al-Mu'ayyad Shaykh, while supporting the sultan's military expedition to restore Mamluk suzerainty following a rebellion there.[8]

As has been mentioned earlier, the Qara Qoyunlu ruler Iskandar sent the heads of his Aq Qoyunlu rival Qara Yoluq 'Uthman and his two sons to Cairo.[9] Three decades later, in 1468, it was the Aq Qoyunlu ruler Uzun Hasan who sent the head of the Qara Qoyunlu ruler Shah Jahan to Sultan Qaytbay,[10] followed the next year by the head of the Timurid sultan Abu Sa'id. The Safavid shah Isma'il sent Sultan al-Ghawri the head of Özbek Khan.[11] Less than a year later, in 1512, al-Ghawri received 10 severed Safavid heads from his Cilician vassal.[12] He also received the head of the Dhul Qadir ruler 'Ala' al-Dawla from the Ottoman sultan Selim I.[13] Fortunately for the Mamluks, Selim did not get hold of al-Ghawri's head, the body having disappeared in Marj Dabiq, otherwise it might have ended up at the Safavid court in Tabriz! The Mamluks themselves were not inexperienced in the skill of severing and preparing heads for display at the gate Bab Zuwayla or as gifts to other rulers. After al-Nasir Muhammad, in 1328, executed the Mongol fugitive Tamurtash, who had come seeking sanctuary in Cairo, he sent his head to his master the Ilkhanid sultan Abu Sa'id in Tabriz. The decapitated body was buried in Cairo.[14]

The Mamluk Assortment of Diplomatic Gifts

Although diplomatic gifts were a highly official matter, the mechanisms of their selection and the persons involved in this action are not documented. While bearing the traditional and universal features of diplomatic practice in the world around them, Mamluk diplomatic gift packages were not composed according to a rigidly set pattern. Rather, variations were common, following the actual circumstances and modes of reciprocation.

The Mamluks offered textiles and animals of varying quality and quantity to most of their diplomatic counterparts. Horses with trappings are mentioned regularly in connection with all gifts. Spices and Chinese porcelain are mentioned mainly but not exclusively in connection with Europe, as were spices, drugs and balsam.

Human beings and weapons are only mentioned as gifts to Muslim courts. Other Muslim courts may have had a different attitude concerning the offering of weapons, as indicated by a gift from a Moroccan ruler to James II of Aragon that included swords, as well as jewellery, silk, fine horses with trappings, a tent and cash.[15] An exception, or rare case, of Mamluk weapons being offered to a Christian monarch is mentioned during the early reign of al-Nasir Muhammad when he sent a sword, bows, crossbows and shields (or mail shirts) to James II of Aragon. This seems to have been special treatment, which is confirmed in the remarkably amicable style of their correspondence. The ban on weapons in the exchange of gifts between Europe and the Muslim world is confirmed on the Christian side by the well-known ecclesiastic ban on the export of strategic goods to Muslims. One of the main accusations brought against Jacques Cœur, the treasurer (*argentier*) of the French King Charles VII, in the course of his trial in 1453, was to have offered a gift of lavish military horse trappings to the Mamluk sultan Jaqmaq and to have sold him military goods.

Apart from bejewelled arms and horse trappings, gemstones and jewellery are not frequently mentioned in the context of Mamluk diplomatic gift exchange, although the chronicles refer to massive quantities of gems, fabulous jewels and bejewelled objects in their descriptions of the treasures and estates of the Mamluk aristocracy and high dignitaries, and the trousseaux of their ladies. Religious orthodoxy, which the Mamluks advertised and emphasised towards other Muslim rulers, might have led them to avoid this kind of extravagance in diplomatic gifts.

Spices and Porcelain

Spices from the Orient and Africa belonged to the vital needs of the medieval world, as the highly lucrative spice trade attests. They included not just seasonings for food, but scents and perfumes and, most importantly, vegetal and animal extracts to be used for medical purposes.

Among the spices offered by the Mamluks were aloewood from Socotra, used both for medical purposes and as scent,[16] and Arabian and other gums,[17] such as benzoic resin from Sumatra, used for medical purposes and as incense.[18] Civet perfume (Arabic: *zibad*), which belonged to the Mamluk diplomatic gifts, was a highly valued secretion of an Indian mammal, for which Renaissance women used to pay high prices.[19] Not only women craved it. King Lear in Shakespeare's play cried 'Give me an ounce of civet, good apothecary to sweeten my imagination.'[20] The civet used to come via Yemen, but it cannot be excluded that it was also bred in Cairo.[21]

Chinese porcelain, which was regularly offered to the rulers of Venice and Florence,[22] came in large quantities from Yemen, and was part of the tribute the Rasulids had to deliver to the Mamluks.[23] Whether the Yemeni gifts could cover all the sultan's needs for porcelain is difficult to tell. Whereas the number of porcelain vessels from Yemen to the Mamluk court ranged in the hundreds (a gift package in 1354 included 400 pieces), the number of porcelain vessels offered by the Mamluks to European monarchs did not exceed 30 pieces per package. The Yemeni sultans themselves owned large quantities of Chinese porcelain. In 1392, at the circumcision celebration of the sultan's sons, 500 porcelain dishes, along with other ceramic ware, were used to serve food.[24] Likewise the Mamluks held important collections of porcelain, as is regularly mentioned in the descriptions of the estates of high dignitaries, in particular during the fifteenth century. But already in 1352, when one of the high-ranking bureaucrats called Ibn Zanbur was arrested for abuse and corruption, the inventory of his confiscated extraordinary estate, whose description fills three pages, revealed 30,000 porcelain dishes and bowls that included blue, transparent white, today called whiteware, and green wares.[25] This large quantity of porcelain, like other valuable things found in Ibn Zanbur's possession, must have been a commercial investment rather than for mere personal use. The Mamluk monopoly of the spice trade entailed the import of Chinese porcelain in large quantities. One of the greatest overseas merchants known as the Karimis, of the early fourteenth century, the Alexandrian 'Abd al-'Aziz al-Halabi navigated between China, Yemen and Egypt trading with silver, porcelain, jade, silk, spices, *mamluks* and slave girls.[26]

At the table of a Mamluk sultan of the fifteenth century, porcelain was present as a matter of course. In a letter to the doge of Venice, Sultan Jaqmaq, who was otherwise reknown for his sober lifestyle, declared that he was sending him the same kind of porcelain he was himself using.[27] On the wedding of Sultan al-Ghawri's son, sugar was offered to the guests in 20 large bowls of Chinese porcelain,[28] and at one of his banquets, food was served in 400 porcelain dishes.[29] When Giovanni Bellini painted the mythological *Feast of the gods* in 1514 (Plate 20), in which the ancient gods are shown eating from blue-and-white porcelain bowls, he depicted only three vessels. According to Spallanzani, the porcelain collection of the Medicis recorded in archival sources grew in number during the second half of the fifteenth century, but remained relatively modest: 62 pieces were registered in 1514. At that time Mamluk diplomatic gifts were the major source of the collection. By the mid-sixteenth century, the collection had grown to 400 pieces.[30] In the meantime the Portuguese, who had become passionate about blue-and-white porcelain, had discovered the ways to acquire it directly from the Far East. It eventually became an important royal gift among European courts.[31]

When Sultan Selim returned from Cairo to Istanbul, carrying with him the treasures of the Mamluks, they included porcelain.[32] Carswell is right in assuming that much of the porcelain that can be seen today in the collection of the Topkapi Museum must have come from this booty.[33] Even after Selim's conquest of Egypt, the inventory of the estate of the first Ottoman governor, Khayrbak, at the time of his death, which revealed that his wealth exceeded that of Sultan Qaytbay, included porcelain alongside gold, textiles and brass objects.[34]

The large quantity of Yüan and Ming porcelain found in Syria and the millions of shards excavated in Fustat in Cairo attest to a long tradition of Egyptian consumption of Chinese porcelain.[35] Art history and archaeology demonstrate the strong impact of Chinese Yüan and Ming blue-and-white porcelain on Mamluk ceramics in Egypt and Syria, and the large-scale imitations of celadon by local potters. Mamluk chroniclers refer to lapis blue porcelain (*lazurd*) as a particularly valuable ware, which may be the Yüan and Ming blue-and-white ware; sometimes also a 'transparent' white ware is mentioned.[36]

As a diplomatic gift, Chinese porcelain was not a Mamluk innovation, however; it had also been offered by earlier Muslim rulers, including the Fatimids.

Mamluks and Craftsmen

The Mamluks gladly received *mamluks* and slave girls as diplomatic gifts, and they also offered them to other Muslim rulers. The *mamluks* were young men like they themselves had been when they had been recruited to join the military establishment. These men might eventually attain high positions. Some of the human gifts offered by the Mamluk sultans included craftsmen and professionals, like the Jewish physician, or the silk weavers sent from Cairo by Sultan Barquq to work for the Rasulid ruler of Yemen, or the masons sent by Qalawun to the Golden Horde to carve Mamluk monumental inscriptions on a Crimean mosque. The practice of offering skilled people was not new: the Fatimids sent musicians to the Kalbids of Sicily and the Zirids of Tunis, and the Byzantine emperor sent mosaics and workmen to the

Umayyad caliph al-Walid for the mosque of Medina and Cordoba.[37]

Eunuchs, slave girls and *mamluks* are not mentioned among the gifts offered to Christian courts. The only reference I found to a human gift sent to a European ruler are the Mongol soldiers captured at the decisive battle of 'Ayn Jalut and sent with their horses to the German king Manfred von Hohenstaufen. In this case the gift conveyed the political message that the Mamluks, who had recently risen to power, were to be reckoned with, and at the same time served to warn European powers against alliance schemes between them and the Mongols. Neither did the Europeans courts send persons as gifts to the Mamluk court, unlike the Byzantines, who offered Turkish slaves to the Fatimid caliphs.[38] Theoretically, Christians were not even supposed to be directly involved in human trade with the Muslims or the transport of *mamluks* trough the Black Sea, although the Genoese controlled this trade from the port of Kaffa and benefited from its taxation, for which they were condemned by the Pope. In practice, Genoese and Venetians were involved in the slave trade and they themselves held slaves in substantial numbers. However, they discriminated between Christians and Muslims, as did the Muslims.[39] The slaves sent from Christian Ethiopia must have come from other African territory.

Giraffes, Elephants and other Animals

While the Mamluks received animals from all the courts they dealt with, they also offered animals to most of their diplomatic partners. Lions, leopards, zebras, ostriches, parrots and falcons are mentioned, but the most prominent gifts were horses, elephants and giraffes. Sultan Barquq reciprocated a gift of horses and dogs from the Duke of Milan Gian Galeazzo Visconti (r. 1378–1402) with leopards.[40] Exotic animals, such as elephants and tigers, came from India and other Asian regions via Yemen or from Africa.

The most sensational exotic animal in Mamluk diplomatic gifts was the giraffe, which was specially acclaimed whenever it was mentioned in European accounts; medieval Egyptians were very aware of its impact abroad. Since antiquity giraffes had come from Africa to Egypt, as imports or tributes. A giraffe is depicted on the wall of a Ptolemaic temple from the reign of Ptolemy II Philadelphus (r. 283–46 BCE) in a triumphal procession in Alexandria,[41] and giraffes were displayed in Julius Caesar's procession in Rome on his return from Africa. The giraffe was well known in the early Muslim world, being mentioned in bestiaries and in geographical and cosmographical literature as originating from Ethiopia. In the Mamluk period, the interest for the giraffe seems to have increased. The scholar al-Damiri wrote a long entry in his book on animals on this beast, which in the interpretation of dreams symbolised the beautiful and unfaithful female.[42]

The great demand for Mamluk diplomatic giraffes was met by the tribute that the Nubians had to deliver. The association of the giraffe with Africa, either Nubia or Ethiopia, is documented in a fourteenth-century Mamluk copy of the bestiary compiled by the Abbasid scholar al-Jahiz in the ninth century. It is an illustrated copy, which is a rare occurrence in the context of this particular text. The illustrations include the image of a luxuriously caparisoned giraffe led by a black groom, which might have been inspired by the arrival of a diplomatic gift from Ethiopia or a tribute from Nubia (Plate 21).[43]

The Fatimids had already held giraffes, not only to be sent as gifts but also to be used in their parades. The caliphs al-Hakim and al-Zahir are reported to have ridden on religious festive occasions in sumptuous processions that included elephants and giraffes. In one of al-Hakim's processions six elephants and five giraffes are mentioned.[44] The caliph al-Zahir sent among his opulent gifts to al-Mu'izz ibn Badis of Tunis a giraffe that made such a great impression that it was praised in a long poem by the court poet Ibn Rashiq.[45] The Ayyubid al-Malik al-Kamil sent a giraffe to the German emperor Friedrich II and it was reciprocated by the aforementioned arctic bear.[46] Al-Zahir Baybars continued this tradition and sent giraffes to Berke of the Golden Horde, Alfonso X of Castile,[47] and Manfred of Sicily. Manfred, who received other gifts at the same time, expressed his particular delight and gratitude over the giraffe.[48] In 1322 al-Nasir Muhammad sent an elephant, a giraffe and four leopards to the Artukid ruler of Mardin and an elephant and a giraffe to the Merinid sultan of Morocco.[49] Faraj sent a giraffe to Timur, which was described in great detail by the Spanish ambassador Clavijo and mentioned by Yazdi in his biography of Timur, the *Zafarname*, where it was also depicted (Plate 4). Qaytbay sent giraffes to Bayazid II, Ferdinand the king of Naples and Lorenzo di Medici.

The arrival of the giraffes in Seville and Florence caused a sensation in these cities. The enthusiasm at the sight of a giraffe crossing the city was not only a European phenomenon: when the Merinid sultan of Fes Abu 'l-Hasan received among other gifts from a king of Mali a giraffe, which Ibn Khaldun describes as 'of strange appearance, formidable shape and unusual among the animals', the sultan sat in a tower of his palace to watch the cortège and the population was called to come and watch the spectacle. A huge crowd flocked in, so that people had to climb on top of each other to admire the beast, and poets composed odes in praise of its beauty.[50]

The elephants of the Mamluks came from India and Africa. Baybars sent an elephant to each of Alfonso X of Castile and Berke of the Golden Horde. Sultan Jaqmaq sent an elephant to each of the Ottoman sultans Murad II and Mehmed II, and al-Ghawri sent one to Selim I. Giovio mentions an elephant and a tiger sent by Sultan Qaytbay to the Duke of Milan, Galeazzo Sforza (r. 1466–76), which has been commemorated in a fresco painting in the courtyard of the ducal castle of Milan, the Castello Sforzesco (Plate 22).[51] The author identifies and praises Qaytbay as the sultan who sent the giraffe to Lorenzo di Medici. A decade later, in his famous series of paintings representing Caesar's triumphs at Hampton Court, Mantegna depicted an elephant with sumptuous trappings that include a band with pseudo-Arabic inscriptions, which may have been seen on Qaytbay's elephant. Qaytbay's image in Renaissance Italy seems to have been largely shaped by the live animals he sent as gifts. It is interesting, however, that no ivory is mentioned among the diplomatic gifts offered by the Mamluks.

Elephants had a place in Egyptian life as well. When in 1510 a small one-year-old elephant arrived from Africa (*Bilad al-Zanj*) at the court of Sultan al-Ghawri, Ibn Iyas commented that the Egyptians had not seen this kind of animal for more than 40 years so that 'Cairo was rocked' by the sight of the beast. Shortly afterwards, another elephant followed, but we are not told how it came and who brought it,[52] and two years later, in 1512, an embassy from India brought two more elephants.[53] Once elephants were available again in Cairo, al-Ghawri used them on many occasions, such as to lead his festive processions as well the processions of emirs on the occasion of the Nile festival, when the dike of the Cairo canal was opened to the yearly flood, and to accompany the departing pilgrimage caravan; they carried banners and were preceded by an orchestra playing drums and trumpets. To impress an Ottoman envoy in 1514, he sent two elephants to lead the diplomatic procession from the Citadel down to the residence of the envoy.[54] 'The three elephants' of the royal menagerie accompanied the sultan on his last procession that took him to the battlefield of Marj Dabiq to meet the Ottoman sultan Selim; Ibn Iyas writes that they were intended to be used in battle.[55]

The use of elephants in warfare seems to have been already known to the Fatimids: A mosque with multiple domes supported by arches, built in the early twelfth century, was called the Mosque of the Elephants because it recalled from afar elephants carrying armoured palanquins, 'like those displayed in festive processions'. The term *mudarra'in*,[56] meaning 'armoured' and normally used in the military context, suggests a martial connection. Usually, however, elephants were used in entertainment to perform fights in spectacles staged for Sultan al-Ghawri, as were lions, bulls and rams.[57]

The death in 1402 of an elephant called Marzuq (meaning 'prosperous') was a matter of public concern in Cairo. When this big elephant belonging to the sultan's menagerie was taken by its groom for a walk to the outskirts of Cairo, they passed over a bridge where

Marzuq stumbled, caught its leg in a breach from which it could not be freed, and died. People flocked in to watch the sad spectacle and many poems were composed in commiseration with the beast's tragic fate.[58]

Among the things that foreign travellers regularly described in their accounts were unfamiliar animals. Pero Tafur (1435–9) saw seven elephants in a menagerie in an undefined place in Cairo and describes them in detail.[59] Felix Fabri mentioned in 1483 the menagerie of the emir and dragoman Taghribirdi, where he saw a civet, a leopard captured in Egypt, ostriches, parrots imported from India, a giraffe, a tamed lion, a monkey and a bear.[60] When the Venetian envoy Domenico Trevisan was invited to visit al-Ghawri's menagerie, he found there three animals he had never seen before: a giraffe, a small elephant and a crocodile.[61]

Exotic animals were kept in a section of the royal stables at the Citadel, which stood under the authority of the *amir akhur* or Master of the Royal Stables. Another emir, the Master of the Hunt (*amir shikar*) was in charge of the birds of prey, which included numerous breeds of eagles and falcons. In the fifteenth century a birds' feeding ground (*mat'am al-tayr*), located in the north-eastern outskirts near the northern cemetery, was a major venue for hunting and equestrian games as well as ceremonial events. The royal menagerie must have contributed to breeding exotic animals for diplomacy. It is likely that giraffes were bred there, as is suggested by a report in 1272 that a giraffe born in the sultan's menagerie at the Citadel was nursed by a cow.[62] The menagerie at the Citadel continued to exist after the Ottoman conquest, as attested by Pierre Belon, who describes a giraffe he saw there in 1547.[63]

The value of the animals lay not only in their exotic or rare nature, but also in the material value of bringing them to the recipient. A giraffe sent from Cairo to Samarqand or Seville had to walk all the way, having previously made a journey from Africa to Cairo. The same applies to the elephants that came from India or Africa. We do not know how exactly zebras or leopards were transported; felines were probably carried as young beasts in cages. The ostriches sent to Timur must also have been carried in cages. As often mentioned in the chronicles, it was not unusual that animals and slaves died on their way, which enhanced the value of those that arrived. In commercial transactions, the price of animals and slaves who died on their way had to be shared by both sides. The transfer of animals required specialised grooms to accompany them. As is occasionally mentioned in the chronicles, these were sometimes part of the gift. We have no details regarding the modalities of animal transport in the Mamluk period. Information about the supply of African animals to Ancient Rome for the arena games conveys a depressing picture of their capture and their shipping (Plate 23). The separation of young animals from their mothers, conditions on board and journey fatigue would lead to high mortality rates.[64] Similar problems still exist today with animal transport, and would have been likely in Mamluk times.

Not all diplomatic gifts of animals had to be imported by the Mamluks; some were native to Egypt, like the special type of sheep mentioned among Qaytbay's gifts to Lorenzo di Medici. This special breed was remarkable for the particularly fat tail that hung to the ground, dragging behind the sheep. The sheep were known to Herodotus and the Arab geographer Yaqut, and to many European travellers who visited Cairo.[65] Thenaud, who writes that the French embassy he was accompanying in 1512 received such sheep for their maintenance from Sultan al-Ghawri, describes their tails as weighing as much as 30 or 40 pounds. He also mentions that the animals were equipped with small carriages that were attached to their horns and were dragged behind them to carry their tail.[66]

After the fall of the Mamluk Sultanate, the Ottomans seem to have inherited the function of sending exotic animals to Europe, for Caterina di Medici is reported to have requested an elephant, a giraffe and other exotic animals as well as Ethiopian slaves from the Ottoman sultan.[67]

Balsam, Theriac and other Local Products

Balsam oil was one of the precious Mamluk gifts,[68] and its value was said to be equivalent to gold. Egyptian balsam was reputed to be of superior quality, unparalleled anywhere else, and the state held the monopoly of its production and trade. The balsam oil was obtained in small quantities by making an incision in a tree, or rather a shrub, grown in a walled heavily guarded garden at Matariyya/'Ayn Shams (Heliopolis) on the northern outskirts of Cairo. It was harvested in a special ceremony attended by state employees and sometimes foreign dignitaries, who then brought it to the royal treasury, from where it was dispatched, only with special authorisation from the sultan, to various hospitals in Egypt and Syria.[69] The balsam was believed to be grown only in this garden, where it was irrigated from a particular well, traditionally associated with the visit of the Holy Family to Egypt; the Virgin Mary is believed to have bathed Christ in its water. Matariyya was therefore one of the 'must' sites to be visited by Christian travellers and pilgrims during their trip to Egypt, and it is regularly described in their accounts. It also belonged to the touristic attractions that foreign ambassadors were invited by Mamluk officials to visit.

Pedro Mártir reports that King James of Cyprus asked Sultan Qaytbay to give him a few bushes of balsam to grow in his country, but that they failed to flourish there. This episode is more likely to have taken place during the reign of Sultan Inal when James was a refugee at this sultan's court. When Pedro Mártir visited the garden in 1512, he found that balsam no longer grew there.[70] An explanation for its disappearance is provided by Arnold von Harff, who wrote his account shortly afterwards, and reported that during the rebellion led by Emir Qansuh Khamsimi'a in 1497 against Qaytbay's son and successor al-Nasir Muhammad, the rebels went to the garden of Matariyya and vandalised its trees and the waterwheels that irrigated them; he witnessed the damage himself and foresaw that there would be no crop there for the next 10 years.[71]

According to the physician Dawud ibn 'Umar al-Antaki, who worked in Ottoman Cairo and wrote in 1599–1600, the balsam had disappeared from Egypt long before his time. This is contradicted by the contemporary traveller Christophe Harant from Prague, who in 1598 described the garden as full of balsam shrubs the product of which was sold to Europe. However, Harant denies that balsam could grow only in Egypt, reporting that it was cultivated in Mecca at that time, in the Arafat hills, and that the *sharif* of Mecca held a monopoly over its production, sending part of its harvest to the Ottoman sultan in Istanbul along with Indian silk, and selling the rest to pilgrims. The Venetian physician Prosper Alpin, who studied the balsam extensively, confirms in 1581–4 that the balsam available in Cairo at that time came from Arabia. Indeed, no balsam oil is known so far to have been offered as a diplomatic gift during the reign of Sultan al-Ghawri, which confirms the report about the destruction of the plantation.

The idea of balsam oil being obtained exclusively from one place with sacral associations was not new, but went back to biblical tradition, where a place near Jericho and the Dead Sea was believed to be the only home of this tree. Its origin was attributed to the Queen of Sheba having brought its roots from Arabia as a gift to King Solomon. As a source of royal revenue, Antony took it away from the Jews and gave it to Cleopatra.[72] Thus, the 'exclusive' production of the balsam was transferred from Jericho, where it was associated with Solomon, to Egypt where it was associated with the Virgin Mary, venerated by Christians and Muslims, before it moved later on to the holy city of Mecca. The sacral attributes raised the commercial, diplomatic and medical value of this plant, which the Mamluk Sultanate exploited well.

Balsam oil was highly cherished by the Christians of Ethiopia, Byzantium and Europe, who purchased it at the highest prices for sacerdotal use, notably for baptism, adding it to the water. Ibn Iyas writes that these rulers used to send valuable gifts to the sultans in order to receive balsam in return. Fabri confirms its great value in

Europe and as a Mamluk gift, and it regularly figures in archival sources among the gifts sent by Mamluk sultans to Europe.[73] Balsam was also valued as a pharmaceutical plant in Greek medicine, and the Egyptians used it as a universal drug against migraine, fevers, dumbness, tooth pain, asthma, cough, plague, stomach, frigidity, sterility, liver, joints and eye diseases, wounds and numerous other disorders. It was an ingredient of the theriac,[74] and was often mixed with other oils, such as aloewood, and was also cooked with sugar to produce a tonic syrup. Also as a diplomatic gift, balsam was sometimes diluted with camphor or other fragrant oils.[75] Women consumed it as a body lotion, in particular when they visited the *hammam*, which was the venue of wellness and cosmetics in medieval Islamic cities.[76]

The theriac for which Egyptian medicine was famous in the premodern period was also a Mamluk gift item, mainly to European monarchs. The theriac, which originated in Greek medicine (*theriake*) and attributed specifically to Galen,[77] was an antidote used against all kinds of snake poison as well as all other diseases. Medieval Muslim culture has dedicated great attention to antidotes; an Arabic manuscript on theriac dated 1119 from Syria or Iraq has been illustrated with fine miniatures. European medieval and Renaissance medicine also used the theriac, albeit in a different composition; it was produced mainly in Venice. In medieval Cairo, the hospital of Sultan Qalawun, one of the greatest hospitals and medical centres of the world, attached to the madrasa and mausoleum of this sultan, was the place where the theriac was produced.[78] It continued to be produced there under the Ottomans, as has been described by the Venetian physician Prosper Alpin,[79] who travelled in 1581–4 to study Egyptian medicine in Cairo, and a century later in great detail by the Ottoman traveller Evliya Çelebi.[80]

The theriac was made with cooked viper flesh mixed with herbs and drugs and processed into pills or capsules. A description is given by the Syrian physician Dawud ibn ‘Umar.[81] Alpin found the Egyptian mixture superior to the Venetian, and Evliya praised it as unique in the world. For fear of fraud and competition, in the Ottoman period the formula was kept secret and it was not allowed to be produced anywhere except in Qalawun's hospital. The preparation of the theriac took place once a year during a formal closed-door ceremony attended by medical authorities. Evliya managed to get special permission to attend it, which Alpin could not. Although Evliya's documentation of the ceremony refers to the Ottoman period, it might well have been the continuation of a Mamluk tradition. Evliya reveals that after eating theriac, he was cured of the impotence he had been suffering from for 27 years![82]

The theriac continued to be produced in the late eighteenth century, as attested by one of the scholars of the French Expedition.[83] It is therefore not surprising that the Mamluks proudly offered this Egyptian specialty, like the balsam, as a gift to European monarchs.

Nuwayri refers to medical drugs (*'aqaqir*) sent by Baybars in 1264–5 to the king of Aragon.[84] Although drugs are often mentioned as gifts to European rulers, it is not clear how frequently such gifts were sent to Muslim rulers. A letter from Sultan Sha'ban in 1364 to the Nasrid ruler of Granada Muhammad Ibn Yusuf mentions a gift of theriac, balsam and 2,000 *dinars*.[85] The Khalji sultan of Malwa Mahmud Shah requested and received balsam, theriac and skink from Qaytbay. When the Ottoman sultan Bayazid I requested a physician from Barquq, medicine was also sent with him.[86]

The Mamluks were not the only ones to offer drugs as diplomatic gifts; in the late sixteenth century the Ottomans sent the Venetians *terra sigillata*,[87] theriac and balsam.[88] The latter probably came from the Arab peninsula. Medical drugs served as diplomatic gifts also in Europe; the gifts sent by Francesco di Medici to Philip II in the late sixteenth century included pharmaceutical products.[89]

Sugar was another local product mentioned as a Mamluk diplomatic gift throughout the period. It was a major agricultural product both in Syria and Egypt and an export item. Beside its nourishing and festive functions it was a generic medical drug.[90]

Emerald was a local speciality of Egypt, the production of

which was a state monopoly. From ancient times, and before the discovery of the Americas, Egypt was the major source of emerald; it was extracted in Bija at a site located in the southern province of Aswan.[91] Although emerald was mentioned in the Fatimid treasuries and early medieval gift exchange, its use seems to have declined in the Mamluk period. When in 1306 a large block of emerald weighing 245 *mithqals* was found and brought to one of the great merchants, he did not manage to sell it at an acceptable price, not even in Yemen, where it was not valued at more than 3,000 *dinars*. The merchant was eventually denounced to the authorities and the stone brought to Sultan al-Nasir Muhammad.[92] However, it was during the reign of this sultan that the mining of emerald was abandoned because of the high costs of its extraction. Emerald was used not only for jewellery but also, as were many other gemstones, for multiple medical purposes.[93]

Religious Gifts

An important aspect in the selection of Mamluk diplomatic gifts was the discrimination between Muslim and Christian recipients. Besides the fact that slaves and weapons were not sent to Christians, some gifts had a specifically religious character.

Perhaps the most spectacular diplomatic gift offered by Mamluk sultans was the Qur'an manuscript believed to have been penned by the third caliph and successor of the Prophet 'Uthman, presented by Baybars to Berke of the Golden Horde and by Sultan Jaqmaq to the Ottoman sultan Murad II.[94] This gift was evidently loaded with religious-political symbolism. In the case of Baybars it honoured the Mongol ruler, who had converted to Islam and become an ally of the Mamluks against the Mongols of Iran. In the second case, Jaqmaq acknowledged the significance of the expansion of Islam in the world, which at that time only the Ottomans were achieving.

It is astonishing that both sultans, who were renowned for their piety, would allow such a valuable relic to leave Cairo, the centre of the Muslim world at that time. Jaqmaq's gift is mentioned only in Ottoman sources and not in Mamluk ones. The two references to a Qur'an manuscript of course raise the question as to the number of copies believed to have been penned by 'Uthman. Even more astonishing is the fact that there was still a copy of an 'Uthman Qur'an manuscript in Cairo in the year 1510, on which Sultan al-Ghawri had the Mamluk recruits swear their oath![95] The sultan is reported to have taken this manuscript with him to the battlefield of Marj Dabiq, where it was reported lost.[96] Yet, a Qur'an manuscript attributed to 'Uthman is at the Topkapi Sarai Museum, another is in a library in Tashkent and another in the library of the shrine of al-Husayn in Cairo. Did the Mamluks have a number of manuscripts attributed to 'Uthman, or were these only fascicles of a composite manuscript? Or did they produce them for diplomatic purposes? Most likely the manuscripts in question were among the oldest known at their time and thus attributed to the caliph 'Uthman.

Otherwise, Qur'an or other manuscripts rarely figure as diplomatic gifts. However, Sultan Barsbay sent a Qur'an manuscript described as *nuskhat yamin* to the Aq Qoyunlu ruler and vassal Hamza ibn Qara Yoluq, on which to swear his allegiance.[97]

Another Islamic gift was water from the sacred well of Zamzam in Mecca offered by a Mamluk envoy to Berke. This envoy had also performed the *'umra*, or smaller pilgrimage, which takes place outside the dedicated holy month of the hajj, as a proxy for Berke.

Textiles

Perhaps even more than their predecessors, the Mamluks attached great importance to textiles in their choice of diplomatic gifts. Although textiles were offered in a variety of forms – such as ceremonial gowns and headgear, various types of garments and furnishings, tents and horse covers and caparisons – ceremonial textiles from Alexandria had a special status in the composition of Mamluk diplomatic gifts, being mentioned alongside military objects and horse trappings as a major and a regular item in all gift packages. The Alexandrian textiles are usually described as products of the

Alexandrian royal manufacture the Dar al-Tiraz. Since the Fatimid period, Alexandria had been a major centre for textile production of silk, linen and cotton, and the seat of Dar al-Tiraz, where the ceremonial gowns with embroidered inscription bands were woven.[98]

The tradition of royal manufacture of ceremonial textiles goes back to pre-Islamic Sassanian court traditions. *Tiraz*, meaning 'embroidery' in Persian, referred in Islamic culture to epigraphic bands on ceremonial gowns; the term was expanded to monumental epigraphy and other crafts as well.[99] Likewise, the Byzantines held state-owned factories for the production of ceremonial gowns.[100] *Tiraz* gowns were characterised by their embroidered honorific inscription bands, in particular around the sleeves, made of silk or gold threads. Although the Umayyads are already mentioned to have established a *dar al-tiraz* for regal textiles, the Abbasids are the first to be associated with the tradition of bestowing robes of honour or *khil'as* to dignitaries.[101] The *tiraz* industry that flourished under the Fatimids served not only the regal custom of bestowing robes of honour on dignitaries, but also seemed to serve the role of supplying the general market with inscribed textiles. The institution, closely related to the Mint, was administered by high-ranking officials at the court and disposed of a large budget. Tinnis and Damietta are mentioned in the Fatimid chronicles as production centres of *tiraz* textiles. Although *tiraz* textiles are mentioned among other Fatimid and Ayyubid diplomatic gifts, the *tiraz* manufacture does not seem to have had the same significance as in Mamluk practice, where it fulfilled an essential function in the culture of honorific robes and diplomatic gifts.

The Dar al-Tiraz as an institution is less well studied in the Mamluk period. Like the Fatimids, the Mamluks held a state monopoly over the manufacture of robes of honour, which were funded by the *diwan al-khass* or Office of the Privy Estate, one of the best endowed and most potent offices in the Mamluk state, which also managed diplomatic gifts and other related expenses.[102] Its production, which stood under the supervision of the Privy Estate, belonged to the Mamluk insignia of royalty alongside the throne, the Mint, the seal, the ceremonial tent, the banners, the *maqsura* or royal enclosure in the mosque, and the mention of the sultan's name in the Friday sermon.[103] Ibn Khaldun describes the *tiraz* as a gold-embroidered band with coloured threads that stand out against the ground colour of the silk or brocade garment. It signalled rank and hierarchy in the process of investiture, as had been done under the Persian kings before Islam. Whereas the Persians used images of kings and representations designed specifically to bestow a regal attribute on textiles, Muslim rulers replaced these with inscriptions bearing their name and other auspicious or documentary texts. Ibn Khaldun adds that the *tiraz* tradition was adopted by all Muslim courts, and he describes the *tiraz* as representing royal themes 'either the images of the kings and their representations or representations and images in that sense'.[104] The increasing significance of silk in Mamluk society is attested by the technological reform introduced in the thirteenth century. Although the drawloom was also used in Spain, it is generally assumed that the Mamluks, who were traditionally using the tapestry loom, imported it from the East, probably from Ilkhanid Iran.[105]

During Qalawun's reign, Damiettta is reported to have produced ceremonial textiles as well as Alexandria, but only the latter continues to be mentioned in the subsequent period. Although the devastation of Alexandria caused by Pierre de Lusignan's raid in 1365 ruined much of the city's industry and markets, the manufacture of ceremonial textiles did not vanish and may have even recovered for a while following state initiatives to promptly restore the damage by consolidating the fortifications and upgrading the city's governor to the status of deputy. When Sultan Sha'ban visited Alexandria three years after the disaster, he inspected the royal textile workshop, which al-Nuwayri describes as rehabilitated, or at least this was partly the case.[106] New causes, however, contributed to its recession. A survey of the Alexandrian textile industry ordered in 1433 indicated that the number of looms operating in the city had diminished in the last four decades from more than 14,000 to a mere 800, a decline that Ibn Taghribirdi blamed on the greed and oppressive methods of the authorities.[107] Piloti, a Venetian merchant who lived in Cairo for two decades in the early fifteenth century, writes that Alexandria's textile industry had declined but it continued to produce silk for the court. This production would have been dedicated specifically to ceremonial and diplomatic purposes. More silk had to be imported from North Africa and Anatolia or came from Damascus. After the Damascus production, which served export, was ruined by Timur's devastation of the city, Alexandria might have taken over some of the Syrian production, at least temporarily.[108]

However, Alexandria may not have remained the sole producer of ceremonial textiles. It seems that the production of at least some of the ceremonial outfit was transferred to the markets of Cairo, where, according to Maqrizi, it was controlled by the sultan, who held a priority right over its disposition.[109] This decentralisation seems to be confirmed by his contemporary Ibn Khaldun's remark that the Mamluks, unlike their predecessors, did not keep the *tiraz* workshop within their palaces, but gave their orders to the weavers.[110] The fact that in 1386 Sultan Barquq sent silk weavers from Alexandria to the sultan of Yemen suggests a decline in the local demand for silk, or a scarcity of raw material that would have left weavers unemployed. The workshop may have returned at some later point. Alexandrian textiles continue through the entire Mamluk period to be mentioned in chronicles and diplomatic correspondence as diplomatic gifts. Although 'Alexandrian' might be interpreted also as a brand that could have been produced anywhere rather than a provenance, al-Zahiri, who held the post of governor of Alexandria in the first half of the fifteenth century, praised the textiles of the city as being unparalleled anywhere else.[111] References to the termination of the Mamluk *tiraz* industry are therefore not correct;[112] rather the Dar al-Tiraz of Alexandria went through a period of recession in the late fourteenth and early fifteenth century, during which time Cairo's markets filled the gap, but eventually royal patronage held production afloat to the end of the Mamluk period.

The general economic decline of the fifteenth century and the shrinking of the Mamluk textile industry in particular, leading to increasing import from Europe, did not preclude production continuing for the ceremonial and diplomatic needs of the court. Royal patronage and luxury requirements do not necessarily mirror the general economy, as the development of other arts and crafts indicates. In spite of serious economic problems, but due to Sultan Qaytbay's and his court's affinity for the arts, carpets and some metalwork of the late fifteenth century belong to the most splendid artistic works of the Mamluk period.

Although no substantial physical evidence of Mamluk *tiraz* gowns survives, we know inscriptions with royal titles and attributes characterised Mamluk ceremonial textiles as well as other items of ceremonial culture and art. The significance of official inscriptions with honorific titles had been articulated in particular during the century when the Qalawunid dynasty ruled (1279–1390). Ibn al-Furat's description of Qalawun's gift to the ruler of the Golden Horde in 1287 is of great interest because it specifies the categories of donated robes according to their inscriptions.[113] Inscribed textiles were thus a matter of state protocol; in the fourteenth century only the emirs who were entitled to an *iqta'*, which is a usufruct tied to an office, were permitted to wear embroidered inscriptions.[114] It was Sultan Qalawun who emphasised the importance of *tiraz* textiles in connection with the reforms he introduced to the military uniform that were meant to enhance hierarchical distinction. In his laudatory biography of this sultan, Shafi' ibn 'Ali dedicates a section composed in poetical terms to the Dar al-Tiraz.[115] Hierarchy was also to be signalled in the elaboration of the silver belts worn by the emirs, which increased in value according to rank. Qalawun's sons and successors al-Ashraf Khalil, al-Nasir Muhammad and his grandson al-Ashraf Sha'ban confirmed and expanded the elaboration of the military outfit.[116] Belts were significant in Islamic ceremonial culture in general and as symbols of military rank.[117] Khalil emphasised hierarchy in the emirs' uniforms by increasing the share of brocaded silk and inscriptions and refining other elements of their outfits.[118] Khalil's concern with matters of military outfit was so passionate that it might even have led to his assassination. According to some chroniclers, his assassination was connected with the embezzlement of the royal textile production of Alexandria. The murderer was his deputy, Emir Baydara, who was being investigated for letting his agents get hold of and divert the textile production of Alexandria that should have been sent to the sultan to supply the army. After being summoned to be questioned by the fuming sultan, who insulted and humiliated him and was on the verge of physically attacking him, Baydara, knowing that he still had to expect the worse reprisals, took the decision, supported by fellow emirs, to kill the sultan. He waited for him to ride out for the hunt accompanied by a small retinue to assault him with his sword.[119] It may be that the textiles of Alexandria were not the sole reason behind the sultan's assassination, rather one among others, but this incident nevertheless points to the significance of Alexandrian textile production to the Mamluk court, and to this sultan in particular.

Succeeding Khalil, al-Nasir Muhammad added to his predecessors' reforms by introducing the golden belt and the belt studded with gemstones to the military uniform. The historian and Ayyubid ruler of Hama, Abu 'l-Fida, describes the gifts he used to receive from Sultan al-Nasir Muhammad to confirm his investiture and vassalage as including horses with complete trappings, various types of falcons, golden belts studded with gemstones, ceremonial textiles and cash. He emphasises the lavish robes and headgear of embroidered silk brocade from the exclusive royal production of Dar al-Tiraz of Alexandria, mentioning the amount of gold that was woven into them. On one occasion the gold embroidered in an ermine-lined robe weighed more than 100 *mithqals*.[120]

The next significant reform in Mamluk outfit took place during the reign of Barquq at the end of the fourteenth century, when he introduced fur as an integral element in Mamluk costume and an obligatory adornment of robes of honour. At that time a fur market flourished in Cairo. According to Maqrizi, fur became so widespread under the subsequent sultans that even ordinary soldiers and minor bureaucrats would wear garments with sable (*sammur*), lynx (*washq*), ermine (*qaqum*) and squirrel (*sinjab*). He adds: 'one may say that there is not a single woman of the well-to-do class who does not wear sable and other furs, and nowadays people use fur on a very large scale'.[121] This had not been the case in the fourteenth century, when fur was far less affordable and ermine was worn only by the sultan and his wives. The new fashion introduced by Barquq, the first Circassian sultan and the one who henceforth shifted the recruitment of *mamluks* from the Crimea to the Caucasus, suggests that fur-adorned costume may have become associated with Circassian Mamluk identity.

However, the Circassian Mamluks were not the only or the first Muslim rulers to crave fur, which had a long tradition in the trade history of the Muslim world.[122] Long before the Mamluks, the Ghaznavids used it to adorn their parade uniforms.[123] Eventually the rules and reforms regarding the costume of the Mamluk establishment were reflected in the textiles offered as diplomatic gifts. Garments and robes of honour with fur, in particular ermine, became a characteristic feature of gifts of the later period. An episode reported by the emir and historian Ibn Shahin al-Zahiri demonstrates that the Mamluks were proud of cultivating their textile culture to an extent that was unparalleled elsewhere, and in particular among their rivals. An envoy of Timur, while looking out from the guesthouse, the Dar al-Diyafa, was astonished and impressed at the sight of the great variety of costumes displayed on the street before him. He expressed his surprise to the Chief of Protocol, the *mihmandar*, commenting that there was no such variety of costume, nor distinction between different groups, in his own country. When the *mihmandar* reported this conversation to Barquq, the sultan told him to brief the envoy that what he saw was only one side of the costume variety in this realm, and that there were still more variations according to occasions and seasons.[124] As Louise Mackie expressed, 'Mamluk society was saturated with textiles', which they proudly displayed. Diplomatic gifts of textiles of the royal manufacture were a vehicle that transmitted this pride abroad.

Although the Mamluk court has not been associated with centralised artistic design workshops in the same way as the Ottoman and the Timurid courts have, what the chronicles and diplomatic letters reveal about the Dar al-Tiraz, calling its textiles sometimes just *'amal al-dar* (work of the Dar), suggests that this manufacture was a centralised royal workshop.

Looking at the history of diplomatic gifts since the Fatimid period, it appears that the Mamluks added a new dimension to the gift practices of their predecessors, and, by the same token, gave a new function to the inherited Dar al-Tiraz by making inscribed textiles a predominant and emblematic feature of their gifts.

Material Witnesses of Mamluk Diplomatic Textiles

Whereas Mamluk artefacts are represented in all major museum collections of the world, the major diplomatic gifts discussed in this book are not. Ceremonial garments exist only in fragmentary form that can hardly provide a significant testimony for the purpose of this study. An exceptional case of a well-preserved Mamluk garment is the brigandine in the name of Sultan Jaqmaq (r. 1438–53) at the Bargello Museum in Florence, mentioned earlier (Plate 6). This has been identified as the *qarqal* that appears in Mamluk chronicles and in lists of diplomatic gifts.[125] Contrary to descriptions in diplomatic correspondence, however, this brigandine does not contain any gold or silver, rather its decorative nails are made of copper that might have been originally gilded, which is surprising for a garment bearing a sultan's name.

The 'mantle for a statue of the Virgin'[126] in the Cleveland Museum of Art (Plate 24) is not original as a garment, neither is it associated with diplomacy. It is made from several pieces of a

Mamluk original, probably of the fifteenth century, made of blue, white, cream and yellow silk with gold. The main pattern consists of pointed medallions inscribed with the words 'glory to our lord the sultan' alternating with chinoiserie blossoms, arranged on a blue floral ground with eight-petal rosettes inscribed with the sultan's title '*al-ashraf*' in the manner of a royal epigraphic blazon.[127] The inscriptions, which refer to an anonymous sultan, identify the textile as royal, and therefore it is likely to have been offered as a diplomatic gift. As it is anonymous, it would have belonged to a lower category.

A striped silk dalmatic inscribed with the repetitive Mamluk formula *al-sultan al-'alim* 'the sultan, the knowledgeable', which is also frequently found on mundane pottery and metalwork of the Mamluk period, might also have reached Europe as a diplomatic gift before it was donated to the church[128] (Plate 25).

Much has been written on Islamic, including Mamluk, artistic effects on Italian art, and this does not need to be repeated here. The fascination with the Islamic Orient, which was inspired by patterns rather than artistic themes, was due mainly to portable objects that reached Europe through trade and sometimes also diplomacy. Much of this fascination was with the Arabic script, a major decorative element in medieval Islamic art. The Italian fascination went as far as to display Arabic and pseudo-Arabic inscriptions on garments, furnishings and religious paraphernalia related to the Madonna and other Christian figures, as numerous publications have already documented.[129] Although the Mamluks were not the only ones to produce inscribed textiles that were purchased in Europe, epigraphy being equally used by the Ilkhanids, Mamluk artefacts outlived the Ilkhanid period for more than one and a half centuries and are more likely, therefore, to have been the major source of inspiration for Italian artists.

A well-known testimony of the iconic significance of the *tiraz*, and in particular of Mamluk inscriptions, is provided by Antonio Pisanello's sketches in 1438–9 depicting what has been described as the apparel of the Byzantine emperor John VIII Palaiologos. One drawing copies a Mamluk inscription in the name of Sultan al-Mu'ayyad Shaykh (r. 1412–21), which has been interpreted as part of a *tiraz* band in a textile, probably a gown, sent by this sultan or his successor Barsbay as a diplomatic gift to the Byzantine emperor.[130] The sketch shows the inscribed band without the textile to which it might have belonged. Considering that it is rather unlikely that a Byzantine emperor would make a public appearance in a gown bearing the name of a Muslim sultan, the band might have been applied to a horse or other textile, or even another kind of object. In any case, Pisanello's drawing confirms that the Mamluks' display of their epigraphic textiles had an impact in the world around them.

The Knight's Outfit

Alongside the epigraphic textiles of Dar al-Tiraz, the major emblematic gift items given by the sultans that constantly figure in historical accounts were luxurious arms and armour, and horses with lavish trappings, notably golden and bejewelled saddles upholstered with velvet and silk. The prominence of military and equestrian items in Mamluk gift packages is not paralleled by any other Muslim court of that period.

The saddle was as a matter of course a prestigious object in premodern societies, and it figures universally as a royal gift. When the sister of the caliph al-Hakim offered him 30 horses, they were equipped with golden saddles, one of them studded with gemstones and another one with rock crystal.[131] The saddles mentioned here were integral elements of the donated horses' outfit, not a separate individual gift.[132] Under the later Mamluks the golden saddle gradually acquired a special iconic status as a diplomatic gift, being mentioned independently from the horse. The golden or bejewelled saddle was a matter of special pride to the Mamluks, having an emblematic status in their aristocracy of cavalrymen. For example, when Sultan Qalawun sent his governor in Syria robes and banners as insignia of royalty, a golden saddle was part of the package.[133]

In the course of the reform of Mamluk costume and military outfit aimed at emphasising hierarchy, al-Ashraf Khalil introduced a type of bejewelled saddle that was named *ashrafiyya* after him.[134] The wrap of the sultan's saddle belonged to the insignia of royalty during the reign of al-Nasir Muhammad.[135]

Although silver elements were previously included in military saddles, in the late fourteenth century Sultan Barquq increased the use of gilded silver and gold in Mamluk saddles, making it a general and characteristic feature.[136] Following the economic crisis of the early fifteenth century, the use of precious metal diminished, but this seems to have been temporary. The golden saddles (*sarj dhahab*) were mostly made of gilded silver, as is revealed on one occasion when Sultan Abu Sa'id Qansuh (r. 1498–1500) appeared dressed entirely in white, with all the trappings, including the saddle of his horse, in 'white silver without gilding'.[137] Pure gold is also occasionally mentioned.[138] The gold or silver would have been applied as sheets on the crescent-shaped front and back of the saddle, following an old Asian tradition that was also valid for Mongol saddles.[139] In a period of crisis during the reign of al-Nasir Ahmad (r. 1342), copper was mixed into the precious metal.[140] In the fifteenth century gemstones were added to the saddle's ornament. Although saddles decorated with rock crystal are mentioned already in the Fatimid period, a crystal saddle (*sarj billawr*) offered in 1457 by the governor of Syria to the sultan was described as a rarity;[141] but eventually this seems to have become more common. In 1511 the governor of Aleppo sent Sultan al-Ghawri a horse with a saddle studded with rock crystal.[142] This sultan, who had a pronounced taste for ceremonial pomp, used to ride in processions, as he did on his return from a visit to Alexandria and on his departure to Aleppo to fight the Ottomans, accompanied by horsemen on saddles adorned with gold and crystal or studded with carnelian and other gemstones.[143] Such saddles were among the Mamluk treasures that fell into Selim's hands.

Golden saddles with brocade and velvet upholstery belonged to the sultan's[144] and the caliph's attire,[145] and to the insignia bestowed by the sultan on his emirs[146] and prominent guests.[147] Unlike the robes of honour, which only the sultan could bestow, the saddle was a gift that emirs frequently offered to the sultan.[148] Mamluk chroniclers usually refer to a brocaded caparison (*kanbush zarkash*) accompanying the saddle, the two items forming a ceremonial set.

It was not before the fifteenth century, however, that the golden saddle became a must as a diplomatic gift. Although al-Zahir Baybars included saddles in his gifts to Berke, this was not yet the established rule, as it appears from the gift selections of al-Nasir Muhammad. The significance of the saddle as a diplomatic gift seems rather to have been established during the reign al-Mu'ayyad Shaykh, in the second decade of the fifteenth century, at the time when the ceremonial bejewelled belt (*hiyasa*), after gradually losing its significance, had totally disappeared.[149] This is probably not due to coincidence but rather to a ceremonial reform. In a letter addressed to the Qara Qoyunlu ruler, Sultan al-Mu'ayyad Shaykh emphasises that the saddles he has sent him are something held in particularly high esteem among his people, 'comparable to luminous crescents, [...] each one being specially wrapped'.[150] The wrapping of the saddle, called *ghashiya*, was made of leather adorned with so much gold that it looked as if it were made entirely of gold.

Pero Tafur reports how he was impressed at the sight of a black horse offered to Sultan Barsbay by one of his emirs. It was equipped with golden bridles and wore a golden saddle with a ruby in the front bow as large as an orange, and three rubies in the rear bow as large as eggs, and a caparison of white brocade bordered with pearls.[151] The Nasrid envoy to the court of Sultan Jaqmaq wrote in the account of his mission about the magnificence of Mamluk saddles, which he described as made of gold inlaid silver and coloured silk, adding that the Mamluks covered their horses with textiles made of golden silk.[152] The Mamluk saddles may have even been a model for others: on one occasion a gift from the Ilkhanid sultan Abu Sa'id is said to have included 'Egyptian style' bejewelled saddles.[153] Mamluk manuals on horsemanship refer to a large variety of saddle types designated by individual names. The list of saddle types is quite long.

Almost at the same time, in the early fifteenth century, as fur became a characteristic feature of Mamluk costume, the golden saddle became the jewel of Mamluk ceremonial outfit. According to Mayer, the belt was the only bejewelled item that Muslim religious opinion allowed a man to wear.[154] The bejewelled saddle was a symbol of status that could not in any way provoke religious concerns, although members of the religious establishment avoided its use, preferring instead the leather saddle.

Judging from the place it held among diplomatic gifts, saddle-making must have been a major industry comparable to the Dar al-Tiraz. Sadly, no Mamluk saddle survives, but golden saddles upholstered with velvet are known from the Ottoman period.[155] Their respective decorative style is, however, distinct from Mamluk aesthetics.

Material Witnesses of Mamluk Military and Equestrian Gifts

Copious literature has been compiled on swords and other white weapons. Although much has been written on Mamluk military and equestrian subjects, art history has hardly been involved in this aspect of Mamluk material culture. The collection of the Topkapi museum in particular includes a number of late Mamluk royal swords that display a large variety of decorative styles and numerous signatures on the blades.[156] In the absence of surviving physical evidence of Mamluk ceremonial horse trappings and horse textiles, some specimens of arms and armour can serve as physical testimony of Mamluk characteristic diplomatic gifts (Plates 7–14). Although there is no evidence so far to identify any extant Mamluk arms or armour as a diplomatic gift, it can be safely assumed that the luxury specimens that are inscribed and decorated with gold overlay would have belonged to the category of diplomatic gifts. Extant armour and weapons confirm the descriptions included in the official lists appended to diplomatic letters, referring to gold decorated steel items. However, neither this material nor the information provided in the literary sources allows a clear distinction between ordinary princely and ceremonial weapons.

Besides the striking effect of the gold decoration on the anthracite surface of the steel, gold would have impressed the adversary and the gift recipient as a sign of opulence.

Compared with the better preserved and more glamorous later military and equestrian equipment of the Ottomans, Moghuls, Safavids and Qajars, Mamluk arms and armour may seem less impressive. Nevertheless, Mamluk military objects are considered by some to be the finest among their Timurid, early Ottoman and Turkmen contemporaries, with which they share many common features, to the extent of making identification sometimes difficult. Seen in their context and their representative and aesthetic functions, Mamluk military and equestrian objects still need a great deal of study.

To the art historian, the most remarkable feature about the craftsmanship of military outfit is its distinct character when compared with contemporary Mamluk metal vessels and furnishings that were produced either of alloys of brass and bronze or copper. Brass was inlaid with silver and sometimes also a bit of gold, and copper vessels were mostly tinned, although some objects show traces of silvering and even gilding. Virtually nothing is known of the Mamluk crafts of silversmiths and goldsmiths.

The artistic differences between military and civil artefacts are obviously dictated by their distinct materials, which require different artisanal skills. Maqrizi, in his description of Cairo's markets in the early fifteenth century, provides the explanation when he writes that the markets of bridles, stirrups, spurs and saddles had their own decorators specialised in the art of their inlay. The silversmiths and goldsmiths of stirrups and other horse trappings would also decorate pen-boxes and inkpots.[157] The metalworkers of horse trappings and armour thus belonged to a group that was separate from that of the coppersmiths. Most likely, different craftsmen would be involved in the production of individual items such as the makers of the steel blades and the bejewelled or inlaid hilts. Apart from the markets in the city, where weapons and equestrian equipment were produced, the *zardakhana* in the Citadel was a military institution for the production, repair and purchase of weapons. It belonged to the royal household, was directly under state control and was headed by an emir with the title of *zardakash*.[158] Like the Dar al-Tiraz it had the status of royal manufacture.

Although steel and iron were the major materials of arms and armour, some helmets and armour from the reign of al-Zahir Baybars were made of painted wood combined with leather and paper.[159]

In spite of the differences in technique and style between military-equestrian artefacts and other metalworking crafts, both categories share the general Mamluk emphasis on inscriptions and blazons that brand Mamluk art through its entire history.

More frequently than other artefacts, arms bear the signatures of their makers. In the list of gifts sent by Sultan Jaqmaq to Mehmed II, the makers of certain items are mentioned. Sometimes the craftsmen's name is preceded by the title *ustadh*, which was commonly used in Iran but not used on other Mamluk artefacts. A cannon maker from Aleppo in the second half of fifteenth century was also named with the title *ustadh*.[160] The title *mu'allim*, which appears frequently on metal vessels, does not seem to have been generally used by arms- and armour-makers.

There were two different techniques used to apply gold decoration onto the steel surface of armour and weapons. One technique consisted of applying or overlaying the patterns over the steel surface, as can be seen on the armour in the name of Sultan Qaytbay (Plates 13a and 13b). The other technique consisted of first applying a gold sheet onto the surface; this would then be scratched to reveal the steel ground forming a linear decorative pattern (Plate

12). However, both techniques were used simultaneously. The border of Qaytbay's armour displays the same engraved pattern seen on the axe of the Bargello at the same time as naturalistic gold painted floral motifs. Both techniques differ from the gold inlay that occasionally appears on Mamluk vessels, which rather echoes the silver inlay work. Moreover, the predominance of floral patterns, which sometimes appear as freehand drawing, is unparalleled in any other craft except perhaps that of book illumination.

Mamluk swords display a variety of techniques in the decoration of hilts and blades, revealing yet other variations of metalwork that have no parallel in copper or alloy metal vessels. Silver, otherwise poorly documented in the Mamluk period, is frequently used in the hilts, usually gilded and engraved. Openwork, sometimes in the shapes of braids or knots, is another characteristic feature of hilt decoration. Standard poles made of sheet metal often display openwork decoration that shows different craftsmanship from that used, for example, on metal lamps. A variety of workshops seem to have contributed to the decoration of regal weapons, something that still needs to be explored in more depth. At this stage, however, it is obvious that these worskhops belonged to a separate craft, probably working exclusively for state commissions. Most likely, similar observations would apply to the *tiraz* textiles.

The earliest arms and armour of artistic quality known from museum collections date from the second half of the fifteenth and early sixteenth century; very few earlier examples are known so far. The helmet in the name of Sultan Barsbay in the Louvre shares the same aesthetics displayed on the chamfron that bears the name of the Great Secretary of Sultan al-Mu'ayyad, after whose death he served under Barsbay (Plates 8a, 8b and 9). In both cases the finely polished and bare steel surface is left undecorated to enhance the magnificent gold overlay of the cartouches inscribed in calligraphic *thuluth* with princely titles accompanied by a blazon.

The oval and pointed helmet is inscribed with the name and titles of Barsbay with his royal epigraphic blazon: a tripartite circle.[161]

The painted inscriptions and cartouches are elegantly drawn in fine lines that make them closer to the art of the book than to the inlaid decoration of metal vessels. The chamfron in the name of Muqbil (d. 1433), the Great Secretary of Sultan al-Mu'ayyad Shaykh, who later became governor of Safad in Syria, is slightly earlier than the helmet;[162] the titles refer to Muqbil's office as the chief secretary of al-Mu'ayyad, which he held until 1421.[163] The decoration is painted and displays a splendid inscription in the front and a blazon (Plate 9).

The suit of armour in the Furusiyya collection (Plates 14a and 14b) bears the name of Inal before he became sultan; his inscribed titles date it to the second quarter of the fifteenth century.[164] It is typically made of a combination of mails and plates. The front part that would cover the belly displays two panels composed of plates of equal size inserted in the mail shirt and densely decorated with a gold overlay design consisting of interlocking ribbons of the kind used in manuscript illumination and metal vessels. The ribbons frame cartouches filled with fine arabesques. The panels are each centred by a medallion with a composite blazon set between an upper and a lower epigraphic rectangle with the name and titles of the emir. The appearance of these front panels is very reminiscent of double frontispieces of late Mamluk manuscripts, and may not be coincidental. On the back, the plates cover the entire length of the shirt from the shoulders to the lower back of the plates; their size is tailored to the body, diminishing towards the bottom. The design of the back consists of three tall panels and two shorter ones. The tall panels are decorated with a pair of double ribbons interlocking in loops framing a vertical series of blazons. With the diminishing size of the plates, the space between the double ribbons vanishes and only one double ribbon remains. The side smaller panels increase in width towards the bottom; they are similarly decorated with double interlocking ribbons framing a vertical series of blazons. A very similar suit of armour in the same collection is in the name of the Timurid ruler Ibrahim Sultan.[165]

The suit of armour in the Naval Museum of Mersin in Turkey is in the name of Sultan al-Ashraf Qaytbay (Plates 13a and 13b). The style of the *thuluth* inscriptions is the same as on other objects related to this sultan. The decoration consists of a central medallion on each of the two front panels, inscribed with the name of the sultan. However, it is not in the circular shape of a blazon, being rather pointed at the top and the bottom and ending in a trilobe arabesque. The decoration that surrounds the medallions is remarkable and unconventional. It consists of flowers with stalks and leaves, densely filling the ground. The flowers are not integrated in an arabesque ground pattern but are rather freely drawn in a naturalistic manner that is not common in Mamluk art.

CHAPTER 9

GIFTS AND MAMLUK IDENTITY

Export

Some countries included their prominent export items and characteristic artefacts in their selection of diplomatic gifts, but this was not always the rule. The Nasrids offered silk and pottery from Malaga and Granada to Sultan Jaqmaq, either as a sign of their artistic identity or perhaps as commercial publicity as well.[1] The Ottoman gifts of silk and silver also reflected their own most prominent productions. The Maghribis offered their main export item, which was horses.

The case of Mamluk diplomatic gifts seems to be different. The artefacts that were exported in significant quantities by the Mamluks, and are recorded in European inventories and are widespread in museums, such as silver inlaid metal vessels, enamelled glass, glazed pottery and carpets, are not mentioned as diplomatic gifts either by the Mamluk chroniclers or in other sources. It is astonishing indeed that al-Nasir Muhammad offered blocks of rock crystal to James II of Aragon but no enamelled glass vessel of Mamluk production, although these were cherished and imported in many parts Europe.

The exception to this rule is the gift package offered by al-Zahir Baybars to Berke Khan of the Golden Horde, which included inlaid and gilded metal lamps and silver inlaid metal vessels. As discussed earlier, Baybars's gift selection was not typical of the general Mamluk gifting pattern, having been superseded since the reign of Qalawun by the simpler yet more emblematic selection of textiles, equestrian and military objects. This would imply that the numerous Mamluk metal vessels bearing European coats of arms and sometimes names of European patrons, such as the brass vessels inscribed with the name of Lusignan rulers,[2] are more likely to have been commissioned on the Mamluk market rather than diplomatic gifts. Likewise, the Mamluk glass and metal vessels inscribed with the names of Rasulid rulers of Yemen must have been ordered on the markets of Egypt and Syria, which seems to be confirmed by the chroniclers, who refer to Mamluk craftsmen working for the Rasulids. Although we know very little about Mamluk gifts to the Ethiopian court, Mamluk metal vessels recently discovered in Ethiopian church treasures include objects of the fourteenth and fifteenth centuries inscribed with honorific titles of emirs. In this case as well, there is no evidence that these objects were Mamluk royal gifts; they could have been private donations by merchants or pilgrims connected to Egypt or the Christian holy sites.[3]

The consistent absence of the kind of Mamluk artefacts that were imported on a large scale by the Europeans in the descriptions of gift packages further suggests the hypothesis that the Mamluk sultans premeditatedly avoided making diplomatic gifts of objects that were common export goods. These objects might not have been considered as suitable or qualified as *tuhaf* in the sense of unusual, special or exclusive objects. It cannot be excluded, however, that some ceramic, glass and metal vessels might have been sent among the gifts as containers of gift items such as spices and scents. For example, balsam is mentioned as being sent in glass flasks; spices are likely to have been contained in the underglaze painted jars known as *albarelli*, found in large quantities in European collections, some of which are inscribed with names of herbs and scents.

The importance of wraps should not be underestimated. Documents and manuscripts are described as being wrapped in silk and silk brocaded textiles, and the wrap of the royal saddle made of gold and leather belonged to the insignia of royalty. Saddles offered as gifts were also presented in a special silk wrap.[4]

Mamluk carpets do not seem to have been offered as gifts either. The workshop of al-Sharif in Fustat, mentioned by Maqrizi in connection with the estate of the mighty emir Qawsun in 1341–2, continued to produce princely carpets half a century later, being mentioned during the reign of Barquq. However, the production seems to have depended on commissions. When Sultan Sha'ban, who had ordered some carpets for a palace in the Citadel, was killed in 1377, the work on the carpets stopped until Barquq commissioned carpets there in 1385 for his funerary complex.[5] In the late fifteenth century Mamluk carpets appear as imports in Europe. Unfortunately, this production is not mentioned in Mamluk chronicles, but is only documented in European collections and archives. Their absence in the lists of diplomatic gifts confirms the hypothesis that Mamluk diplomatic gifts had to be distinct from export goods. I have so far found only one mention of carpets presented as a diplomatic gift; this was among the gifts offered by Sultan Jaqmaq to the doge of Venice in 1442, referring to two pairs of carpets. It is not known, however, whether they were a local production or imports or recycled gifts. If it is the case that these carpets were a local production and not imported or recycled, they would have had a special value because at that time Mamluk carpets had not yet been exported on a large scale. This gift would have heralded the revival of this craft. However, Jaqmaq cannot be associated with any significant artistic initiative. The Ottomans, however, used to offer lavish gifts of carpets; in 1464 Mehmed II sent Ferdinand of Naples as many as a hundred pieces.[6]

The fact that export items were avoided as diplomatic gifts is not contradicted by the importance of state-manufactured Alexandrian luxury textiles in diplomatic gift packages. The gifts of Alexandrian textiles of Dar al-Tiraz embroidered with honorific inscriptions were most likely a non-commercial royal production. They would not have been common export or commercial goods but a rather exclusive production for the court, which continued to be supplied even when the commercial textile manufacture declined in fifteenth century.

The absence of publicity for Mamluk commercial artefacts would not exclude that another kind of more subtle publicity might have been involved in the selection of Mamluk gifts: spices, scents and Chinese porcelain advertised the worldwide commercial network of the Mamluks and their monopoly of Far East trade. Although porcelain and spices had always been used by Muslim rulers as diplomatic gifts, prior to Vasco da Gama the Europeans could mainly get them through the Mamluks. Spices, scents and porcelain were valuable gifts that delighted and gained the favour of the recipient at the same time as they enhanced the status of the giver in the sense of noblesse oblige.

Weapons, armour, horses and *mamluks* sent by the sultans could not have been associated with any kind of commercial publicity, rather the Mamluk sultans had to import horses and *mamluks* at high costs. It is difficult to tell, however, whether balsam and theriac had any significant commercial value in the global trade context. The balsam irrigated by the sacred water of the Virgin's well might have recalled Mamluk supremacy over the Christian holy places. The theriac, for which Egyptian medicine was and continued to be famous, may have been for the Mamluks a matter of scientific pride. The hospital of Qalawun, the major medical institution of the Muslim world at that time, was famous in Europe and continued to be mentioned in all traveller accounts even long after the fall of the Mamluk Sultanate.

Although horses were the main export and gift item from North Africa to the Mamluk court, al-Nasir Muhammad sent horses along with textiles to the Maghribi rulers. This implies that horses were swapped, which would allow new breeds and cross-breeds, and enrich the royal stable collections.

The main intention of a diplomatic gift was to please the royal counterpart, even amuse him, to gain his favour as a means to smooth the way for negotiations. This would be consistent with the tone of some diplomatic letters that include amicable and even warm terms of friendship and brotherhood between monarchs.

The traditional and consistent use of the term *tuhaf* and its derivatives in the context of gift-giving in diplomatic correspondence, implying fascination and wonder, confirms that the primary intention behind the selection of gifts was to impress the recipient with something out of the ordinary and provoke wonder and excitement. Impressing and stimulating the admiration of the counterpart was an effective means of self-representation. This kind of decorum, which seems to have had priority over straightforward self-representation or commercial publicity, explains the great significance of animals as diplomatic gifts through history. In a letter from 1411 the Byzantine emperor wrote to the Mamluk sultan that he was sending him a falconer with five falcons, knowing his passion for these birds.[7] In one of his letters to al-Nasir Muhammad, James II of Aragon wrote that he had selected precious things from his country with which he wished to please the sultan.[8] The desire to please Qaytbay was obvious when the king of Naples Ferdinand of Aragon offered him a shipload of weapons, breaking the Pope's ban. With this unconventional gift he was obviously ingratiating himself with the sultan, whose support he needed to promote his own son to the throne of Cyprus.[9]

The fact that the Mamluks composed their gift packages with the main intention of pleasing and impressing rather than directly promoting commerce is further confirmed by the fact that their assortment of diplomatic gifts was not much different from that of gifts exchanged within the Mamluk court itself, except perhaps in terms of quantity. The sultans offered foreign monarchs the same things that they appreciated themselves. The remittance, also described as gift, that the governors of Damascus brought to the sultans included similar selections, albeit in larger quantities and yet more lavish. In 1396 Barquq received from his deputy in Damascus falcons, young *mamluks*, horses, camels, a lavish Qur'an manuscript, a bejewelled sword, a diadem, gold-embroidered textiles, golden saddles and other golden horse trappings, a horse outfit and brocaded caparisons, fur, candy sugar, fruits, sweets and other edibles.[10] The composition of gift packages within the Mamluk court was a mixture of delightful and valuable things selected to please. Once they reached the royal treasury, the emirs' gifts might have been recycled as diplomatic gifts.

There is an evolution in the patterns of diplomatic gift-giving within the period of the Mamluk Sultanate between the mid-thirteenth and the early sixteenth centuries. The first substantial diplomatic gift reported in Mamluk chronicles, which earned one of the most detailed descriptions therein, offered by al-Zahir Baybars to Berke Khan of the Golden Horde, displayed a remarkable variety of items spanning Venetian textiles, Chinese porcelain, exotic animals, and various Mamluk artefacts, weapons and equestrian items, sugar, crockery and female cooks, forming a combination that remained singular in Mamluk diplomatic practice. Two decades later, the gifts of Sultan Qalawun to the Golden Horde reveal a new trend: the bulk of the package consisted of ceremonial epigraphic textiles produced in Alexandria and Damietta. The gifts of the reign of al-Nasir Muhammad are usually described in more cursory terms that seem to reflect their rather simple composition, even when they must have been particularly lavish. The first gifts he sent to the Ilkhanid sultan Abu Sa'id in 1320 to celebrate the new entente between the two courts were worth the unusually high amount of 40,000 *dinars*, but consisted merely of ceremonial textiles and bejewelled belts. None of the arts that reached the peak of craftsmanship during al-Nasir's reign are documented as diplomatic gifts.

Whereas al-Nasir Muhammad is usually viewed as the glamorous innovator of Mamluk visual culture, in the light of the patchy information available, it appears rather that his father al-Mansur Qalawun introduced the new pattern of diplomatic gifts characterised by less diversity and more ceremoniousness. The new concept was focused on Mamluk-specific ceremonial outfits of robes, belts and lavishly equipped horses. These objects, which were inscribed and adorned with blazons, reflected Qalawunid pride in military insignia and regalia,[11] as it continued to be demonstrated by al-Ashraf Khalil and al-Nasir Muhammad. The development of a Qalawunid official style of gift-giving anticipates the development of the visual arts during the reign of al-Nasir, when a homogeneous 'official style' had taken shape, featuring large inscriptions of princely titles alongside blazons as major iconographic and aesthetic elements.

The reigns of Sultan al-Zahir Barquq and his Circassian successors introduced their own ceremonial vision in the second half of the Mamluk period. The chronicles do not explicitly report a premeditated and clearly defined scheme of reform aimed at repudiating the existing rules established by their predecessors, but rather, as things moved on, new choices were made by individual sultans, reflecting their respective vision of representation. Unlike in the fourteenth century, when a dynastic continuity had a cumulative effect that created a 'Qalawunid' visual culture, the reforms of the fifteenth century appear more individual and less programmatic. It was during this period that the ceremonial saddle acquired an iconic significance.

By the end of the Mamluk period, costume, insignia of royalty and ceremonial choreography had evolved and along with them the culture and aesthetics of diplomatic gift-giving. While maintaining the basic pattern of diplomatic gift packages established by their predecessors in the fourteenth century, taste changed and details were modified. This evolution is mirrored in the history of Mamluk art.

The reign of Sultan Jaqmaq in the mid-fifteenth century seems to stand out in this evolution. As in other aspects of his rule and self-representation, which still need to be thoroughly investigated, this unconventional ruler seems to have adopted an individual attitude in the selection of his gifts. The Qur'an manuscript attributed to 'Uthman for Murad II and the cock-shaped crystal ewer for the Ethiopian monarch are unusual.

It is interesting to note that books are rarely mentioned as Mamluk gifts throughout the entire period of the sultanate, although scholarship belonged to the main objectives of princely patronage. Books would have been addressed of course only to Muslim counterparts. Although the Mamluks were keen to host foreign scholars on a large scale in their religious institutions, thus exerting their influence on the intellectual and religious life of the Muslim world, this aspect of their policy was not involved in their selection of diplomatic gifts.

The gifts exchanged within the Mamluk aristocracy along with the diplomatic gifts they offered reveal a dimension of aesthetic affinities that has been so far overlooked. There is also discrepancy between the modern definition of Mamluk art, as it is discussed in scholarship and displayed in museums, and what Mamluk society valued most among the artefacts it produced. From the perspective of the chroniclers, architecture and ceremonial spectacles with all the material culture they involved, were, beside the art of the book, the major artistic expressions of their time. The chronicles also show that in the Mamluk households of the high dignitaries and wealthy urban bourgeoisie there was a *tuhaf* culture, which cherished imported valuable things from all over the world, reflecting the taste of a society that owed its prosperity to the international spice trade.

The Iconography of Mamluk Gifts

The aim to please the recipient through diplomatic gifts did not preclude the involvement of self-representation in the selection process. Just as their parades and processions displaying glorious uniforms and horse trappings enhanced the glamour of the Mamluks in their cities, diplomatic gifts were a vehicle of self-representation abroad. This is expressed implicitly through traditional and exotic gifts that reveal the far-reaching access of the sultans to objects that others could not as easily acquire, and explicitly through gifts that mirrored the Mamluk identity as a military aristocracy of cavalrymen.

Epigraphic textiles of Dar al-Tiraz, armour, horses with their trappings and human gifts projected in the Muslim world the image of the Mamluks as they showed themselves in the elaborate ceremonial spectacles they staged for their subjects and foreign visitors. These gifts portrayed the Mamluks in their glorious outfits in the same way as an image would. Ceremonial robes, armour and horse trappings, notably saddles, were the most prominent gifts bestowed by a Mamluk sultan on his dignitaries. They symbolised status within the Mamluk establishment as well as vis-à-vis foreign courts and vassals.

Among the few illustrated manuscripts of the Mamluk period were the treatises of *furusiyya*, or equestrian and military exercise, a subject to which the Mamluks made substantial contributions.[12] Although the significance of this literature was mainly to document equestrian and martial skills, some illustrations in *furusiyya* manuals show horses of different colours, as they were praised in Mamluk poetry and diplomatic letters, wearing diverse, elaborate and colourful caparisons. Horsemanship with its tournaments, parades and paraphernalia was the theatre of Mamluk performance. It should be recalled that only Mamluks – that is, members of the ruling military aristocracy – were officially entitled to ride horses. When in the later period civil servants began to ride horses as well, they provoked anger in Mamluk circles and a sense of degeneration among historians, in particular Ibn Taghribirdi, who was himself the son of an emir. The chroniclers leave no doubt that the greatest spectacle, the most beautiful and artful thing that people had the opportunity to admire in Cairo, against Cairo's splendid architectural background, were Mamluks in their lavish outfits riding their horses with ceremonial trappings in solemn processions and parades. Chroniclers of that time reveal very little about what we describe as Mamluk arts and crafts, but they loved to dwell on descriptions of ceremonials and their material culture. For them this was Mamluk art.

For religious reasons the Mamluk court did not demonstrate much affinity with the patronage of illustrated manuscripts that might have been used as gifts to convey a pictorial self-image. However, the emblematic objects they sent depicted a glorious 'picture' of themselves as soldiers. This parallel does not equate the saddle and the gown with a painting, but rather it points to the element of self-representation in diplomatic gift exchange. Certainly, gifts of textiles were ubiquitous long before the Mamluks, but the consistent combination of epigraphic gowns of the Dar al-Tiraz with arms, armour and saddles, and sometimes *mamluks*, conveyed a Mamluk identity. Arms and armour would remind the recipients, and in particular the rivals and adversaries among them, of Mamluk military exploits, while the ceremonial saddle would symbolise their aristocracy of horsemen. These objects would bear Mamluk blazons, which in the medieval Muslim world were a feature exclusive to Mamluk visual culture. The blazon was an emblem of Mamluk identity and symbol of prestige through merit. When Renaissance Venetian artists depicted scenes showing the Mamluk court, they emphasised the presence of blazons in multiple places.

As is often documented in various sources, the appearance of the Mamluk embassies in foreign capitals contributed to disseminating a glamorous image of the sultanate. When the envoy Taghribirdi went to Venice in 1506, he attended the various social events to which he was invited accompanied by a retinue in military formation and gala attire.[13] This spectacle conveyed an ephemeral picture of the Mamluk court to the doge in Venice.

The late Mamluk period corresponded to an age of increasing visual documentation in the world around the sultanate. The fact that Timurid painters accompanied their embassies to document their travel experience with illustrations indicates the curiosity for visual documentation at the courts of that time.[14] It had been common since the fifteenth century that European rulers would send painted portraits of themselves as equivalents to their presence, or as a way of introducing themselves.[15] This practice was emulated by Mehmed the Conqueror and other Ottoman sultans. European embassies in the late fifteenth and early sixteenth centuries are likely to have included artists or draftsmen among their group to complement oral and written accounts with pictorial documentation. The bishop of Mainz Bernhard von Breydenbach, on his visit to Egypt and the Holy Land in 1483, was accompanied by Erhard Reuwich of Utrecht, who illustrated his account with woodcuts, which were repeatedly copied by later artists.[16] Although the portraits of Qaytbay and al-Ghawri made by Giovio in the sixteenth century, now in the Uffici in Florence, are not sufficiently documented, it cannot be totally excluded that, rather than being based only on verbal descriptions, they may have been copied from originals made during the rule of these sultans with their acquiescence, or perhaps ordered for their exclusive use. Giovio commented briefly on his portrait of Qaytbay that it was based on the portrait seen (or perhaps found?) in Cairo by the Ottoman sultan Selim during his conquest of Egypt. The Mamluks may have been aware of pictorial significance in the visual culture around them and interacted with it.

The combination of Mamluk-specific and emblematic objects with the more conventional gifts that had been exchanged worldwide since ancient times created a complex and balanced picture. Combined with the objects of Mamluk identity, the traditional gifts of animals, spices and *tuhaf* bestowed a historical aura, a pedigree, to the Mamluk martial image, placing the sultans in the legacy of the ancient kings and ideals of the 'Mirror for Princes' literature, to enhance their status in the eyes of the world.

CONCLUSION

As has been demonstrated in the first part of this book, the modalities of diplomatic gift exchange in the period between the thirteenth and the sixteenth centuries belonged predominantly to a shared universal culture that went back almost to the beginning of history. The patterns behind the composition of gift packages, as shown in the second part of this volume, also depended on specific geo-political and economic factors and the resources available regionally – for example, the exotic animals, spices and porcelain from Asia acquired and offered by the Mamluks, the turquoise they received from the Timurids, and the fur and falcons offered by European and Ottoman monarchs.

The third part of this book shows the tension between the traditional and universal features of diplomatic gifts, such as animals and textiles, and princely self-representation. The kind of self-representation involved here was less a personal or individual image of the monarch than an image of royalty defined by the traditional virtues associated with the kings of the past and described in the 'Mirror for Princes' literature. The personal portrayal of a royal patron is rather a phenomenon that emerged in Renaissance diplomacy, where paintings and royal portraits were offered as diplomatic gifts, inspiring the Ottomans and later Muslim rulers to use similar media. In the earlier age Byzantine, Abbasid and Fatimid courts, the quantity, lavishness and impressive character of the gifts weighed more than straightforward references to the person of the gift-giver. The diversity and exoticism of a gift package would have conveyed the image of a universal ruler, which was essential at that time. In the age of the Mamluks, the proportions of the gifts packages were no longer the same as they had been under their predecessors and changes also occurred during their period.

Recycled, imported and exotic gifts further indicate that cultural self-representation was not predominant in the selection of medieval gifts. To represent themselves personally the monarchs used instead explicit formulation in written and probably also oral diplomatic messages. The size of the embassy, the status of the ambassador and the diplomatic paraphernalia would have expressed the more specific identity of the gift-giver.

However, scrutiny of diplomatic gifts within a specific political framework, as has been undertaken here with the Mamluk Sultanate, shows that the shared culture of diplomatic gifts did not prevent the Mamluks from articulating and emphasising their political identity by adding their own cachet to traditional gift items, and it may be assumed that this was the case at other courts as well.

NOTES

Introduction

1 Marcel Mauss, *Le Don* (Paris, 1925).

2 The forthcoming *European History Yearbook* 17 (2016) is dedicated to this subject. Harriet Rudolph/Gregor Metzig (eds), *Lost in Translation? Material Culture Studies and the History of Diplomacy.*

3 Forthcoming publication of this conference: Frédéric Bauden and Malika Dekkiche (eds), *Mamluk Cairo, a Crossroad for Embassies: Studies on Mamluk Diplomacy and Diplomatics,* (Brill, 'Islamic History and Civilization') Leiden/Boston, 2017.

4 See the articles by al-Waqqad on general Mamluk gift practice and Wansbrough on Mamluk diplomacy with Europe, which also refers to gifts. Curatola and Spallanzani provide archive material on gifts exchanged with Italy. Kanat and Muhanna focus on Mamluk–Ottoman gift exchanges and Muslu dedicates a chapter in her book on Ottoman–Mamluk diplomacy to this subject, using archival sources. A paper presented by Vallet at the conference *Mamluk Cairo: Crossroad of Embassies* deals with the significance of Rasulid gifts to the Mamluks. Broadbridge in her book *Kingship* refers to the significance of gifts as a medium of diplomacy in Mongol–Mamluk relations. Cutler's studies on gift exchange between Byzantium and the Orient in late Antiquity and the early medieval period are also relevant to Mamluk diplomatic gift practice, notably for comparison. The exhibition catalogue *Gifts of the Sultans*, ed. by Komaroff deals with various types of gifts but includes no reference to the Mamluk case.

5 See previous note.

Chapter 1

1 Not including Chinese cities.
2 Labib, *Handelsgeschichte*, pp. 70–121, 327–36, 390–401.
3 Ibid., p. 93.
4 Maqrīzī, *Sulūk*, I, p. 282.
5 Ibn Shaddād, *Tārīkh al-Malik al-Ẓāhir*; Ṣayrafī, *Inbā'*, p. 363.
6 Maqrīzī, *Sulūk*, I, p. 586.
7 Maqrīzī, *Sulūk*, II, p. 533.
8 Labib, *Handelsgeschichte*, pp. 105–7.
9 Lane-Poole, pp. 269–72.
10 Coulon, 'Western Trade'.
11 See Meloy, 'Imperial Strategy'.
12 Labib, *Handelsgeschichte*, p. 399–401.
13 Ibid., p. 90; Khazrajī, I, pp. 185, 235.
14 Labib, *Handelsgeschichte*, pp. 93–4, 397–9.
15 Ṣayrafī, *Inbā'*, p. 362.

Chapter 2

1 Queller, pp. 191–6.
2 See, for example, on this practice at the court of Aragon, Péquignot, pp. 285–7, 292.
3 Queller, pp. 202–4.
4 Maqrīzī, *Sulūk*, II, pp. 892–3.
5 Ibn al-Furāt, I, p. 222.
6 Pagani, pp. 181–2.
7 Drocourt, pp. 89–92; Queller, p. 175; Nizāmulmulk, pp. 299–300.
8 Mattingly, pp. 30–4.
9 Ciseri, pp. 29–30.
10 Wansbrough, 'A Mamluk Ambassador', p. 515.
11 Ibid., p. 516.
12 Maqrīzī, *Sulūk*, IV, p. 1208.
13 Holt, *Diplomacy*, pp. 131–3; Ibn ʿAbd al-Ẓāhir, *Tashrīf*, p. 117.
14 Ibn Taghrībirdī, *Ḥawādith*, p. 118.
15 Musabbiḥī, p. 42.
16 ʿAynī, *ʿIqd*, IV, p. 132; Ibn Iyās, IV, pp. 231, 319, 383–4.
17 Broadbridge, pp. 56, 101.

18 Ibn Iyās, IV, pp. 124, 384.
19 Ibid., IV, pp. 268–9.
20 Pagani, p. 186.
21 Behrens-Abouseif, 'Sultan al-Ghawri', pp. 74–5.
22 Qalqashandī, IV, p. 22.
23 Ibid., IV, pp. 58–9.
24 Casanova, p. 699, n. 2.
25 Maqrīzī, *Sulūk*, IV, p. 346.
26 Ibid., IV, p. 366.
27 Maqrīzī, *Khiṭaṭ*, IV, p. 702.
28 Schefer, p. LXXIX, n. 2.
29 Labib, *Handelsgeschichte*, pp. 79, 85.
30 Ṣayrafī, *Nuzha*, IV, pp. 306–8; Ibn Taghrībirdī, *Nujūm*, XV, pp. 364–6; Sakhāwī, *Tibr*, pp. 96–8; Ibn Iyās, IV, pp. 385–6.
31 Ibn Taghrībirdī, *Ḥawādith*, pp. 336, 339, 345–8, 571–3; passim, *Nujūm*, XVI, pp. 132–4, 143, 147–8, 150–1.
32 See F. Forcellini's detailed account in *Strane peripazie d'un bastardo di Casa Aragona* and Nino Cortese's short version of this account. I thank Benjamin Arbel for these references.
33 Maqrīzī, *Sulūk*, IV, p. 738.
34 See the contributions of Rosenthal *et al.* to the 'Hiba' in the *Encyclopaedia of Islam*, 2nd edn, vol. 3.
35 Mauss, *Essai*; Caillé, *Anthropologie*.
36 Häberlein and Jeggle, 'Einleitung', pp. 13–14.
37 Ibid., p. 15.
38 Maqrīzī, *Sulūk*, II, pp. 536–7.
39 Ibn Khaldūn, *Taʿrīf*, p. 370.
40 Hirschbiegel and Ewert, pp. 57–8.
41 Yazdī, for example, uses both terms regularly to describe diplomatic gifts at the Timurid court.
42 Dunlop (ed.), *Bronnen tot de geschiedenis der Oostindische Compagnie in Perzië, 1611–1638*, p. 182. In a letter to the governor-general in Batavia on 6 April 1626 Pieter van den Broecke in Surat writes that the Great Mogul has asked him that one of his servants, who is a painter, and five or six other persons, be allowed to sail on the VOC's ships to Europe to buy 'toffas' or curiosities for him. Van den Broecke declined. The glossary, p. 811, gives: *toffas*: Persian: *tuḥfa* = gift. The letter states 'toffas

ofte curieuscheyt', toffas or curiosities. I thank Timon Screech for this reference.

43 See Morony, 'Gift Giving in the Iranian Tradition'.

44 See Nizāmulmulk, Chapter 21.

45 Rudolph, p. 83.

46 Ibn al-ʿAbbās, pp. 93–6.

47 Ẓāhirī, pp. 64, 69.

48 Ibn Razīn, p. 128.

49 See pp. 100–2.

50 Wansbrough, 'A Mamluk Ambassador', p. 516, and n. 2.

51 Kaplony, p. 366; Häberlein and Jeggle, 'Einleitung', pp. 13–14. On reciprocity in early Islamic diplomacy, see Cutler, 'Significant Gifts', p. 82.

52 ʿAynī, *ʿIqd*, IV, pp. 136, 167; Dawādārī, *Kanz*, IX, pp. 56, 70; Zettersteen (ed.), p. 100.

53 Qalqashandī, V, pp. 255, 392; VII, pp. 364–6, 383–4, 392–3; VIII, p. 73.

54 Qalqashandī, VII, pp. 364–5.

55 Ibid., VII, pp. 383–4; Ibn al-Furāt, I, pp. 231–2.

56 Qalqashandī, IX, pp. 106–14.

57 Qaddūmī, p. 102.

58 Qalqashandī, II, pp. 52, 98, 118.

59 Ibn ʿAbd al-Ẓāhir, *Tashrīf*, pp. 92–3.

60 Maqrīzī, *Sulūk*, II, p. 246.

61 Ibid., II, p. 7; Ibn Iyās, I/1, p. 419; ʿAynī, *ʿIqd*, IV, pp. 377, 463.

62 The *khirqāh* from the Persian *khargāh* is a circular trellis tent. See O'Kane, p. 250.

63 Maqrīzī, *Sulūk*, II, p. 490.

64 Walker, pp. 169, 180–2; Mayer, pp. 56–64; see also Flood, pp. 76–84.

65 Yazdī, II, p. 357.

66 Maqrīzī, *Sulūk*, II, p. 336; Qalqashandī, IV, p. 464.

67 Hambley, p. 215. Some authors looking at objects alone have confused gowns and robes with the specific 'robe of honour' mentioned in texts, which has the specific meaning of bondage.

68 For Shahrukh's gifts see below, p. 74; Ibn Ḥajar, *Inbā'*, V, p. 130; Persian sources mention a crown sent with the *khilʿa.* Broadbridge, p. 195; Yazdī, II, pp. 356–7.

69 This passage of Ibn Iyās is not in Muṣṭafā's edition, but is cited by Salīm, II, pp. 239–40 and Bauden, p. 14, n. 84, referring to R.L. Devonshire, *Extraits de l'Histoire de l'Egypte*, Cairo 1933.

70 Ibn Iyās, IV, p. 218.
71 Maqrīzī, *Itti'āẓ*, II, p. 228.
72 Nuwayrī, XXXII, p. 304.
73 Ibn Iyās, IV, pp. 266, 268, 271.
74 Waqqād, p. 223; 'Umarī, *Ta'rīf*, p. 63; Qalqashandī, VIII, p. 35.
75 See Chapter 2, n. 70.
76 Broadbridge, p. 36.
77 Ibid., p. 182; Qalqashandī, VII, pp. 309–10.
78 Cf. Broadbridge, p. 88.
79 A letter from Sultan Qalāwūn to the Rasulid sultan of Yemen, mentioned below, associates diplomatic gifts with the Public Treasury.
80 Ibn Iyās, II, p. 158.
81 Maqrīzī, *Sulūk*, IV, p. 1189.
82 Ibn Iyās, IV, p. 269.
83 Waqqād, pp. 221–2; Atiya, pp. 28–30; Bauden, p. 13.
84 Cutler, 'Gifts', pp. 257–8.
85 Péquignot, pp. 280, 282.
86 Dawādārī, *Kanz*, VIII, p. 84.
87 Ibn Iyās, V, p. 12. I could not find a reference to the embassy of 712/1312.
88 Ibid., V, p. 8.
89 Broadbridge, p. 111, n. 47; Dawādārī, *Kanz*, IX, p. 315.
90 Ṣayrafī, *Inbā'*, p. 12; Ibn Taghrībirdī, *Ḥawādith*, XVI, p. 675.
91 Ibn Iyās, II, p. 113; Maqrīzī, *Sulūk*, IV, p. 741.
92 Ibn Ḥajar, *Inbā'*, VII, pp. 192, 207, 220.
93 Broadbridge, p. 55; Maqrīzī, *Sulūk*, I, p. 514; Dawādārī, *Kanz*, VIII, p. 97–8; Ibn Abī 'l-Faḍā'il, *Nahj*, pp. 112–13.
94 I am not sure about this translation of *kurr/karr* found in the dictionary of Fīrūzābādī. Blochet translates the term as horse, but the use of this term elsewhere in the context of Yemeni gifts does not confirm this meaning. Ibn Abī 'l-Faḍā'il, *Nahj*, p. 297; Dawādārī, *Kanz*, VIII, pp. 220–4.
95 Ṣayrafī, *Nuzha*, III, pp. 350–1.
96 Maqrīzī, *Sulūk*, II, p. 210.
97 See p. 97.
98 Ahwānī, p. 105.
99 See, for example, Maqrīzī, *Sulūk*, I, p. 621 and IV, p. 524; Curatola, 'Marin Sanudo', p. 175.

100 See p. 58.
101 Ibn Taghrībirdī, *Ḥawādith*, pp. 471–3.
102 Ibn Iyās, IV, p. 266.
103 Ibid., IV, p. 252.
104 See Cutler, 'Significant Gifts', p. 92 on the historical significance of gifts.
105 Gottschalk, p. 144.
106 Ibn ʿAbd al-Ẓāhir, *Rawḍ*, p. 290; Maqrīzī, *Sulūk*, I, p. 563.
107 Maqrīzī, *Sulūk*, I, p. 702. See also n. 6; Anonymous, ms. ar. 4440, fol. 65.
108 Nuwayrī, XXXIII, p. 12.
109 Muhanna, p. 191; Ṣayrafī, *Nuzha*, III, pp. 128–9.
110 Bloom, p. 98.
111 Allsen, pp. 50, 88–9.
112 Broadbridge, p. 135; Maqrīzī, *Sulūk*, II, p. 264.
113 Darrag, p. 401, n. 1; Ibn Ḥajar, *Inbā'*, VIII, p. 194.
114 Darrag, p. 401, n. 1.
115 Ibn Iyās, I/2, p. 462.
116 Muhanna, p. 192; Ṣayrafī, *Nuzha*, I, p. 366.
117 Ibn Iyās, V, p. 60.
118 Raby, 'Sérénissime', pp. 96–7, 100–1.
119 Kubersky-Piredda, pp. 152–3.

Chapter 3

1 Baybars al-Manṣūrī, *Tuḥfa*, p. 103.
2 Maqrīzī, *Sulūk*, I, p. 713; Nuwayrī, XXXI, p. 103–5; Qalqashandī, VIII, pp. 77–8; Labib, *Handelsgeschichte*, p. 84.
3 Qalqashandī, V, p. 37.
4 Vallet, 'Du système', p. 274.
5 Maqrīzī, *Sulūk*, I, pp. 563, 595, 702–3; II, p. 107; Ibn ʿAbd al-Ẓāhir, *Rawḍ*, p. 290.
6 Levathes, p. 149.
7 Ibn ʿAbd al-Ẓāhir, *Rawḍ*, p. 290; Vallet, 'Du système', pp. 282–3.
8 Ibn ʿAbd al-Ẓāhir, *Rawḍ*, p. 299.
9 Abū 'l-Fidā, IV, p. 15; Baybars al-Manṣūrī, *Zubda*, pp. 208–9; Maqrīzī, *Sulūk*, I, pp. 702–3; Ibn al-Furāt, VII, pp. 28–9.
10 Ibn al-Furāt, VIII, pp. 28–9; Maqrīzī, *Sulūk*, I, p. 729; Vallet, 'Du système', p. 285.

11 Ibn ʿAbd al-Ẓāhir, *Tashrīf*, pp. 117–18.
12 Dāwūd ibn ʿAli, I, p. 207.
13 Ibid., I, p. 80.
14 Khazrajī, I, pp. 298–9; Yamānī, pp. 335–6.
15 Vallet, '*Umara' wa-muluk*'.
16 ʿAynī, ʿ*Iqd*, III, p. 210. The editor writes the word '*hudna*' meaning truce instead of '*hadiyya*', both spelled the same except for the dots. This must be a misreading of the manuscript; the sentence only makes sense when read with '*hadiyya*'.
17 ʿAynī, ʿ*Iqd*, IV, pp. 377, 463–8; Maqrīzī, *Sulūk*, II, p. 7; Ibn Iyās, I/1, p. 419. Unlike Ibn Iyās, who dates this episode to 706/1305–06, and ʿAynī, who places it between 705/1305–06 and 707/1307, and Khazrajī, who reports the envisaged attack on Yemen and its eventual cancellation among the events of the year 1307 (I, pp. 307–8), Maqrīzī relates it among the events of 704/1304–5.
18 ʿAynī, ʿ*Iqd*, IV, pp. 463–8.
19 Qalqashandī, VII, pp. 344–52.
20 Maqrīzī's text seems to suggest that this part was delivered in cash, while the sultan's gift was in kind. This may have changed at a later stage in favour of gifts in kind only.
21 Broadbridge, pp. 101–2.
22 Qalqashandī, V, p. 35–8.
23 Maqrīzī, *Ittiʿāẓ*, p. 222.
24 According to the dictionary of Fīrūzābādī, *al-Qāmūs al-muḥīṭ*, II, p. 130.
25 Dawādārī, *Kanz*, IX, p. 217; Baybars al-Manṣūrī, *Tuḥfa*, p. 238.
26 ʿUmarī, *Taʿrīf*, p. 49; Nuwayrī, XXXIII, p. 307; Qalqashandī, VII, p. 372.
27 Vallet, 'Du système', p. 273.
28 Qalqashandī, VII, pp. 364–5.
29 A *qinṭār* was equivalent to 7,200 *dīnārs*.
30 Maqrīzī, *Sulūk*, II, pp. 892–3.
31 Ibid., II, p. 916.
32 Atıl, *Levni and the Surname*, pp. 174, 192, 194, 198, 212.
33 Ibn Iyās, I/1 pp. 572–3.
34 Ibn Iyās, I/2, p. 42.
35 Qalqashandī, VIII, pp. 74–5.
36 Khazrajī, II, pp. 167–8.
37 ʿAynī, ʿ*Iqd*, ed. Shukrī, pp. 409–10 and Ṣayrafī, *Nuzha*, I, pp. 444–5 have the most detailed accounts, which I am using here; see also

Maqrīzī, *Sulūk*, III, pp. 874–5; Ibn Taghrībirdī, *Nujūm*, XII, pp. 66–7; Ibn Iyās, I/2, p. 487.
38 Labib, *Handelsgeschichte*, pp. 334–6; Heyd, II, pp. 580–1, 639, 644–8.
39 Maqrīzī adds four other chamfrons.
40 Large *shamsī* and *ḥabl ṭarī*.
41 Heyd, II, pp. 571–4.
42 Dāwūd ibn ʿUmar, I, p. 244.
43 Ibid., I, p. 218.
44 Ibid., I, p. 254.
45 Alpin, II, p. 290.
46 Heyd, II, p. 632–3.
47 *Mūmiā*: Dāwūd ibn ʿUmar, I, p. 325; Alpin, pp. 387, 411; Heyd, II, pp. 635–6.
48 Dāwūd ibn ʿUmar, I, p. 266.
49 Ibid., I, pp. 326–7.
50 *Khūlanjān*: Dāwūd ibn ʿUmar, I, p. 148; Heyd, II, pp. 616–17.
51 Dāwūd ibn ʿUmar, I, p. 74.
52 Ibid., I, p. 278.
53 Ibid., I, p. 283; Heyd, II, pp. 624–5.
54 *Tūtiā*: Dāwūd ibn ʿUmar, I, pp. 98–9; Heyd, II, pp. 674–6.
55 *Sunbul*: Dāwūd ibn ʿUmar, I, pp. 201–2; Alpin, II, p. 382.
56 This item is not mentioned by Dāwūd ibn ʻUmar in his list of pharmaceutical drugs.
57 Dāwūd ibn ʿUmar, I, pp. 265–6.
58 Ibid., I, p. 334.
59 Ṣayrafī, *Nuzha*, II, p. 362; ʿAynī, *ʿIqd*, ed. Qarmūṭ (1985), pp. 260–1.
60 Ṣayrafī, *Nuzha*, IV, p. 174. Rosewater was a Yemeni speciality. Labib, *Handelsgeschichte*, p. 130.
61 Khazrajī, II, p. 242.
62 Vallet, 'Du système', p. 296. The appendix of this article presents abundant documentation on Mamluk–Rasulid gift exchange.
63 See Porter, 'Die Kunst der Rasuliden' and 'Enamelled Glass'.
64 See Chapter 3, n. 26.
65 Shujāʿī, p. 257.
66 Maqrīzī, *Sulūk*, IV, p. 756.
67 Ibid., IV, p. 773
68 Ṣayrafī, *Nuzha*, III, pp. 350–1; Maqrīzī, *Sulūk*, IV, p. 977.
69 Ibn Iyās, III, p. 99.

70 Ibid., IV, pp. 284, 288, 293, 325, 379; V, pp. 35, 40.
71 Clavijo, pp. 157–8.
72 Anonymous, ms. ar. 4440.
73 Dāwūd ibn ʿUmar, p. 65. Ibn Baṭṭūṭa mentions *saqunqur* as a dish eaten in Siyustan in today's Pakistan: II, p. 453.
74 Ibn Iyās, IV, p. 297.
75 Dāwūd ibn ʿUmar, I, p. 194; Damīrī, II, p. 32; Rogers, 'The Palace', pp. 274, 283 mentions skink as an ingredient of an Ottoman theriac. Dāwūd ibn ʿUmar mentions an Indian and an Egyptian species of skink.
76 Anonymous, ms. ar. 4440, fols 191–4v.
77 Sakhāwī, *Ḍaw'*, III, p. 58; Ibn Taghrībirdī, *Manhal*, IV, pp. 243; passim, *Nujūm*, XVI, pp. 320–4; passim, *Ḥawādith*, pp. 567–8. John Meloy's contribution to the conference 'Cairo: Crossroad of Embassies' discusses this episode in the context of the Red Sea connection; the publication of the papers is forthcoming.

Chapter 4

1 The Kārimīs were an association of wholesale merchants from India, Africa and Mamluk lands involved in the spice trade.
2 Mercier and Lepage, p. 36.
3 See also Werthmuller, pp. 69–70.
4 Mercier and Lepage, p. 38.
5 Ibid., p. 39.
6 Nuwayrī, XXX, pp. 211–13; Qalqashandī, VIII, pp. 119–20; Ibn ʿAbd al-Ẓāhir, *Tashrīf*, pp. 170–1.
7 Maqrīzī, *Sulūk*, II, p. 270.
8 Ibn Abī 'l-Faḍā'il, *Histoire*, II, p. 387.
9 Ibn Iyās, I/2, p. 379.
10 Ṣayrafī, *Nuzha*, IV, p. 225; Maqrizi, *Suluk*, IV, p. 1234 cf Ibn Hajar, *Inba'*, IX, pp. 142–5.
11 Ibid., IV, p. 281; ʿAynī, *ʿIqd*, ed. Qarmūṭ (1989), p. 604; Sakhāwī, *Tibr*, pp. 67–8.
12 Ibid., p. 71.
13 Ibn Iyās, III, pp. 179–80.
14 Ibid., V, pp. 10–12.
15 Labib, *Handelsgeschichte*, pp. 95–6.
16 Lane-Poole, pp. 41, 271.

17 Maqrīzī, *Itti^cāẓ*, II, p. 134.
18 Maqrīzī, *Sulūk*, II, pp. 7–8; Ibn Iyās, I/1, p. 418; see also p. 441.
19 Qalqashandī, VIII, p. 83.
20 Ibn ʿAbd al-Ẓāhir, *Tashrīf*, p. 175.
21 ʿAynī, *ʿIqd*, ed. Shukrī, p. 449.
22 Ibn Khaldūn, *Taʿrīf*, pp. 375–81; Ibn Khaldūn, *ʿIbar*, V, pp. 479–80, 501.
23 Ibn Ḥajar, *Inbāʾ*, III, p. 250.
24 Ibn Khaldūn, *ʿIbar*, VII, pp. 226–7; Baybars al-Manṣūrī, *Tuḥfa*, p. 192; Canard, pp. 43–6.
25 Maqrīzī, *Sulūk*, II, p. 15 n. 25.
26 The text is not easy to understand; my translation is conjectural.
27 Canard, pp. 47–56; Ibn Abī ʾl-Faḍāʾil, *Ägypten und Syrien*, pp. 69–70; Shujāʿī, pp. 29–30; Maqrīzī, *Sulūk*, II, pp. 447–8.
28 Ibn Khaldūn, *Taʿrīf*, p. 374; passim, *ʿIbar*, VII, pp. 264–5.
29 The lists are published in French translation by Canard, pp. 56–60.
30 See Qalqashandī, II, p. 104.
31 Probably another green stone, emerald being at that time mainly or exclusively mined in Egypt.
32 Qalqashandī, VII, pp. 392–3, 398–9.
33 Ibn Khaldūn, *ʿIbar*, V, pp. 440–1; passim, *Taʿrīf*, p. 373.
34 This was not the first Mamluk tent-mosque to be mentioned; half a century earlier al-Ẓāhir Baybars had ordered a tent-mosque to be made and pitched near his own tent. It had doors, mihrabs and even a *maqṣūra* or loggia for the sultan to pray separately. Ibn ʿAbd al-Ẓāhir, *Rawḍ*, pp. 181–2.
35 Ibn Khaldūn, *Taʿrīf*, p. 374; passim, *ʿIbar*, V, p. 441.
36 Ṣayrafī, *Nuzha*, IV, pp. 324–5; Ibn Taghrībirdī, *Ḥawādith*, p. 19; Ibn Iyās, I/2, p. 500; ʿAynī, *ʿIqd*, ed. Qarmūṭ (1989), p. 643.
37 Nuwayrī, XXXIII, p. 69; Dawādārī, *Kanz*, IX, pp. 316–17; Qalqashandī (based on al-ʿUmarī), V, pp. 287, 289, 294–6; Maqrīzī, *Sulūk*, II, p. 255.
38 This is the subject of a paper presented by Rémi Dewière at the conference 'Mamluk Cairo: Crossroad of Embassies' in Liège in September 2012, publication forthcoming.
39 Qalqashandī, VIII, pp. 7–8, 116–18.
40 Dāwūd ibn ʿUmar, I, p. 184.
41 Nuwayrī, XXXIII, pp. 308–9; Maqrīzī, *Sulūk*, II, pp. 321–2. The two versions of this episode are not identical. I have simplified the story here for the mere purpose of documenting the need for mercury.

Chapter 5

1 ʿAynī, *ʿIqd*, I, pp. 361–2; Nuwayrī, XXX, p. 88; Ibn ʿAbd al-Ẓāhir, *Rawḍ*, pp. 172–3; also Syedah Fatima Sadeque (ed. and trans.), *Baybars I of Egypt*, pp. 82–3, 322–3; Dawādārī, *Kanz*, VIII, p. 97; Ibn Abī 'l-Faḍā'il, *Nahj*, pp. 111–12; Baybars al-Manṣūrī, *Zubda*, p. 84. The most detailed accounts are by Ibn ʿAbd al-Ẓāhir and Nuwayrī. The translation of some terms included in this list is problematic. My translation diverges from Sadeque's and my list merges the items of the various accounts. I have reordered the sequence according to items.

2 Qalqashandī describes *mashāʿil* as ceremonial lanterns carried before the sultan, made of iron like cages but open at the top and lit with straw. II, p. 137.

3 Qalqashandī refers to lighting implements with iron ribs and shades of white linen. II, p. 137.

4 This item is problematic. *Manjāniqāt*, pl. of *manjanīq*, means mangonel, a war machine and a type of catapult. I could not find any other meaning for this word. Baybars al-Manṣūrī's text is the only source that associates *manjāniqāt bi aghshiyya* with *shamʿ* meaning candles or wax, which may be a corruption of the text. Sadeque translates it as painted 'bowls' for candles without explaining.

5 The *qaljūrī* or *qalajūrī* or *kalatshūrī* is a light and flexible type of European sword. ʿAbd al-ʿAzīz, *Khizāna*, p. 29; Nicolle, 'Silāḥ', p. 740. According to Qalqashandī it was a non-Arab type of sword. Qalqashandī, III, p. 473.

6 ʿAbd al-ʿAzīz, *Khizāna*, p. 37; Nicolle, 'Silāḥ', p. 740.

7 Fahīm, p. 209; ʿAbd al-ʿAzīz, *Khizāna*, p. 86. Ibn ʿAbd al-Ẓāhir mentions here the item '*julūd li'l qurūd al-b.l.q.?*', which is translated by Sadeque as 'leather of dabbled monkeys'.

8 The *khawārizmī* is a type of light saddle for archers, which the Mamluks rarely used. ʿAbd al-ʿAzīz, *Khayl*, p. 86.

9 Ibid., p. 91.

10 The porcelain is mentioned by Ibn Abī 'l-Faḍā'il, but not by Ibn ʿAbd al-Ẓāhir and Dawādārī.

11 Qalqashandī, II, p. 138.

12 See p. 28.

13 Dawādārī, *Kanz*, IX, p. 128, 280; ʿAynī, *ʿIqd*, IV, p. 346; Maqrīzī, *Sulūk*, II, p. 177; Ṣayrafī, *Nuzha*, I, p. 106.

14 Baybars al-Manṣūrī, *Zubda*, p. 228.
15 Holt, p. 314.
16 Ibn al-Furāt writes that it was addressed to Berke, which must be a mistake since Berke was dead at that time, and the Golden Horde was ruled by Töde Möngke (r. 1280–7). There are also other unclear passages that must be due to a corruption of the text. Ibn al-Furāt, VIII, p. 51.
17 The terminology used is difficult to understand.
18 Ibn Baṭṭūṭa mentions that this mosque was founded by al-Nāṣir Muḥammad. I, p. 358.
19 Dawādārī, *Kanz,* IX, pp. 280–1. There seems to be a confusion in Dawādārī's description here, which might refer to two different gift packages.
20 Nuwayrī, XXXII, pp. 254–5, 323–6; Maqrīzī, *Sulūk*, II, p. 164.
21 Maqrīzī, *Sulūk*, II, p. 177.
22 Broadbridge, pp. 133–6.
23 Ibn ʿAbd al-Ẓāhir, *Rawḍ*, p. 399; Broadbridge, p. 36.
24 See Broadbridge, Chapter 3.
25 Ibn Abī 'l-Faḍā'il, *Ägypten und Syrien*, p. 11.
26 Nuwayrī, XXXIII, p. 12; Ibn Abī 'l-Faḍā'il, *Ägypten und Syrien*, pp. 11–12.
27 Abū 'l-Fidā, IV, p. 90. A *tumān* was according to him worth 10,000 *dirhams* = *c.*5,000 *dīnārs*.
28 Ibn Abī 'l-Faḍā'il, *Ägypten und Syrien*, p. 15.
29 Maqrīzī, *Sulūk*, II, p. 210.
30 Zettersteen (ed.), p. 173.
31 Little, p. 396.
32 ʿAynī, *ʿIqd*, Topkapi Palace Museum, Sultan Ahmet III collection, TSMK.A.2911/A-17, p. 298.
33 Maqrīzī, *Sulūk*, II, p. 243.
34 Qalqashandī, II, p. 14.
35 Dawādārī, *Kanz*, IX, p. 315; Abū 'l-Fidā, IV, p. 93.
36 ʿAynī, *ʿIqd*, Dār al-Kutub, mns 8203 *jim*, microfilm no 30350, fol. 22.
37 Dawādārī, *Kanz*, IX, p. 351; Nuwayrī, XXXIII, pp. 280–1; Abū 'l-Fidā, IV, p. 100. A few years earlier, in 723/1323, Nuwayrī reported that the Mongol regent Choban had asked for the princess' hand and the sultan had replied that she was only five years old. XXXIII, p. 63.

38 Perhaps pairs.
39 Dawādārī, *Kanz*, IX, p. 361.
40 Ibid., IX, p. 372.
41 Little, pp. 398, 400.
42 Rogers, 'Mamluk–Mongol Relations'; Meinecke, 'Werkstätte', pp. 85–144; Haddon, pp. 95–114.
43 James, p. 92–5.
44 Smith, 'Djalāyir, Djalāyirid'; Maqrīzī, *Sulūk,* III, pp. 799f., 807ff.
45 Maqrīzī, *Sulūk*, III, pp. 376–7; Ṣayrafī, *Nuzha*, I, p. 377; Ibn Iyās, I/2, p. 465.
46 Ibn Iyās, I/2, p. 327.
47 Maqrīzī, *Sulūk*, III, p. 797; Ibn Ḥajar, *Inbā'*, III, pp. 206–7; Broadbridge, pp. 177–80.
48 Translation by the author of this book.
49 On this encounter, see Fischel, pp. 44–65.
50 Ibn Khaldūn, *Taʿrīf*, pp. 421–2.
51 Ibid., p. 423.
52 Ibid., p. 425.
53 Yazdī, II, p. 357.
54 Maqrīzī, *Sulūk*, III, p. 1111; Ibn Ḥajar, *Inbā'*, V, p. 130; Ibn Iyās, I/2, p. 678.
55 Clavijo, p. 156.
56 Van Ghistele writes that he saw many ostriches in Egypt and that their meat was appreciated as a fine dish. pp. 142, 147.
57 Clavijo, p. 86.
58 Yazdī, II, p. 425; Komaroff, *Gifts of the Sultans*, pp. 218–19, 288.
59 Mankalī Bughā al-Ṣalāḥī later became Inspector of the Markets of Cairo (*muḥtasib*), and chamberlain. Ibn Taghrībirdī, *Manhal*, XI, pp. 286–6.
60 Qalqashandī, II, p. 14.
61 Kauz, pp. 117, 119.
62 Ṣayrafī, *Nuzha*, III, p. 197.
63 Ibid., III, p. 300; Ibn Taghrībirdī, *Nujūm*, XV, p. 48–9; Maqrīzī, *Sulūk*, IV, p. 927; Ibn Iyās, II, p. 158.
64 Ibn Taghrībirdī, *Nujūm*, XV, pp. 73–4; Ṣayrafī, *Nuzha*, III, p. 343.
65 Broadbridge, p. 103.
66 Shujāʿī, p. 232; Vallet, *'Umara' wa-muluk*.

67 Maqrīzī, *Sulūk*, IV, p. 1209; Ṣayrafī, *Nuzha*, IV, pp. 198, 200, 203; Ibn Taghrībirdī, *Nujūm*, XV, p. 342–3. Ibn Taghrībirdī and Maqrīzī mention 100 pieces of turquoise.
68 Maqrīzī, *Sulūk*, IV, p. 1211; Ṣayrafī, *Nuzha*, IV, pp. 202–3.
69 Ṣayrafī, *Nuzha*, IV, pp. 306–8; Ibn Taghrībirdī, *Nujūm*, XV, pp. 364–6; Sakhāwī, *Tibr*, pp. 96–8; Ibn Iyās, IV, pp. 385–6.
70 Maqrīzī, *Sulūk*, III, p. 947; Ibn Taghrībirdī, *Nujūm*, XII, p. 115.
71 Anonymous, ms ar. 4440, fol. 114.
72 Ṣayrafī, *Nuzha*, III, p. 326; Ibn Taghrībirdī, *Nujūm*, XV, p. 70.
73 Ṣayrafī, *Nuzha*, III, p. 337; Ibn Iyās, II, p. 166.
74 Ibn Taghrībirdī, *Ḥawādith*, p. 103.
75 Ibid., pp. 102–3. The Mamluk gifts are only mentioned in the edition of ʿIzz al-Dīn, p. 321, not in Popper's.
76 Ibn Taghrībirdī, *Ḥawādith*, p. 137.
77 Ibn Taghrībirdī, *Ḥawādith*, p. 302.
78 Ibid., pp. 321, 473–4.
79 Sakhāwī, *Tibr*, p. 384.
80 Anonymous, ms. ar. 4440, fols. 161v.–71v.
81 Petry, *Protectors*, pp. 45–9; Ibn Taghrībirdī, *Nujūm*, XVI, p. 384; passim, *Ḥawādith*, pp. 662–3.
82 Maqrīzī, *Sulūk*, IV, p. 1069.
83 Ibn Taghrībirdī, *Ḥawādith*, p. 419.
84 Ibid., pp. 513–15.
85 Ibid., pp. 712–14; Ṣayrafī, *Inbā'*, pp. 74–5. Abū Saʿīd was captured and executed in a battle in Azerbaijan in 1468 while helping the Qara Qoyunlus against their Aq Qoyunlu rivals led by Uzun Hasan.
86 Ṣayrafī, *Inbā'*, p. 428, Ibn Iyās, III, p. 70.
87 Ibn Taghrībirdī, *Ḥawādith*, pp. 699–700; Ṣayrafī, *Inbā'*, p. 51.
88 Ṣayrafī, *Inbā'*, p. 199.
89 Ibid., p. 428.
90 Ibn Taghrībirdī, *Nujūm*, XV, p. 47.
91 Ṣayrafī, *Inbā'*, p. 12.
92 Ibn Taghrībirdī, *Ḥawādith*, p. 675.
93 Ibid., p. 225.
94 Ṣayrafī, *Inbā'*, p. 163.
95 Conermann, pp. 165–6.
96 Ibn Iyās, IV, p. 252. See above.

97 On Safavid–Mamluk relations, see Petry (based on Ibn Iyās) *Twilight*, pp. 174–8.
98 Ibn Iyās, IV, p. 123.
99 Ibid., IV, p. 191.
100 Ibid., IV, pp. 207, 219, 221–8.
101 Basil was used as a perfume.
102 Ibn Iyās interprets the disdain for narcissus and myrtle as reference to al-Ghawri's recently founded garden at the hippodrome beneath the Citadel.
103 English translation by the author of this book.
104 Ibn Iyās, IV, pp. 222–8.
105 Ibid., IV, pp. 262, 265–6.
106 The Baalbaki fabric mentioned here is unlikely to have come from Baalbak, which was part of Mamluk territory, but most likely the term refers to the type of textile for which Baalbak was famous.
107 Pagani, p. 200.
108 Ibn Iyās, IV, pp. 184, 265.
109 Ibn Ḥajar, *Inbā'*, III, p. 248.
110 Ibn Iyās, IV, p. 201.
111 Maqrīzī, *Sulūk*, III, p. 574.
112 Ibn Iyās, I/2, p. 462; Maqrīzī, *Sulūk*, III, p. 790; Kanat, p. 45.
113 Muhanna, p. 190.
114 Kanat, p. 48.
115 Piloti, pp. 109–10; Ibn Ḥajar, *Inbā'*, III, pp. 323–4.
116 Maqrīzī, *Sulūk*, III, p. 1069.
117 Fabri, pp. 419, 432–3. I thank Sami De Giosa for drawing my attention to this episode.
118 Anonymous, ms. ar. 4440, fol. 51.
119 Regarding the sets of nine, see p. 93.
120 Muhanna, p. 191; Ferīdūn, I, p. 146.
121 Ṣayrafī, *Nuzha*, II, p. 466.
122 Muhanna, p. 191; Ṣayrafī, *Nuzha*, III, pp. 128–9.
123 Muhanna, p. 191.
124 Maqrīzī, *Sulūk*, IV, p. 1189; Ṣayrafī, *Nuzha*, IV, p. 177; Ṣayrafī mentions 30 *mamluks* and a variety of furs; Maqrīzī mentions 10 *mamluks* and only sable.
125 Muhanna, p. 192; Ferīdūn, I, p. 207. I have modified here Muhanna's reading and translation of Ferīdūn's text.

126 Ferīdūn's text mentions *maljūrī*, which is a corruption of *qaljūrī*. See p. 62–3 for Baybars' gifts to Berke.
127 For *qarqal* see Qalqashandī, IV, p. 11; Muhanna, p. 204, n. 44; Mayer, pp. 37, 39–41; C. Tonghini, cat. 194, pp. 330–1 in Curatola (ed.), *Eredità*; Nicolle, *Military Equipment*, pp. 57–60.
128 Ibn Iyās mentions the term *ʿarqiyya* as a type of horse cover.
129 The text shows d.r.k.a.s., which is perhaps *durbash*, a spear or a kind of axe. Nicolle, 'Silāḥ', p. 740; passim, *Military Equipment*, pp. 57–60. Another possibility is that *dikhas* is a kind of shield. ʿAbd al-ʿAzīz, *Khizāna*, p. 60.
130 According to Ṣayrafī, *kamkha* is a type of silk fabric that used to be spread before the sultan's horse in processions. *Nuzha*, I, p. 295, II, p. 73; the material was known as camocan in Europe. Heyd, II, pp. 697–8.
131 This textile was known in Europe as nacco or nacchetto, Heyd, II, pp. 698–9. In Arabic the term also means carpet.
132 Ṣayrafī, *Nuzha*, IV, p. 179.
133 The manuscript is at the Biblioteca Nazionale Marciana in Venice (Gr. 516, fols. 2v–3r). See Redford, pp. 394–5.
134 Kanat, p. 41, n. 25; Muhanna, p. 193; ʿAynī, *ʿIqd*, ed. Qarmūṭ (1989), pp. 631–2; Ṣayrafī, *Nuzha*, IV, pp. 311–12; Sakhāwī, *Tibr*, pp. 98–9; Ibn Iyās, II, p. 247.
135 Sakhāwī, *Tibr*, p. 99.
136 Muhanna, p. 193, ʿAynī, *ʿIqd*, ed. Qarmūṭ (1989), p. 642; Ṣayrafī, *Nuzha*, IV, p. 324.
137 Ibn Taghrībirdī, *Ḥawādith*, p. 195; passim, *Nujūm*, XVI, p. 71; Muhanna, p. 193.
138 Muhanna, p. 194, Ferīdūn, I, p. 139. I have modified here Muhanna's reading and translation of Ferīdūn.
139 In the text *zadghānī* maces are mentioned. It is probably a corruption of *buzdughānī* maces, mentioned by Nicolle, 'Silāḥ', p. 739.
140 See note 131 of this chapter.
141 Muhanna, p. 194.
142 Ibn Taghrībirdī, *Ḥawādith*, pp. 257, 263.
143 This letter is published in Ibn Taghrībirdī, *Ḥawādith*, pp. 263–9, but only the version included in the Anonymous ms. ar. 4440 includes an appended list of gifts, fol. 82v.
144 Nicolle, 'Silāḥ', p. 742.

145 Ibn Iyās mentions *ʿarqiyya* as a brocaded textile for horses, apart from the caparison. I/2, p. 111, IV, pp. 417–18.
146 The word lacks diacritical marks.
147 The term *fūṭa*, normally meaning towel, was a textile of Alexandrian silk used to wrap official documents. Maqrīzī, *Sulūk*, I, p. 578, n. 1 by Ziyāda, referring to Quatremère.
148 Ibn Taghrībirdī, *Ḥawādith*, pp. 471–2.
149 Ibid., p. 473.
150 Ibn Iyās, III, p. 215.
151 Muhanna, p. 195; Ibn Ṭūlūn, I, p. 147; Ibn al-Ḥimṣī, p. 228.
152 Muhanna, p. 195; Ibn Ṭūlūn, I, p. 154.
153 Ibn Iyās, III, p. 316.
154 Ibn al-Ḥimṣī, pp. 430, 433–4.
155 Curatola, 'Appendix', pp. 370–1.
156 Ibn Iyās, IV, pp. 289, 324.
157 Ibid., IV, pp. 365–6.
158 Ibid., IV, pp. 383–4.
159 Ibid., IV, pp. 385–6.
160 Ibid., IV, pp. 462–3.
161 Ibid., V, p. 61.
162 Ibid., V, p. 65.
163 Ibid., V, p. 68.
164 *Lāzurd* literally means lapis blue, but it may refer here to the commonly imported blue-and-white porcelain. The 'transparent' ware may be white ware. Ibn Iyās, V, pp. 330–1.
165 Maqrīzī, *Sulūk*, III, p. 1069; Ibn Iyās, I/2, p. 633; Ṣayrafī, *Nuzha*, II, p. 466; III, pp. 128–9, 131–2; IV, p. 324; Muhanna, pp. 191–3.
166 Clavijo, p. 146.
167 Kanat, citing Hammer-Purgstall, p. 37, n. 9.
168 Muhanna, p. 191.

Chapter 6

1 Nuwayrī, XXX, p. 100.
2 Ibid., XXXI, p. 126.
3 Ibid., XXXI, pp. 126–7.
4 Martínez Montávez, p. 346.
5 Ibid., p. 350.

6 Ibn al-Furāt, VII, p. 246.
7 Alarcón y Santón and García de Linares (eds and trans.), p. 346. I am using the Arabic text, not the editor's translation, which is problematic. It is interesting to note that the terms used in the correspondence with Aragon to describe some gifts differ from those used in other texts.
8 It cannot be excluded that the term 'Venetian' here (*bunduqī*) might refer to a type of textile rather than a provenance.
9 One of the meanings of *ḥalaqa* (pl. *ḥalaq*), according to Lane's dictionary, is mail shirt. Another meaning is shield. ʿAbd al-ʿAzīz, *Khizāna*, p. 60.
10 It is not clear from the Arabic text whether 'ginger and 3 boxes/caskets' is meant, or '3 boxes of ginger'; the latter is more likely.
11 See p. 25.
12 Labib, *Handelsgeschichte*, pp. 353–6, 365–6, 395.
13 Ibn ʿAbd al-Ẓāhir, *Tashrīf*, p. 156.
14 Atiya, p. 17.
15 The island is located near the coast of Tripoli. Nuwayrī, XXXII, p. 19.
16 Ibid., XXXII, pp. 77–8; ʿAynī, *ʿIqd*, IV, pp. 304–8; Maqrīzī, *Sulūk*, I, pp. 950–1.
17 ʿAynī, *ʿIqd*, IV, p. 321.
18 Atiya, p. 23, n. 1.
19 ʿAynī, *ʿIqd*, IV, p. 379.
20 Atiya, pp. 28–32.
21 Ibid., p. 33. I have revised here Atiya's chronology on the grounds of the later published chronicles of ʿAyni and Nuwayrī.
22 Atiya, pp. 29–32.
23 Ibid., p. 44.
24 Ibid., pp. 44, 47, 60.
25 Alarcón y Santón and García de Linares (eds and trans.), pp. 361–2. Some of the technical terms in the Arabic text cannot be identified and may have been misread by the editors.
26 The production of Dār al-Ṭirāz is commonly described in diplomatic correspondence as '*ʿamal al-dar*', as is the case here.
27 Translated by the editors as 'belts', p. 364.
28 The word used here is *sajjāda*, usually meaning prayer rug.
29 The editor read *q.sh.y.*, which is probably a misreading of *qusiyy*, the plural of *qaws*.

30 See p. 96 and n. 6.
31 The term *zaynat al-fumm* literally means 'ornament of the mouth'.
32 *Blau clar* may not be just the colour, but a type of textile. De Capmany de Montpalau i Surís, IV, p. 75; Péquignot refers to a slightly different list, p. 279.
33 Atiya, p. 62.
34 Ibn Zamrak, p. 139. I thank Wali Akef for this information.
35 Ahwānī, p. 105.
36 Pedro Mártir, p. 82.
37 Ibid., pp. 176–82, 186, 206; Schefer, 'Introduction', pp. 44–52.
38 Pedro Mártir, pp. 142–4.
39 Labib, *Handelsgeschichte*, p. 444.
40 Ibn Iyās, I/2, pp. 35–7; Maqrīzī, *Sulūk*, III, pp. 118–19.
41 Ṣayrafī, *Nuzha*, III, p. 120.
42 Ibn Taghrībirdī, *Ḥawādith*, pp. 336, 339, 345–8, 571–3; passim, *Nujūm*, XVI, pp. 132–4, 143, 147–8, 150–1.
43 Ibn Taghrībirdī, *Nujūm*, XVI, p. 136.
44 See Chapter 2, n. 32.
45 Heyd, II, pp. 580–1.
46 Spallanzani, *Ceramiche*, p. 195.
47 Fabri, p. 430.
48 Van Ghistele, pp. 40–1.
49 Forcellini, p. 180.
50 Cortese, p. 13.
51 Ibn Taghrībirdī, *Nujūm*, XVI, p. 148; passim, *Ḥawādith*, pp. 577–8.
52 Behrens-Abouseif, 'Mamluk Artistic Relations with Latin Europe', forthcoming.
53 Spallanzani, *Ceramiche*, pp. 194–5.
54 Khushqadam was enthroned in June that year following Īnāl's death. Al-Mu'ayyad Aḥmad, the son of Īnāl, ruled for only four months in 1461.
55 Spallanzani, *Ceramiche*, p. 195.
56 Gabrieli, p. 431.
57 Spallanzani, *Ceramiche*, p. 196.
58 Probably a *kanbūsh zarkash* in Mamluk terminology.
59 Spallanzani, *Ceramiche*, p. 196; Curatola, 'Marin Sanudo', p. 174. Spallanzani dates the arrival of the gift to 1498; Curatola dates it to

April 1499. In the first case, the donor might by al-Nasir Muhammad, the son of Qāytbāy, whose reign ended in October 1498.

60 Spallanzani, *Ceramiche*, p. 196; Curatola, 'Marin Sanudo', p. 175; passim, 'Appendix', p. 370; There is also a discrepancy here between the two accounts. According to Spallanzani this gift was dedicated to the Venetian governor of Cyprus, whereas Curatola writes only that it was handed to the Venetian ambassador during his visit to Cairo.

61 Curatola, 'Appendix', p. 370.

62 F. Lane, *Venice*, pp. 289–94; Turner, 'Spices'.

63 Ibn Iyās, IV, pp. 257, 259.

64 Pagani, pp. 186–7, 191.

65 Howard, p. 84.

66 Curatola, 'Marin Sanudo', p. 175.

67 Ṣayrafī, *Inbā'*, p. 436.

68 Tafur, p. 165.

69 McCray, pp. 14–19; Raby, 'Sérénissime', p. 105.

70 On export to Florence, see Spallanzani, *Vetri*, pp. 17–22.

71 Maqrīzī, *Sulūk*, II, p. 86.

72 Ibid., IV, p. 325.

73 Curatola, 'Marin Sanudo', p. 175; Raby, 'Sérénissime', p. 103.

74 Heyd, II, pp. 478–80, 487–90; Labib, *Handelsgeschichte*, pp. 361–3.

75 Heyd, II, p. 490.

76 Wansbrough, 'Venice and Florence'; Labib, *Handelsgeschichte*, p. 198.

77 '*Vasi di confectione, mirabolani e giengituo*', Fabrionus, p. 337. *Mirabolani* is the mirabelle prune. *Giengituo* is very likely to be a corruption or misspelling of '*gengiovo*', a medieval Italian term for ginger. It is *zanjabīl* in Persian and Arabic. The Mamluks received ginger jam from Yemen.

78 Spallanzani, *Ceramiche*, p. 57; Rogers, 'Gorgeous East', pp. 71–2; Landucci, pp. 52–3; Giovio, p. 199.

79 Lloyd, p. 49.

80 Ibid., p. 52.

81 Ibid., pp. 58–62.

82 Ibid., pp. 50–1.

83 Ibid., p. 50.

84 See Joost-Gaugier, 'Lorenzo the Magnificent and the Giraffe as a Symbol of Power'.

85 Cf. Ibid., p. 95.

86 Spallanzani, *Metalli*, p. 1; passim, *Ceramiche*, p. 57, n. 74; Corti, p. 255.
87 The subject of Jacques Cœur is copiously documented. However, information about his Mamluk connections, although they played a major role in his career, is rather patchy.
88 Clément, pp. xxxi, xxxvi–xxxvii.
89 Cordellier-Delanoue, pp. 60–1, 80; Clément, pp. xvi–xviii; Mollat, pp. 128–9; Heers, pp. 128–32, 155–67; Nicolle, *Military Equipment*, pp. 37–8.
90 Clément, pp. 140–1.
91 The very rare term *mabouguet* is used here. Its definition as a variety of a mixture of fine musks is given in the *Dictionnaire du Moyen Français* (available at www.atil.fr.dmf).
92 Ibn Iyās, IV, p. 255; Thenaud, p. 43.

Chapter 7

1 See Qaddūmī's edition.
2 Gift exchange of this period has been copiously documented by Cutler in numerous publications.
3 Qaddūmī, pp. 471–80; Kaplony, pp. 201–2.
4 Morony, p. 36.
5 Qaddūmī, p. 63.
6 *Einhard: The Life of Charlemagne*, trans. Samuel Epes (New York, 1880). Online: *Medieval Sourcebook: The Life of Charlemagne*, Fordham University, The Jesuit University of New York. Available at www.fordham.edu/halsall/basis/einhard.asp. Scholz, pp. 81–3; Thorpe, p. 184–5; Herrin, p. 105; Garver, p. 240.
7 Wazzān (Leo Africanus), II, pp. 173–4; Lloyd's translation lacks some of the items mentioned in the Arabic translation I use, p. 54.
8 Barthold, pp. 283–4.
9 Ibid., p. 272.
10 Mayer, p. 63.
11 Ibn Khaldūn, *Muqaddima*, pp. 295–6.
12 Bumke, I, pp. 168–71.
13 Abū Shāma, I, p. 253.
14 Bumke, I, p. 171.
15 See pp. 56–7.
16 Jardine and Brotton, pp. 153–5; Bayreuther, 'Pferde in der Diplomatie'.

17 Bayreuther, pp. 235, 250.
18 See Chaiklin, ‘The Merchant’s Ark’.
19 Lloyd, pp. 39–40.
20 Häberlein and Jeggle, ‘Einleitung’, pp. 26–7.
21 Clarke, pp. 18–20.
22 Gschwend, pp. 8–12.
23 Nuwayrī, XXXIII, pp. 280–1.
24 Maqrīzī, *Sulūk*, III, p. 254; Ibn Ḥajar, *Inbā’*, I, p. 156; Ibn Iyās, I/2, pp. 157–8.
25 Herrin, p. 105.
26 Raby, ‘Sérénissime’, 103–4; Rogers, *Islamic Art and Design*, pp. 49, 51.
27 Maqrīzī, *Ittiʿāẓ*, II, p. 194; Qaddūmī, p. 109.
28 Ibn Muyassar, p. 44.
29 Maqrīzī, *Ittiʿāẓ*, II, p. 43.
30 Qaddūmī, p. 109.
31 An Egyptian *mann* was equivalent to 819 grams. Hinz, p. 30.
32 Maqrīzī, *Ittiʿāẓ*, II, p. 177; Qaddūmī, p. 108 gives a more detailed version of the description.
33 Qaddūmī, pp. 105–6.
34 Musabbiḥī, I, p. 22; Qaddūmī, p. 105.
35 Maqrīzī, *Ittiʿāẓ*, II, p. 132.
36 Musabbiḥī, I, pp. 22, 29.
37 Dāwūd ibn ʿUmar, I, p. 62.
38 Ibn Abī ’l-Faḍā’il, *Nahj*, XIV, p. 229.
39 Abū Shāma, I, pp. 243–4.
40 Ibn Wāṣil, I, p. 226.
41 Nuwayrī, XXIX, p. 42.
42 Cutler, ‘St Francis’, p. 47. The article includes other information on Ayyubid–Christian gift exchange.
43 Maqrīzī, *Sulūk*, I, p. 260.
44 Nuwayrī, XXIX, p. 202.

Chapter 8

1 Mansouri, p. 160.
2 Martin, pp. 102, 106.
3 Ibid., p. 103.
4 Ṣayrafī, *Nuzha*, IV, pp. 276, 279.

5 Ṣafadī, VIII, pp. 351–4.
6 ʿAynī, *ʿIqd*, II, p. 88.
7 Ibid., IV, p. 379.
8 ʿAynī, *ʿIqd*, ed. Qarmūṭ (1985), p. 246.
9 Ṣayrafī, *Nuzha*, III, p. 326; Ibn Taghrībirdī, *Nujūm*, XV, p. 70.
10 Ibn Taghrībirdī, *Nujūm*, XVI, p. 384; passim, *Ḥawādith*, VIII, p. 662–3.
11 Ibn Iyās, IV, pp. 207, 219, 221.
12 Ibid., IV, p. 262.
13 Ibid., IV, p. 462.
14 Nuwayrī, XXXII, p. 257.
15 Péquignot, pp. 282–3.
16 Heyd, II, p. 563; Alpin, pp. 429, 433, 438.
17 Alpin, pp. 383, 407–8.
18 Labib, *Handelsgeschichte*, p. 334.
19 Lloyd, pp. 75–6.
20 Ibid., p. 73.
21 Ṣayrafī, *Nuzha*, II, p. 362.
22 Spallanzani, *Ceramiche*, pp. 56–7, 194–5.
23 Ibn ʿAbd al-Ẓāhir, *Rawḍ*, p. 290.
24 Khazrajī, II, p. 195.
25 Ibn Iyās, I/1, p. 545.
26 Yamānī, pp. 231–2.
27 Spallanzani, *Ceramiche*, p. 194.
28 These large bowls are called *sulṭāniyya*. Ibn Iyās, IV, p. 407.
29 Ibn Iyās, IV, p. 151.
30 Spallanzani, *Ceramiche*, pp. 56, 67.
31 Carswell, p. 129.
32 Ibn Iyās, V, p. 307.
33 Carswell, p. 67; Atasoy and Raby, p. 96.
34 Ibn Iyās, V, p. 492.
35 Carswell, pp. 65–8, 112–13.
36 Ibn Iyās, V, pp. 182, 331.
37 Creswell, II, pp. 154–65.
38 Qaddūmī, p. 110.
39 Heyd, II, pp. 557–8.
40 Wolff, pp. 26–7.
41 Laufer, pp. 18–25. This book contains interesting information on the subject.

42 Damīrī, II, pp. 8–10.
43 See Löfgen, p. 27 and the included article by Lamm, pp. 34–8.
44 Musabbiḥī, p. 80; Maqrīzī, *Ittiʿāẓ*, II, p. 58.
45 See the translation of this poem by Qaddūmī, pp. 106–8.
46 Laufer, p. 70.
47 Martínez Montávez, pp. 346, 350.
48 ʿAynī, *ʿIqd*, I, p. 290; Ibn ʿAbd al-Ẓāhir, *Rawḍ*, pp. 88, 124–5.
49 Zettersteen (ed.), p. 220.
50 Ibn Khaldūn, *ʿIbar*, VII, p. 310.
51 Giovio, p. 200.
52 Ibn Iyās, IV, p. 187.
53 Ibid., IV, p. 284, 288, 293, 325, 379; V, pp. 35, 40.
54 Ibid., IV, pp. 388–9.
55 Ibid., IV, p. 293.
56 Maqrīzī, *Khiṭaṭ*, IV/1, pp. 146–7.
57 Ibn Iyās, IV, pp. 269, 379.
58 Ibid., I/2, pp. 648–51.
59 Tafur, pp. 78–9.
60 Fabri, pp. 409–10, 414–25.
61 Pagani, pp. 196–7.
62 Maqrīzī, *Sulūk*, I, p. 604.
63 Belon, p. 118.
64 Mackinnon, pp. 12–14.
65 Van Ghistele, p. 140; Pagani, p. 210; Belon, pp. 98b–99a, see n. 213.
66 Thenaud, p. 43.
67 Raby, 'Sérénissime', p. 101.
68 Maqrīzī, *Khiṭaṭ*, I, pp. 624–6; Qalqashandī, III, p. 283; Ibn Iyās, III, p. 149; Piloti, pp. 28–34; Tafur, pp. 77–8; Breydenbach, pp. 41–4; Fabri, pp. 387–98; Harant, pp. 86–97; Heyd, II, pp. 575–80; Labib, *Handelsgeschichte*, pp. 324–5; Wolff, pp. 199–202; Milwright.
69 Dāwūd ibn ʿUmar, p. 82; Alpin, pp. 382, 412, 432, 437, 439.
70 Pedro Mártir, p. 188.
71 Von Harff, p. 87.
72 'Balsam', in www.jewishencyclopaedia.com; Milwright, p. 197.
73 Spallanzani, *Ceramiche*, pp. 194–5; Curatola, 'Appendix', pp. 370–1.
74 Alpin, pp. 331–3, 382, 402–3, 412, 438; Dāwūd ibn ʿUmar, I, p. 82. For its botanic identification and medical use, see Milwright.

75 Ferīdūn, I, p. 207; Atiya, p. 30.
76 Harant, pp. 93–4.
77 See Leiser and Dols, 'Evliya Chelebi's Description of Medicine in Seventeenth Century Egypt'.
78 Nuwayrī, *Nihāyat al-arab*, X, pp. 133–45; Ibn Iyās also refers to the vipers as normally prepared at the hospital of Qalāwūn, III, p. 358.
79 Alpin, pp. 375–7.
80 Evliya, pp. 145–51.
81 Dāwūd ibn ʿUmar, I, pp. 92–6.
82 Evliya, p. 150.
83 Rouyer, 'Notice'.
84 Nuwayrī, XXX, p. 222.
85 Qalqashandī, VII, p. 415.
86 Ibn Iyās, I/2, p. 462.
87 A medical clay believed to be a cure against poison.
88 Raby, 'Sérénissime', p. 118, n. 89.
89 Kubersky-Piredda, p. 150.
90 See detailed account by Tsugitaka, pp. 87–107.
91 Al-ʿUmarī, pp. 11–12; Labib, *Handelsgeschichte*, pp. 312–14.
92 Ibn Abī 'l-Faḍā'il, *Nahj*, XIV, pp. 114–16.
93 Qalqashandī, II, pp. 109–10.
94 Muhanna, pp. 192–3; Ṣayrafī, *Nuzha*, IV, p. 179.
95 Ibn Iyās, IV, p. 180.
96 Ibid, V, p. 71.
97 Maqrīzī, *Sulūk*, IV, p. 1069.
98 Labib, *Handelsgeschichte*, pp. 135, 308–9.
99 On the origins of the *Ṭirāz* institution, see Stillman and Sanders, 'Ṭirāz'.
100 Cutler, 'Gifts', p. 271.
101 Stillmann, 'Khilʿa'; Hambley, 'From Baghdad'.
102 Ẓāhirī, pp. 107–8.
103 Ibn Khaldūn, *Muqaddima*, pp. 294–5; Hīla (ed.), p. 1094. The enumeration of the insignia of royalty during the reign of al-Nāṣir Muḥammad, however, as documented by Qalqashandī, based on ʿUmarī, is slightly longer. Besides the throne, the *maqṣūra*, the Ṭirāz textiles with the sultan's name and titles, the flags and banners, they also included the royal orchestra, the parasol, the leather saddle wrap, a horse neck textile, a pair of mounted parade

pages and ceremonial tents. Qalqashandī, IV, p. 7. It is not quite clear whether the shorter fifteenth-century list indicates a change of protocol or is rather due to oversight by the authors.

104 Ibn Khaldūn's words are not quite clear: *ṣuwar al-mulūk wa ashkāluhum aw ashkāl wa ṣuwar muʿayyana li-dhalika*, *Muqaddima*, p. 294.

105 Mackie, p. 128; Walker, p. 180.

106 Nuwayrī al-Sakandarī, cited by Sālim, pp. 559–60.

107 Ibn Taghrībirdī, *Nujūm*, XV, p. 38.

108 Jacoby, pp. 78–80; Piloti, p. 36.

109 Mayer, pp. 33, 56–64; Walker, p. 169; Atıl, *Renaissance*, pp. 223–5; Maqrīzī, *Khiṭaṭ*, III, p. 327.

110 Ibn Khaldūn, *Muqaddima*, p. 295.

111 Ẓāhirī, p. 41.

112 Mack, p. 56; Walker, p. 169.

113 Ibn al-Furāt, VIII, p. 51.

114 Qalqashandī, IV, p. 41.

115 Shāfiʿ ibn ʿAlī, p. 365.

116 For Shaʿbān see Ibn Iyās, II/1, p. 182.

117 Alexander, *Arts of War*, pp. 14–19.

118 ʿAynī, *ʿIqd*, III, p. 211.

119 Nuwayrī, XXXI, pp. 259–60; ʿAynī, *ʿIqd*, I, pp. 201–4.

120 Abū 'l-Fidā, IV, pp. 63, 68, 79, 87.

121 Qalqashandī, IV, p. 40; Maqrīzī, *Khiṭaṭ*, III, pp. 342–3. Maqrīzī does not mention squirrel (*sinjāb*), which was also very commonly used at that time; Ẓāhirī, p. 109.

122 Martin, pp. 11–14.

123 Ibid., p. 18.

124 Ẓāhirī, p. 88.

125 See pp. 86, 88–9.

126 Atıl, *Renaissance*, pp. 223–5.

127 Several sultans in the fifteenth century bore this title.

128 Mack, fig. 32, and p. 41; Adelson, p. 133; Sievernich and Budde (eds), pp. 172–3.

129 See examples discussed by Mack, Chapter 3.

130 Barnbach, pp. 526–31; Vickers, pp. 417–24; Mack, pp. 153–4.

131 Maqrīzī, *Ittiʿāẓ*, II, p. 15.

132 Ibid., II, p. 17; III, pp. 75, 218, 308–9, 343.

133 ʿAynī, *ʿIqd*, II, p. 33.
134 Maqrīzī, *Khiṭaṭ*, III, pp. 327, 703–4.
135 Qalqashandī, II, p. 133; Maqrīzī, *Khiṭaṭ*, III, p. 636.
136 Maqrīzī, *Khiṭaṭ*, III, pp. 325–6; Qalqashandī, II, p. 135.
137 Ibn Iyās, III, pp. 432–3.
138 Qalqashandī, IV, p. 41.
139 See Kramarowsky, 'Mongol Horse Trappings'.
140 Ibn Iyās, I, p. 503.
141 Ibid., II, p. 344.
142 Ibid., IV, p. 200.
143 Ibid., IV, p. 417; V, pp. 23, 36, 41, 75.
144 Ibid. I/1, pp. 437, 546; I/2, pp. 173, 344, 372, 459; II, p. 197; III, p. 333.
145 Ibid., III, p. 152.
146 Ibid., I, 546; I/2, p. 573, 651, 704; II, p. 472; III, pp. 16, 31, 361, 420.
147 Ibid., I/2, p. 465; III, p. 185.
148 Ibid., I/2, pp. 484–5; IV, p. 417.
149 Maqrīzī, *Khiṭaṭ*, III, pp. 329–30.
150 Anonymous, ms. ar. 4440, fol. 114v.
151 Tafur, p. 75.
152 Ahwānī, p. 101.
153 Broadbridge, p. 111, n. 47; Dawādārī, *Kanz*, IX, p. 315.
154 Mayer, p. 26.
155 *Chevaux et cavaliers*, pp. 156–9.
156 On this subject see, for example, Alexander, 'Swords' and Yücel, *al-Suyūf al-islāmiyya wa-ṣināʿātuhā*.
157 Maqrīzī, *Khiṭaṭ*, III, pp. 324–6.
158 Qalqashandī, IV, pp. 11–12; XI, p. 345.
159 Nicolle, *Military Equipment*, see Chapter 4.
160 Ibn Taghrībirdī, *Ḥawādith*, p. 474.
161 Atıl, *Renaissance*, pp. 112–13.
162 Ibn Ḥajar, *Inbā'*, VIII, pp. 336–7.
163 Meinecke, 'Heraldry and Furūsiyya', in Alexander (ed.), *Furusiyya*, pp. 152–3.
164 Mohamed, pp. 298–9.
165 Ibid., pp. 300–1.

Chapter 9

1 Ahwānī, p. 105.
2 Makariou, p. 263–70.
3 Oral communication by Dr Tania Tribe (SOAS), who showed me a tray in the name of an emir of the Mamluk sultan al-Ṣāliḥ (r. 1351–4) at the church of Ganneta Maryam. See also Mercier and Lepage, pp. 317–21 on Mamluk princely vessels from the fourteenth century and the first quarter of the fifteenth century in Ethiopian church collections.
4 See p. 170.
5 Maqrīzī, *Khiṭaṭ*, III, p. 238; passim, *Sulūk,* II, p. 592; Ṣayrafī, *Nuzha*, I, pp. 114, 135.
6 Raby, 'Court and Export', p. 35.
7 Qalqashandī, VIII, p. 122; Maqrīzī, *Sulūk*, IV, p. 178.
8 Péquignot, p. 279.
9 Van Ghistele, p. 40.
10 Maqrīzī, *Sulūk*, III, p. 870.
11 Maqrīzī, *Khiṭaṭ*, III, p. 327.
12 Atıl, *Renaissance*, pp. 262–3; R. Smith, 'Horsemanship'; al-Sarraf 'Furūsiyya Literature'.
13 Wansbrough, 'A Mamluk Ambassador', pp. 515–16.
14 Necipoğlu, pp. 29–30.
15 Cropper (ed.), 'Introduction', p. 13; Chiarini, 'Personaggi e Ritratti'.
16 Lloyd, p. 87; Raby, *Venice*, p. 66; Mack, pp. 163–4.

Bibliography

Primary Sources and Travellers' Accounts

Abū 'l-Fidā, al-Mu'ayyad ʿImad al-Dīn, *al-Mukhtaṣar fī-tārīkh al-bashar*, 4 vols (Cairo, n.d.).

Abū Shāma, Shihāb al-Dīn, *ʿUyūn al-rawḍatayn fī akhbār al-dawlatayn al-nūriyya wa 'l-ṣāliḥiyya*, ed. Aḥmad al-Baysūmī, 2 vols (Damascus, 1991).

Alpin, Prosper, *La Médecine des Egyptiens, 1581–1584*, ed. and trans. R. de Fenoyl, 2 vols (Cairo, 1980).

Anglería, Pedro Mártir de, *see* Mártir, Pedro de Anglería.

Anonymous, ms. ar. 4440, Bibliothèque Nationale de France.

al-ʿAynī, Badr al-Dīn Maḥmūd, *al-Sultān Barqūq mu'asis dawlat al-mamālīk al-sharākisa min khilāl makhṭūṭ ʿIqd al-Jumān fī tārīkh ahl-al-zamān, li-Badr al-ʿAynī*, ed. Imān ʿUmar Shukrī (Cairo, 2002).

———, *ʿIqd al-Jumān fī tārīkh ahl-al-zamān*, ed. Muḥammad Muḥ. Amīn, 4 vols (Cairo, 1987–92).

———, *ʿIqd al-Jumān fī tārīkh ahl-al-zamān (815–824)*, ed. ʿAbd al-Razzāq al-Ṭanṭāwī al-Qarmūṭ (Cairo, 1985); [824–50/1421–47] (Cairo, 1989).

Baybars al-Manṣūrī al-Dawādār, *Zubdat al-fikra fī tārīkh al-hijra*, ed. Donald S. Richards (Beirut, 1998).

———, *Kitāb al-tuḥfa 'l-mamklūkiyya fī 'l-dawla 'l-turkiyya*, ed. ʿAbd al-Ḥamīd S. Ḥamdān (Cairo, 1987).

Belon, Pierre du Mans, *Le Voyage en Egypte 1547*, annotated by Serge Sauneron (Cairo, 1969).

Breydenbach, Bernard de, *Les Saintes Pérégrinations (1483)*, ed. and trans. F. Larrivaz S.J. (Cairo, 1904).

Clavijo, Ruy Gonzalez de, *Narrative of the Embassy of Ruy Gonzalez de Clavijo to the Court of Timour at Samarcand A.D. 1403–6*, trans. Clemens R. Markham F.R.G.S. (London, 1859) (repr. Elibron Classics, 2005).

al-Damīrī, Kamāl al-Dīn Muḥammad, *Ḥayāt al-ḥayawān al-kubrā*, ed. Aḥmad Ḥ. Basaj, 2 vols (Beirut, 1994).

Dāwūd ibn ʿUmar al-Anṭākī, *Tadhkirat ūlā 'l-albāb wa 'l-jāmiʿ li 'l-ʿajab al-ʿujjāb*, 2 vols (Cairo, 1952).

al-Dawādārī, Ibn Aybak, *Kanz al-durar wa jāmiʿ al-ghurar*, vol. 9, ed. H. R. Römer (Cairo, 1960).

Evliya Çelebi, *Seyahatnamesi*, vol. 10, eds S.A. Kahraman, Y. Dagli, R. Dankoff (Istanbul, 2007).

Fabri, Félix, *Le Voyage en Egypte 1483*, trans. Gisèle Hurseaux, ed. R.P. Jacques Masson (Cairo, 1975).

Fabronius, Angelus, *Laurentii Medicis Magnifici Vita*, vol. 2, Pisa 784 (repr. Nabu Public Domain).

Ferīdūn, Aḥmed, *Münşe'āt ül-selāṭīn*, 2 vols (Istanbul, 1848).

al-Fīrūzābādī, Muḥammad ibn Yaʿqūb, *al-Qāmūs al-muḥīṭ*, 4 vols (Būlāq, 1884–5).

Giovio, Paolo, *Gli elogi vite brevemente scritte d'homini illustri di guerra, antichi et moderni, di Mons Paolo Giovi vescovo di Nocera ... tradotte per M. Domenichi, Ludovico* (Florence, 1554).

Harant, Christophe, *Le Voyage en Egypte 1598*, eds and trans. Claire and Antoine Brejnik (Cairo, 1972).

Harff, Arnold von, *Die Pilgerfahrt des Ritters Arnold von Harff* (Cologne, 1860).

al-Hīla, Muḥammad al-Ḥabīb (ed.), 'al-Nuẓum al-idāriyya bi-miṣr fī 'l-qarn al-tāsiʿ min khilāl rawḍat al-adīb wa nuzhat al-arīb li-Muḥammad ibn Ẓuhayr al-Ḥanafī', in *Abḥāth al-nadwa '-l-dawliyya li-tārīkh al-qāhira māris-abrīl 1969* (Cairo, 1971), pp. 1043–95.

Ibn al-ʿAbbās, Ibn ʿAbd Allāh, al-Ḥasan, *Āthār al-uwal fī tartīb al-duwal* (Cairo, n.d.).

Ibn ʿAbd al-Ẓāhir, *al-Rawḍ al-zāhir fī sīrat al-malik al-Ẓāhir*, ed. ʿAbd al-ʿAzīz al-Khuwayṭir (Riyadh, 1976).

———, *Tashrīf al-ayyām wa 'l-ʿuṣūr fī sīrat al-malik al-Manṣūr*, ed. Murād Kāmil (Cairo, 1961).

Ibn Abī 'l-Faḍā'il, al-Mufaḍḍal, *al-Nahj al-sadīd wa 'l-durr al-farīd fīmā baʿda tārīkh Ibn al-ʿAmīd*, ed. E. Blochet, *Histoire des Sultans Mamlouks, Patrologia Orientalis*, vols 12, 14 (1920), 20 (1985).

———, *Ägypten und Syrien zwischen 1317 und 1341 in der Chronik des Mufaḍḍal b. Abī l-Faḍā'il*, ed. Samira Kortantamer (Freiburg, 1973).

Ibn Baṭṭūṭa, *Riḥlat Ibn Baṭṭūṭa al-musammā tuḥfat al-nuẓẓār fī gharā'ib al-amṣār wa ʿajā'ib al-asfār*, 2 vols (Beirut, 1985).

Ibn al-Furāt, al-Muḥammad ibn ʿAbd al-Raḥīm, *Tārīkh Ibn al-Furāt*, vols 4 (1–2), V/1, ed. Ḥasan al-Shammāʿ (Basra, 1967, 1969, 1970); vols 7, 8, 9/1 ed. Qusṭanṭīn Zurayq (Beirut, 1942, 1939, 1936).

Ibn Ḥajar al-ʿAsqalānī, *Inbā' al-ghumr bi-abnā' al-ʿumr*, 9 vols (Beirut, 1986).
Ibn al-Ḥimṣī, *Ḥawādith al-zamān wa wafayāt al-shuyūkh wa 'l-aqrān* (Beirut, 2000).
Ibn Iyās, *Badā'iʿ al-zuhūr fī waqā'iʿ al-duhūr*, ed. M. Muṣṭafā (Wiesbaden/ Cairo, 1961–75).
Ibn Khaldūn, ʿAbd al-Raḥmān ibn Muḥammad, *al-Taʿrīf bi-Ibn Khaldūn* (Beirut, 1979).
———, *Kitāb al-ʿibar wa diwān al-mubtadā wa 'l-khabar*, 7 vols (repr. Beirut, 1867).
———, *al-Muqaddima* (Beirut, n.d.).
Ibn Muyassar, *al-Muntaqā min akhbār miṣr li-Ibn Muyassar*, ed. Ayman Fū'ād Sayyid, *Textes Arabes et Études Islamiques*, 17 (Cairo, 1981).
Ibn Razīn al-Kātib, *Ādāb al-mulūk*, ed. Jalīl al-ʿAṭiyya (Beirut, 2001).
Ibn Shaddād, *Tārīkh al-Malik al-Ẓāhir*, ed. Aḥmad Ḥuṭayṭ (Beirut, 1983).
Ibn Taghrībirdī, *al-Nujūm al-zāhira fī mulūk miṣr wa 'l-qāhira*, 16 vols (Cairo, 1963–71).
———, *Ḥawādith al-duhūr fī madā 'l-ayyām wa 'l-shuhūr*, ed. W. Popper (Berkeley, 1931); (*University of California Publications in Semitic Philology* VIII/1–3) (Berkeley, 1930–42); also ed. Muḥammad Kamāl al-Dīn ʿIzz al-Dīn (Cairo, 1990).
———, *al-Manhal al-ṣāfī wa 'l-mustawfā baʿd al-wāfī*, 12 vols (Cairo, 1956–2005).
Ibn Ṭūlūn, Muḥammad, *Mufākahat al-khillān fī ḥawādith al-zamān*, ed. Muḥammad Muṣṭafā, 2 vols (Cairo, 1962).
Ibn Wāṣil, Jamāl al-Dīn Muḥammad, *Mufarrij al-kurūb fī akhbār Banī Ayyūb*, ed. Jamāl al-Dīn al-Shayyāl, 5 vols (Cairo, 1960).
Ibn Zamrak, *Dīwān Ibn Zamrak al-Andalusī*, ed. Muhammad Tawfīq al-Nayfar (Beirut, 1997).
al-Khālidī, Abū Bakr Muḥammad, *al-Tuḥaf wa 'l-hadāyā* (Cairo, 1956).
al-Khazrajī, *al-ʿUqūd al-lu'lu'iyya fī tārīkh al-dawla al-rasūliyya*, 2 vols (Cairo, 1911).
Landucci, Luca, *Diario fiorentino dal 1450 al 1516 di Luca Landucci* (repr. from the collections of the University of California Libraries) (Florence, 1883).
Leo Africanus, *see* al-Wazzān.
al-Maqrīzī, Taqiyy al-Dīn Aḥmad, *Kitāb al-mawāʿiẓ wa 'l-Iʿtibār bi dhikr al-khiṭaṭ wa 'l-āthār*, ed. Ayman Fū'ād Sayyid, 4 vols (London, 2002–3).
———, *Kitāb al-sulūk li-maʿrifat duwal al-mulūk*, eds M. Ziyāda and S. ʿĀshshūr, 4 vols (Cairo, 1934–73).

———, *Itti'āẓ al-ḥunafā' bi akhbār al-a'imma al-fāṭimiyyīn al-khulafā'*, ed. Jamāl al-Dīn al-Shayyāl, 3 vols (Cairo, 1967–73).

Mártir, Pedro de Anglería, *Una embajada de los Reyes Católicos a Egipto según la 'Legatio Babylonica' y el 'Opus epistolarum' de Pedro Mártir de Anglería*, ed. and trans. Luis García y García (Valladolid, 1947).

al-Musabbiḥī, Muḥammad ibn 'Ubayd Allāh, *Akhbār miṣr*, eds Ayman F. Sayyid and Thierry Bianquis, *Textes Arabes et Études Islamiques* 13/1 (Cairo, 1978).

Nizāmulmulk, *Das Buch der Staatskunst Siyāsatnāma*, ed. and trans. Karl Emil Schabinger Freiherr von Schowingen (Zurich, 1987).

al-Nuwayrī al-Sakandarī, Muḥammad ibn Qāsim, *Kitāb al-Ilmām*, ed. A.S. Aṭiyya, 4 vols (Hyderabad, 1970).

al-Nuwayrī, Shihāb al-Dīn Aḥmad, *Nihāyat al-arab fī funūn al-'arab*, vol. X (Cairo, 1351/1933), vol. 30, eds Muḥ.'Abd al-Hādī Sha'īra and Muḥ. Muṣṭafā Ziyāda (Cairo, 1990); vol. 31, ed. al-Bāz al-'Arīnī (Cairo, 1992); vol. 32, ed. Fahīm Muḥ.'Ulwī Shaltūt (Cairo, 1998); vol. 33, ed. Muṣṭafā Ḥijāzī and Muḥammad Muṣṭafā Ziyāda (Cairo, 1997).

Pagani, Zaccaria, *Voyage du magnifique et très illustre chevalier et procurateur de Saint Marc Domenico Trevisan*, ed. Ch. Schefer (Paris, 1884), repr. in *Le voyage d'outre-mer Egypte, Mont Sinay, Palestine de Jean Thenaud suivi de la relation de l'ambassade de Domenico Trevisan au près du Soudan d'Egypte 1512* (Paris, 1884) (repr. Elibron Classics, 2006).

Piloti, Emmanuel, *L'Egypte au Commencement du Quinzième Siècle d'après le traité d'Emmanuel Pilot de Crète*, annotated by P-H Dopp (Cairo, 1950).

al-Qalqashandī, Abū 'l-'Abbās Aḥmad, *Ṣubḥ al-a'shā fī ṣinā'at al-inshā*, 14 vols (Cairo, 1914–28).

al-Ṣafadī, Ibn Aybak, *al-Wāfī bi'l-wafayāt*, VIII, ed. Muhammad. Y. Najm (Wiesbaden, 1982).

al-Sakhāwī, Muḥammad ibn 'Abd al-Raḥmān, *al-Ḍaw' al-lāmi' li-ahl al-qarn al-tāsi'*, 12 vols (Cairo, 1934–7).

———, *al-Tibr al-masbūk fī dhayl al-sulūk* (Cairo, 1896).

al-Ṣayrafī, al-Jawharī, 'Alī ibn Dāwūd, *Inbā' al-haṣr bi-abnā' al-'aṣr*, ed. Ḥasan al-Ḥabashī (Cairo, 1970).

———, *Nuzhat al-nufūs wa 'l-abdān fī tawārīkh al-zamān*, ed. Ḥasan al-Ḥabashī, 4 vols (Cairo, 1970–94).

Schäfer, B., *Beiträge zur mamlukischen Historiographie nach dem Tode al-Malik al-Nāṣir's* (Freiburg, 1971).

Shāfi' ibn 'Alī, *Šāfi' Ibn 'Alī's Biography of the Mamluk Sultan Qalāwūn*, ed. Paulina B. Lewicka (Warsaw, 2000).

al-Shujāʿī, Shams al-Dīn, *Tārīkh al-malik al-Nāṣir Muḥammad ibn Qalāwūn al-Ṣāliḥī*, ed. Barbara Schäfer (Wiesbaden, 1978).
Tafur, Pero, *Pero Tafur Travels & Adventures 1435–39*, ed. and trans. Malcolm Letts (London, 1926).
Thenaud, Jean, *Le voyage d'outre-mer Egypte, Mont Sinay, Palestine de Jean Thenaud*, ed. Ch. Schefer (Paris, 1884) (repr. Elibron Classics, 2006).
al-ʿUmarī, Ibn Faḍl Allāh, *Masālik al-abṣār fī mamālik al-amṣār*, ed. Ayman Fu'ād al-Sayyid (Cairo, 1985).
———, *al-Taʿrīf bi 'l-muṣṭalaḥ al-sharīf* (Cairo, 1893–4).
Van Ghistele, Joos, *Le Voyage en Egypte 1882/1483* (Cairo, 1986).
al-Wazzān, al-Ḥasan ibn Muḥammad (Leo Africanus), *Waṣf Ifriqyā*, ed. and trans. Muḥammad Ḥijjī and Muḥammad al-Akhḍar, 2 vols (Beirut, 1983).
al-Yamānī, ʿAbd al-Bāqī ibn ʿAbd al-Mājid, *Bahjat al-zaman fī tārīkh al-Yaman* (Sanaa, 1408/1988).
Yazdī, Sharaf al-Dīn ʿAlī, *Zafarnāmeh*, ed. Muḥammad ʿAbbāsī, 2 vols (Tehran, 1957).
al-Ẓāhirī, Khalīl ibn Shāhīn, *Zubdat kashf al-mamālik*, ed. Paul Ravaisse (Paris, 1893) (repr. Frankfurt, 1993).
Zettersteen, K.V. (ed.), *Beiträge zur Geschichte der Mamlukensultane in den Jahren 690 –741 der Hiğra nach arabischen Handschriften* (Leiden, 1919).

Studies

ʿAbd al-ʿAzīz, Nabīl Muḥ., *Khizānat al-silāḥ li-mu'allif majhūl. Dirāsa ʿan khazā'in al-silāḥ wa muḥtawayātihā ʿalā āṣr al-ayyubīyyīn wa 'l-mamālīk* (Cairo, 1978).
———, *al-Khayl wa riyāḍatuhā fī ʿāṣr al-salāṭīn al-mamālīk* (Cairo, 1976).
ʿAbd al-ʿAzīz, Sālim, *Tārīkh al-Iskandariyya wa haḍāratihā fī 'l-ʿaṣr al-islāmī* (Alexandria, 1982).
Adelson, C., 'Dalmatic', in Levenson (ed.), *Circa 1492.*
al-Ahwānī, ʿAbd al-ʿAzīz, 'Sifāra siyāsiyya min Gharnāṭa ilā 'l-Qāhira fī 'l-qarn at-tāsiʿ al-hijrī (sanat 844)', *Majallat Kulliyyat al-Ādāb – Jāmiʿat al-Qāhira*, 16 (1954), pp. 95–120.
Alarcón y Santón, Maximiliano and Ramón García de Linares (eds and trans.), *Los Documentos Árabes Diplomáticos del Archivo de la Corona de Aragón* (Madrid/Granada, 1940).
Alexander, David (ed.), *Furusiyya: The Horse in the Art of the Near East* (exhibition catalogue), 2 vols, 2nd edn (Riyadh, 2012).

———, 'Swords from Mamluk and Ottoman Treasuries', in Linda Komaroff (ed.), *Pearls from Water, Rubies from Stone: Studies in Islamic Art in Honor of Priscilla Soucek, Artibus Asiae*, 16/2, Part 1 (2006), pp. 13–34.

———, 'Armi de Ceremonia e Armi da Guerra', in *Islam Specchio d'Oriento: Rarità e Preciosi nelle Collezioni Statali Fiorentine* (Florence, 2002).

———, *The Arts of War: Arms and Armours of the 7th to the 19th Centuries (The Nasser D. Khalili Collection of Islamic Art)*, vol. 21 (Oxford, 1992).

Allsen, Thomas T., *Commodity and Exchange in the Mongol Empire: A Cultural History of Islamic Textiles* (Cambridge, 1997).

Amari, Michele, *I diplomi arabi del R. Archivio Fiorentino, testo originale con la traduzione letterale e illustrazioni* (Florence, 1863–7).

Arcangeli, Catarina Schmidt and Gerhard Wolf (eds), *Islamic Artefacts in the Mediterranean World: Trade, Gift Exchanges and Artistic Transfer* (Venice, 2010).

Atasoy, Nurhan and Julian Raby, *Iznik: The Pottery of Ottoman Turkey* (London, 1989).

Atıl, Esin, *Levni and the Surname: The Story of an Eighteenth-Century Ottoman Festival* (Istanbul, 1999), pp. 174, 192, 194, 198, 212.

———, *Renaissance of Islam: The Arts of the Mamluks* (Washington DC, 1981).

Atiya, Aziz Suryal, *Egypt and Aragon, Embassies and Diplomatic Correspondence between 1300 and 1330 A.D.* (Leipzig, 1938).

Barnbach, Carmen C., 'Studies of Emperor John VIII Palaiologos and his Retinue' (cat. 318A,B) in Evans (ed.), *Byzantium, Faith and Power, 1261–1557*, pp. 526–31.

Barthold, W., *Turkestan down to the Mongol Invasion*, 3rd edn (London, 1968).

Bauden, Frédéric, 'Les relations diplomatiques entres les sultans mamlouks circassiens et les autres pouvoirs de Dar al-islam', *Annales Islamologiques*, 41 (2007), pp. 1–16.

Bayreuther, Magdalena, 'Pferde in der Diplomatie der frühen Neuzeit', in Häberlein and Jeggle (eds), *Materiele Grundlagen der Diplomatie*, pp. 227–56.

Behrens-Abouseif, Doris, *Cairo of the Mamluks: A History of Architecture and its Culture* (London, 2007).

———, 'Sultan al-Ghawri and the Arts', *Mamluk Studies Review*, 6 (2002), pp. 69–75.

———, 'Mamluk Artistic Relations with Latin Europe', forthcoming.

Belozerskaya, Marina, *The Medici Giraffe* (New York/Boston/London, 2006).

Bierman, Irene, 'Art and Politics: The Impact of Fatimid Use of Ṭirāz Fabrics', PhD dissertation (Chicago, 1980).
Bloom, Jonathan, 'Fatimid Gifts', in Komaroff (ed.), *Gifts of the Sultans*, pp. 95–109.
Bosworth, C.E., *The New Islamic Dynasties: A Chronological and Genealogical Manual* (Edinburgh, 2004).
Broadbridge, Anne F., *Kingship and Ideology in the Islamic and Mongol Worlds* (Cambridge, 2008).
______, 'Diplomatic Conventions in the Mamluk Sultanate', *Annales Islamologiques*, 41 (2007), pp. 97–118.
Bumke, Joachim, *Höfische Kultur. Literatur und Gesellschaft im hohen Mittelalter*, 2 vols, 6th edn (Munich, 1992).
Caillé, A., *Anthropologie du Don* (Paris, 2007).
Canard, M., 'Les relations entre les Mérinides et les Mamelouks au XIVe siècle', *Annales de l'Institut d'Études Orientales*, 5 (1939–1941), pp. 41–81.
Capmany de Montpalau i Surís, Antoni de, *Memorias Historicas sobre la Marina, Comercio y Artes de la Antigua Ciudad de Barcelona*, 4 vols (Madrid, 1792).
Carswell, John, *Blue and White: Chinese Porcelain around the World* (London, 2000).
Casanova, Paul, *Histoire et Description de la Citadelle du Caire (Mémoires de la Mission Archéologique du Caire)* (Italy, 1894), pp. 509–617, VI/5 (1897), pp. 619–781.
Chaiklin, Martha, 'The Merchant's Ark: Live Animal Gifts in Early Modern Dutch–Japanese Relations', *World History Connected* (2012). Available at http://worldhistoryconnected.press.illinois.edu/9.1/chaiklin.html (accessed 4 January 2014).
Chevaux et cavaliers arabes dans les arts d'Orient et d'Occident (exhibition catalogue) (Paris, 2003).
Chiarini, Marco, 'Personaggi e ritratti: I Medici, l'Italia e l'Europa', in Cropper (ed.), *The Diplomacy of Art*, pp. 45–50.
Ciseri, Ilaria, 'Diplomazia dell Effimero', in Cropper (ed.), *The Diplomacy of Art*, pp. 21–43.
Clarke, T.H., *The Rhinoceros from Dürer to Stubbs 1515–1799* (London, 1986).
Clément, Pierre M., *Jacques Cœur et Charles VII* (Paris, 1853).
Conermann, Stephan, 'Ibn Aǧās (d. 881/1476) "Tā'rīkh al-Amīr Yašbak aẓ-Ẓāhirī": Biographie, Autobiographie, Tagebuch oder Chronik?', in Stephan Conermann and Anja Pistor-Hatam (eds), *Die Mamlūken:*

Studien zur ihrer Geschichte und Kultur. Zum Gedenken an Ulrich Haarmann (1842–1999) (Schenefeld, 2003), pp. 123–78.

Cordellier-Delanoue, M., *Jacques Cœur* (Tours, 1847).

Cortese, Nino, 'Don Alfonso d'Aragon ed il Conflitto tra Napoli e Venezia per la Conquista di Cipro', *Rivista Abruzzese*, 4 (1916), pp. 5–15.

Corti, Gino, 'Relazione di un viaggio al Soldano d'Egitto e in Terra Santa (1488–89)', *Archivio Storico Italiano*, 76/2 (1958), pp. 247–66.

Coulon, Daniel, 'Western Trade and Seafaring to the Levant, 13th to 15th Centuries', in *Mediterraneum: Splendour of the Medieval Mediterranean, 13th–15th Centuries* (exhibition catalogue) (Barcelona, 2004), pp. 269–303.

Creswell, K.A.C., *Early Muslim Architecture* (Oxford, 1932).

Cropper, Elizabeth (ed.), *The Diplomacy of Art: Artistic Creations and Politics in Seicento Italy. Papers from a Colloquium held at the Villa Spelman, Florence, 1998. Villa Spelman Colloquia*, vol. 7 (Milan, 2000).

Curatola, Giovanni, 'Marin Sanudo, Venezia, I Doni Diplomatici', in Arcangeli and Wolf (eds), *Islamic Artefacts in the Mediterranean World*, pp. 173–81.

———, 'Appendix', in *Venise et l'Orient 828–1797*, pp. 370–1.

——— (ed.), *Eredità dell'Islam: Arte Islamics in Italia* (exhibition catalogue) (Venice, 1993).

Cutler, Anthony, 'St Francis and the "Noble Heathen": Notes on Gift Practice in the Ayyubid Area', in Arcangeli and Wolf (eds), *Islamic Artefacts in the Mediterranean World*, pp. 45–51.

———, 'Significant Gifts: Patterns of Exchange in Late Antique, Byzantine and Early Islamic Diplomacy', *Journal of Medieval and Early Modern Studies*, 38/1 (2008), pp. 79–101.

———, 'Gifts and Gift Exchange as Aspects of the Byzantine, Arab, and Related Economics', *Dumberton Oakes Papers*, 55 (2001), pp. 247–78, 51.

Darrag, Aḥmad, *L'Egypte sous le Règne de Barsbay 825–841/1422–1438* (Damascus, 1961).

Description de l'Égypte (Etat Moderne), 2nd edn (Paris, 1822).

Dozy, R.P.A., *Dictionnaire Détaillé: Noms des Vêtements chez les Arabes* (Amsterdam, 1845).

Drocourt, Nicolas, 'L'ambassadeur maltraité', in *Les relations diplomatiques au Moyen Âge*, pp. 87–109.

Dunlop, H. (ed.), *Bronnen tot de geschiedenis der Oostindische Compagnie in Perzië, 1611–1638* [Sources for the History of the East India Company in Persia] (The Hague, 1930).

Encyclopaedia of Islam, 2nd edn (Leiden/London, 1986–2004).

Evans, Helen C. (ed.), *Byzantium, Faith and Power, 1261–1557* (exhibition catalogue) (New York/New Haven/London, 2004).

Fahīm, Maḥmūd Nadīm Aḥmad, *al-Fann al-ḥarbī li 'l-jaysh al-miṣrī fī 'l-ʿaṣr al-mamlūkī al-baḥarī* (Cairo, 1983).

Fischel, Walter J., *Ibn Khaldun in Egypt: His Public Functions and his Historical Research (1382–1406)* (Berkeley/Los Angeles, 1967).

Flood, Finbarr B., *Objects of Translation: Material Cultural and Medieval 'Hindu–Muslim' Encounter* (Princeton/Oxford, 2009).

Forcellini, F., *Strane peripazie d'un bastardo di Casa Aragona* (Naples, 1915). Originally published in *Archivio storico per le provincie napoletane*, 37 (1912), pp. 553–63; 38 (1913), pp. 87–114, 441–82; 39 (1914), pp. 172–214, 268–98, 459–94, 767–87.

Gabrieli, Francesco, 'Venezia e i Mamelucchi', in Pertusi (ed.), *Venezia e l'Oriente fra Medioeve e Rinascimento* (Florence, 1966), pp. 417–32.

Garver, Valerie L., *Women and Aristocratic Culture in the Carolingian World* (New York, 2009).

Gottschalk, Hans L., *Al-Malik al-Kamil von Egypten und seine Zeit* (Wiesbaden, 1958).

Gschwend, Annemarie Jordan, *The Story of Süleyman: Celebrity Elephants and Other Exotica in Renaissance Portugal* (Zurich, 2010).

Häberlein, Mark and Christof Jeggle (eds), *Materielle Grundlagen der Diplomatie: Schenken Sammeln und Verhandeln im Spätmittelalter und Früher Neuzeit* (Munich, 2013).

Haddon, Rosalind W., 'Mamluk Influences on Mamluk Ceramics in the Fourteenth Century', in Doris Behrens-Abouseif (ed.), *The Arts of the Mamluks in Egypt and Syria: Evolution and Impact* (*Mamluk Studies* 1) (Bonn, 2012), pp. 95–114.

Hambley, Gavin R.G., 'From Baghdad to Bukhara, from Ghazna to Delhi: The Khilʿa Ceremony in the Transmission of Kingly Pomp and Circumstance', in Stewart Gordon (ed.), *The Medieval World of Investiture* (London, 2011), pp. 193–222.

Heers, Jacques, *Jacques Cœur 1400–1456* (Paris, 2008).

Herrin, Judith, 'Constantinople, Rome and the Franks in the Seventh and Eighth Centuries', in Jonathan Shepard and Simon Franklin (eds), *Byzantine Diplomacy: Papers from the Twenty-Fourth Spring Symposium of Byzantine Studies* (Cambridge, 1990; Aldershot, 1992), pp. 91–107.

Heyd, Wilhelm, *Histoire du commerce du levant au moyen âge*, 2 vols (Leipzig, 1885–6).

Hinz, Walther, *Islamische Masse und Gewichte umgerechnet ins metrische System* (*Handbuch der Orientalistik*, Ergänzungsband I/1) (Leiden, 1955).

Hirschbiegel, Jan and Ulf Christian Ewert, 'Mehr als nur der schöne Schein: Zu einer Theorie der Funktion von Luxusgegenständen im zwischenhöfischem Gabenaustausch im späten Mittelalters', in Häberlein and Jeggle (eds), *Materielle Grundlagen der Diplomatie*, pp. 33–58.

Holt, Peter, 'An-Nasir Muhammad b. Qalawun (684–741): His Ancestry, Kindred and Affinity', in U. Vermeulen and D. De Smet (eds), *Egypt and Syria in the Fatimid, Ayyubid and Mamluk Eras, Orientalia Lovaniensia Analecta* (Leuven, 1995), pp. 313–24.

——, *Early Mamluk Diplomacy (1260–1290). Treaties of Baybars & Qalawun with Christian Rulers* (Leiden/New York/Koln, 1995).

Howard, Deborah, 'Venise et les Mamlûks', in *Venise et l'Orient 828–1797*, pp. 73–89.

Humphreys, Stephen, 'Egypt in the World System of the Later Middle Ages', in Carl F. Petry (ed.), *Cambridge History of Egypt*, vol. 1, *Islamic Egypt, 640–1517* (Cambridge, 1998), pp. 71–88.

Jacoby, David, 'Oriental Silks go West: A Declining Trade in the Later Middle Ages', in Arcangeli and Wolf (eds), *Islamic Artefacts in the Mediterranean World*, pp. 71–88.

James, David, *Qur'ans of the Mamluks* (London, 1988).

Jardine, Lisa and Jerry Brotton, *Global Interests: Renaissance Art between East and West* (London, 2000).

Joost-Gaugier, Christiane, 'Lorenzo the Magnificent and the Giraffe as a Symbol of Power', *Artibus et Historiae*, 8/16 (1987), pp. 91–9.

Kanat, Cüneyt, 'Osmanlı ve Memulûk Devletleri'nin Birbirlerine Gönderdiği Armağanlar', in *Uluslarasi Osmanlı Tarihi Sempozyumu (8–10 Nisan 1999)* (Izmir, 2000), pp. 27–34.

Kaplony, Andreas, *Konstantinopel und Damaskus: Gesandschaften und Verträge zwischen Kaisern und Kalifen 639–750* (Berlin, 1996).

Kauz, Ralph, 'Gifts between Iran, Central Asia, and China under the Ming Dynasty, 1368–1644', in Komaroff (ed.), *Gifts of the Sultans*, pp. 115–21.

Komaroff, Linda, 'The Art of Giving at the Islamic Courts', in Komaroff (ed.), *Gifts of the Sultans*, pp. 17–30.

—— (ed.), *Gifts of the Sultans: The Arts of Giving at the Islamic Courts* (Los Angeles/New Haven/London, 2011).

Kramarowsky, Mark, 'Mongol Horse Trappings in the Thirteenth and Fourteenth Centuries', in Alexander (ed.), *Furusiyya*, I, pp. 48–53.

Kubersky-Piredda, Susanne, 'Ein Hofnarr als Agent: Zum diplomatischen Geschenkwesen am Hof Philipps II', in Häberlein and Jeggle (eds), *Materielle Grundlagen der Diplomatie*, pp. 123–74.

Labib, Subhi, 'al-Iskandariyya', in *Encyclopaedia of Islam*, 2nd edn, vol. 4 (Leiden, 1978), pp. 131–7.

——, *Handelsgeschichte Ägyptens im Spätmittelalter (1171–1517)* (Wiesbaden, 1965).

Lamm, Carl Johann, 'The Miniatures: Their Origin and Style', in Löfgen (ed.), *Ambrosian Fragments of an Illuminated Manuscript Containing the Zoology of al-Ğāḥiz*.

Lane, Edward William, *An Arab-English Lexicon* (Edinburgh/London, 1863).

Lane, Frederic C., *Venice: A Maritime Republic* (Baltimore/London, 1973).

Lane-Poole, Stanley, *A History of Egypt in the Middle Ages*, 5th edn (London, 1936).

Laufer, Berthold, *The Giraffe in History and Art* (Chicago, 1928).

Leiser, Gary and Michael Dols, 'Evliya Chelebi's Description of Medicine in Seventeenth Century Egypt', *Sudhoffs Archiv*, 71 (1987), pp. 197–216.

Levathes, Louise, *When China Ruled the Seas: The Treasure Fleet of the Dragon Throne, 1405–1433* (Oxford, 1994).

Levenson, Jay A. (ed.), *Circa 1492: Art in the Age of Exploration* (exhibition catalogue) (Washington/New Haven/London, 1992).

Little, Donald P., 'Notes on Aytamiš, a Mongol Mamluk', in *Die islamische Welt zwischen Mittelalter und Neuzeit: Festschrift für Hans Robert Roemer zum 65. Geburtstag* (Beirut, 1979), pp. 387–401.

______, 'Diplomatic Missions and Gifts Exchanged by Mamluks and Ilkhans', in Linda Komaroff (ed.), *Beyond the Legacy of Genghis Khan* (Leiden/Boston, 2006).

Lloyd, Joan Barclay, *African Animals in Renaissance Literature and Art* (Oxford, 1971).

Löfgen, Oskar, *Ambrosian Fragments of an Illuminated Manuscript Containing the Zoology of al-Ğāḥiz* (Uppsala/Leipzig, 1946).

Lopez, Roberto S., *The Commercial Revolution of the Middle Ages* (Cambridge, 1996).

McCray, W. Patrick, 'Glassmaking in Renaissance Italy: The Innovation of Venetian Cristallo', *Journal of the Minerals, Metals and Materials Society*, 50/5 (1998), pp. 14–19.

Mack, Rosamond E., *Bazaar to Piazza: Islamic Trade and Italian Art, 1300–1600* (Los Angeles/London, 2002).

Mackie, Louise, 'Towards an Understanding of Mamluk Silks: National and International Considerations', *Muqarnas*, 2 (1984), pp. 127–46.

Mackinnon, Michael, 'Supplying Exotic Animals for the Roman Amphitheatre Games: Ancient Textual, Historical an Ethnographic Data', *Mouseion* III/6 (2006), pp. 1–25. Available at www.alexandriaarchive.org/bonecommons/archive/files/mackinnon---mouseion---exotic-animals_5699c70e61.pdf (accessed 4 January 2014).

Makariou, Sophie (ed.), *Islamic Art at the Musée du Louvre* (Paris, 2012).

Mansouri, M.T., *Recherches sur les relations entre Byzance et l'Egypte (259–1453) d'apres les sources arabes* (Tunis, 1992).

Martin, Janet, *Treasures of the Land of Darkness: The Fur Trade and its Significance for Medieval Russia* (Cambridge, 2004).

Martínez Montávez, Pedro, 'Relaciones de Alfonso X de Castilla con el Sultán Mameluco Baybars y sus Sucesores', *al-Andalus*, 27 (1962), pp. 343–76.

Mattingly, Garrett, *Renaissance Diplomacy* (Boston, 1988).

Mauss, Marcel, *Essai sur le don, forme et raison de l'échange dans les sociétés archaïques*. Introduction by Florence Weber (Paris, 2012).

Mayer, L.A., *Mamluk Costume* (Geneva, 1952).

Meinecke, Michael 'Die mamlukischen Fayencemosaikdekorationen: Eine Werkstätte aus Tabriz in Kairo', in *Kunst des Orients*, XI (1976–7), pp. 85–144.

———, 'Heraldry and Furūsiyya', in Alexander (ed.), *Furusiyya*, I, pp. 152–7.

Meloy, John L., 'Imperial Strategy and Political Exigency: The Red Sea Spice Trade and the Mamluk Sultanate in the Fifteenth Century', *Journal of the American Oriental Society*, 123/1(2003), pp. 1–19.

Mercier, Jacques and Claude Lepage, *Lalibela: Wonder of Ethiopia: The Monolithic Churches and their Treasures* (London, 2012).

Milwright, Marcus, 'The Balsam of Maṭariyya: An Exploration of a Medieval Panacea', *Bulletin of the School of Oriental and African Studies* (BSOAS), 2 (2003), pp. 193–209.

Mohamed, Bashir, *The Arts of the Muslim Knight: The Furusiyya Art Foundation Collection* (Milan, 2007).

Mollat, Michel, *Der königliche Kaufmann, Jacques Cœur oder der Geist des Unternehmertums*, trans. Wolfgang Kaiser (Munich, 1991).

Mordtmann, J.H. and V.L. Ménage, 'Dhu 'l Kaḍr', in *Encyclopaedia of Islam*, 2nd edn, vol. 2, pp. 239–40.

Morony, Michael, 'Gift Giving in the Iranian Tradition', in Komaroff (ed.), *Gifts of the Sultans*, pp. 33–47.

Muhanna, Elias, 'The Sultan's New Clothes: Ottoman–Mamluk Gift Exchange in the Fifteenth Century', *Muqarnas*, 27 (2010), pp. 189–208.

Muslu, Cihan Yüksel, *The Ottomans and the Mamluks: Imperial Diplomacy and Warfare in the Islamic World* (London, 2014).
Necipoğlu, Gülru, 'Serial portraits', in *The Sultan's Portrait: Picturing the House of Osman* (exhibition catalogue) (Istanbul, 2000), pp. 29–30.
Nicolle, David, *Late Mamluk Military Equipment* (Damascus, 2011).
——, 'Silāḥ', in *Encyclopaedia of Islam*, 2nd edn (supplement 11–12) (Leiden, 2004), pp. 735–46.
——, 'Armes et armures islamiques', in *Chevaux et cavaliers arabes dans les arts d'Orient et d'Occident* (exhibition catalogue) (Paris, 2003), pp. 95–9.
Nicolle, David and Angus McBride, *The Mamluks (1250–1517) (Men-at-Arms 259)* (Oxford, 1993).
O'Kane, Bernard, 'From Tents to Pavilions: Royal Mobility and Persian Palace Design', *Ars Orientalis*, 23 (1993), pp. 249–68.
Péquignot, Stéphane, *Au Nom du Roi: Pratique Diplomatique et Pouvoir Durant le Règne de Jacques II D'Aragon (1291–1327)* (Madrid, 2009).
Petry, Carl, *Twilight of Majesty: The Reigns of the Mamlūk Sultans al-Ashraf Qāytbāy and Qānṣūh al-Ghawrī in Egypt* (Seattle/London, 1993).
——, *Protectors or Praetorians? The Last Mamlūk Sultans and Egypt's Waning as a Great Power* (New York, 1994).
Porter, Venetia, 'Enamelled Glass Made for the Rasulid sultans', in Rachel Ward (ed.), *Gilded and Enamelled Glass from the Middle East* (London, 1998), pp. 91–5.
——, 'Die Kunst der Rasuliden', in Werner Daum (ed.), *Yemen 3000 Jahre Kunst und Kultur dues glücklichen Arabien* (exhibition catalogue) (Frankfurt, 1987), pp. 225–36.
al-Qaddūmī, Ghāda al-Ḥijjāwī, *Book of Gifts and Rarities: Kitāb al-hadāyā wa 'l tuḥaf* (Cambridge MA, 1996).
Queller, Donald E., *The Office of Ambassador in the Middle Ages* (Princeton, 1967).
Raby, Julian, 'La Sérénissime et la Sublime Porte: Les Arts dans l'Art Diplomatique 1600', in *Venise et L'Orient 828–1797*, pp. 91–119.
——, 'Court and Export: Part 1. Market Demands in Ottoman Carpets 1450–1550', *Oriental Carpet and Textile Studies*, 2 (1986), pp. 29–38.
—— *Venice, Dürer and the Oriental Mode* (*Hans Huth Memorial Studies* I) (London, 1982).
Redford, Scott, 'Byzantium and the Islamic World, 1261–1557', in Evans (ed.), *Byzantium, Faith and Power, 1261–1557*, pp. 389–96.
Les relations diplomatiques au Moyen Âge: Formes et enjeux. XLIe Congrès de la SHMESP (Paris, 2011).

Rogers, J.M., '"The Gorgeous East": Trade and Tribute in Islamic Empires', in Levenson (ed.), *Circa 1492*, pp. 69–81.

——, 'The Palace, Poisons and the Public: Some Lists of Drugs in Mid-16th Century Ottoman Turley', in Colin Heywood and Colin Imber (eds), *Studies in Ottoman History in Honour of Professor V.L. Ménage* (Istanbul, 1994), pp. 273–95.

——, 'To and Fro: Aspects of Mediterranean Trade and Consumption in the Fifteenth and Sixteenth Centuries', in *Villes au Levant: Hommage à André Raymond. Revue du monde musulman et de la Méditerranée*, 56 (1990–2), pp. 57–74.

——, *Islamic Art and Design* (London, 1983).

——, 'Evidence for Mamluk–Mongol Relations', in *Colloque international sur l'histoire du Caire (1969)* (Cairo, 1972), pp. 385–403.

Rosenthal, F., 'Hiba', in *Encyclopaedia of Islam*, 2nd edn, vol. 3 (Leiden, 1986), pp. 342–5.

Rouyer, P.C., 'Notice sur les médicaments usuels des Égyptiens', in *Description de l'Égypte, Recueil des observations et des recherches qui ont été faites en Égypte pendant l'expédition de l'armée française*, 2nd edn (Paris, 1822), vol. 11, pp. 436–8.

Rudolph, Harriett, 'Fürstliche Gaben? Schenkakte als Elemente der politischen Kultur im Alten Reich', in Häberlein and Jeggle (eds), *Materielle Grundlagen der Diplomatie* (Munich, 2013), pp. 79–101.

Sadeque, Syedah Fatima, *Baybars I of Egypt* (Dacca, 1956).

Sālim, ʿAbd al-ʿAzīz, *Tārīkh al-iskandariyya wa ḥaḍāratihā fī 'l-ʿaṣr al-islāmī* (Alexandria, 1982).

Salīm, Maḥmūd Rizq, *ʿAṣr salāṭīn al-mamālīk wa nitājuhu 'l-ʿilmī wa 'l-adabī*, 7 vols (Cairo, 1965).

al-Sarraf, Shihab, 'Furūsiyya Literature of the Mamlūk Period', in Alexander (ed.), *Furusiyya*, vol. 1, pp. 118–35.

Schefer, Charles, 'Introduction', in *Le Voyage D'Outre-Mer: Égypte, Mont Sinay, Palestine de Jean Thenaud suivi de la Relation de l'Ambassade de Domenico Trevisan auprès du Soudan d'Egypte 1512* (Paris, 1884) (repr. Elibron Classics, 2006).

Scholz, Bernhard Walter, *Carolingian Chronicles: Royal Frankish Annals and Nithard's Histories*, trans. Barbara Rogers (Ann Arbor, 1970).

Schulz, Warren, 'Mansā Mūsā's Gold in Mamluk Cairo: A Reappraisal of a World Civilization Anecdote', in Judith Pfeiffer and Sholeh A. Quinn (eds), *History and Historiography of Post-Mongol Central Asia and the Middle East: Studies in Honor of John A. Woods* (Wiesbaden, 2006), pp. 428–47.

Sievernich, Gereon and Hendrik Budde (eds), *Europa und der Orient 800–1900* (exhibition catalogue) (Berlin, 1989), pp. 172–3.

Smith, J.M., jr, 'Djalāyir, Djalāyirid', in *Encyclopaedia of Islam,* 2nd edn (Leiden, 1982), II, p. 402.

Smith, Rex G., *Medieval Muslim Horsemanship: A Fourteenth-Century Arabic Cavalry Manual* (London, 1978).

Spallanzani, Marco, *Vetri Islamici a Firenze Nel Primo Rinascimento* (Florence, 2012).

———, *Metalli Islamici a Firenze nel Rinasciamento* (Florence, 2010).

———, *Ceramiche Orientali a Firenze Nel Rinascimento* (Florence, 1997).

Stillman, N. A., 'Khilʿa', *Encyclopaedia of Islam,* 2nd edn, vol. 5 (Leiden, 1986), pp. 6–7.

Stillman, Yedida K. and Paula Sanders, 'Ṭirāz', *Encyclopaedia of Islam,* 2nd edn, vol. 10 (Leiden, 2000), pp. 534–8.

Thorpe, Lewis, *Einhard and Notker the Stammerer: Two Lives of Charlemagne,* 7th edn (Baltimore, 1969).

Tsugitaka, Sato, 'Sugar in the Economic Life of Mamluk Egypt', *Mamluk Studies Review,* 8/2 (2004), pp. 87–107.

Turner, Jack, 'Spices and Christians', in Jay A. Levenson (ed.), *Encompassing the Globe: Portugal and the World in the 16th & 17th Centuries* (exhibition catalogue) (Washington DC, 2007).

Vallet, Eric, 'Du système mercantile à l'ordre mamelouke: Les ambassades entre l'Egypte mamelūke et Yemen rasūlide (VII–IXe/XIIIe–XVe siècle)', in *Les relations diplomatiques au Moyen Âge. Formes et enjeux. XLIe Congrès de la SHMESP* (Paris-Sorbonne, 2011), pp. 269–301.

———, *'Umara' wa-muluk. La place des émirs dans la diplomatique mamluko–rasulide (XIIIe–XVe siècle)'*, paper presented at the conference *Mamluk Cairo: A Crossroad for Embassies,* University of Liège, 6–9 September 2012.

Venise et l'Orient 828–1797 (exhibition catalogue) (Paris, 2006).

Vickers, Michael, 'Some Preparatory Drawings for Pisanello's Medallion of John VIII Palaeologus', *Art Bulletin,* 60/3 (1978), pp. 417–24.

Walker, Bethany J., 'Rethinking Mamluk Textiles', *Mamluk Studies Review,* 4 (2000), pp. 167–215.

Wansbrough, John, 'Hiba (Mamluk Egypt)', in *Encyclopaedia of Islam,* 2nd edn, vol. 3 (Leiden, 1986), p. 346.

———, 'Venice and Florence in the Mamluk Commercial Privileges', *Bulletin of the School of Oriental and African Studies (BSOAS)*, 28 (1965), pp. 483–523.

——, 'A Mamluk Ambassador to Venice in 913/1507', *Bulletin of the School of Oriental and African Studies (BSOAS)*, 26/3 (1963), pp. 503–21.
al-Waqqād, Maḥāsin Muḥammad, 'al-Hadāyā wa 'l tuḥaf zaman salāṭīn al-mamālīk al-baḥariyya 648–784 1250–1382', *Ḥawliyyāt Kullyiat Ādāb ʿAyn Shams*, 28 (2000), pp. 185–240.
Werthmuller, Kurt J., *Coptic Identity and Ayyubid Politics in Egypt 1218–1250* (Cairo/New York, 2010).
Wolff, Anne, *How Many Miles to Babylon? Travels and Adventures to Egypt and Beyond from 1300 to 1640* (Liverpool, 2003).
Yücel, Ünsal, *al-Suyūf al-islāmiyya wa-ṣināʿātuhā*, trans. Taḥsīn ʿUmar Ṭahaoghlū (Kuwait, 1988).

INDEX

Abaqa (khan of the Golden Horde) 25, 65
Abu 'l-Hasan (Merinid sultan) 55, 56–7, 142
Abu Sa'id (Ilkhanid sultan): Arghun Shah al-Nasiri 134; diplomatic gifts 18, 29, 66–7, 68; envoys 67, 68–9; gifts from Mamluk Sultanate 174; *kiswa* of the Ka'ba 75; al-Nasir Muhammad 7; recycled gifts 32; saddles 162–3
Abu Sa'id (Timurid sultan): severed heads 135; Uzun Hasan 79
Africa 140, 141, 142
Ahmad ibn Uways (Dhul Qadir ruler) 69–70
'Ala' al-Dawla (Dhul Qadir ruler) 31, 81, 82, 89, 92, 135
Alexandria 102–3, 112, 152, 153–4, 156, 174
Alexandrian textiles: Barsbay 79; Dar al-Tiraz 151; gifts to Golden Horde 63; gifts to Jaqmaq 78; gifts to Timurids 73; importance 171; not sent as gift 108
Alfonso (illegitimate son of Ferdinand of Aragon) 16, 105, 106–7
Alfonso X of Castile 96, 141, 142
'Ali ibn Dawud, al-Mujahid (Rasulid sultan) 42
alliances: Aq Qoyunlus and Mamluk Sultanate 79; diplomatic gifts 17, 77; Mamluk Sultanate 9; Ottomans and Mamluks 9–10, 84; Safavids 82; al-Zahir Baybars 7; al-Zahir Baybars and Berke Khan 62
Alpin, Prosper 147, 148–9
ambassadors (envoys) 30, 42, 74, 92–3, 114
Anatolia 8, 9, 23, 77
animals: death 145; diplomatic gifts 63, 68–9, 77, 121, 125–7; exotic 144, 174, 181; gifts from Aq Qoyunlus 79; gifts from Aragon 100; gifts from Byzantium 128; gifts from Dhul Qadirs 81; gifts from Fatimids 129; gifts from Mamluk Sultanate 86, 136, 140–5; gifts from Morocco 55, 56; gifts from Ottomans 93; gifts from Safavids 83–4; gifts to Eastern Turkestan 123–4; gifts to Europe 96, 131; gifts to Florence 113; gifts to France 117; gifts to Golden Horde 62; gifts to Mamluk Sultanate 129–30; gifts to Ottomans 90; importance 132; Mamluk Sultanate 126; Nubian embassies 52; significance 173
Aq Qoyunlus: attacked by Jahan Shah 78; diplomatic gifts 22, 24, 25; eastern Anatolia 9;

Aq Qoyunlus *cont.*: *kiswa* of the Ka'ba 75; Mamluk Sultanate 79–80; Qara Qoyunlus 77; Qur'an 151; recycled gifts 31; severed heads 135
Aragon 6, 7, 95–102
armour: ceremonial 129; Coeur, Jacques 117; decoration 166; diplomatic gifts 163, 164, 172, 177; elephants 143; Furusiyya collection 167; al-Ghawri 91; gifts 160; horses 42; iconography 176, 178; insults 25; Jahan Shah 78; mail shirts 86, 106, 167; material culture 165; Mehmed II 88; military support 64–5; Murad II 87; Qalawun 63; Safavids 83; Uzun Hasan 80; al-Zahir Baybars 32
arms: diplomatic gifts 64–5, 178; gifts from Aq Qoyunlus 80; gifts from Naples 106; gifts from Qara Qoyunlus 78; gifts from Safavids 83; inscriptions 165; Mamluk Sultanate 164; publicity 172 *see also* axes; swords
axes 86, 88, 106, 116
Aytamish (emir) 67–8, 69
Ayyubids 127–32
Azerbaijan 12–13, 69, 78

Bahmanids 9, 46, 89–90
balsam oil: diplomatic gifts 146–50, 170; gifts from Mamluk Sultanate 99–100, 106, 136; gifts to Castile 96; gifts to France 117; gifts to Mamluk Sultanate 88; gifts to Venice 107–8; Jaqmaq 51, 87; Mahmud 47; Medici, Lorenzo di 113; al-Nasir Muhammad 54; Nur al-Din Zanji 130; Qaytbay 48; uses 148; value 172
Barquq, al-Zahir (sultan): Ahmad ibn Uways 69–70; animals 140; craftsmen 139, 154; diplomatic correspondence 43–4; diplomatic gifts 21, 25–6, 53, 59, 173–4; gift selections 175; gifts from Jalayirids 70; gifts from Timurids 71; Ibn Zamrak 100; marriage 70; Ottomans 85; Palace of Hospitality 15; Qara Muhammad 77; requested gifts 32; saddles 161; textiles 156–8
Barsbay, al-Ashraf (sultan): Aq Qoyunlus 79; conquers Cyprus 104; diplomatic correspondence 74; diplomatic gifts 24, 25, 27, 29; Florence 112; gifts from Ottomans 86; helmets 166–7; Iskandar 78; Palace of Hospitality 15; Pisanello, Antonio 160; Qur'an 151; recycled gifts 32; requested gifts 32; torture 16
Bayazid I (Ottoman sultan) 32, 84–5, 125, 134
Bayazid II (Ottoman sultan): 'Ala' al-Dawla 89; diplomatic gifts 29–30, 90–1; al-Ghawri 84; gifts 93; giraffes 142; tents 125
Baybars, al-Zahir (sultan): alliances 7; Berke Khan 28, 62, 169–70, 174; Charles of Anjou 95; court visitors 6; diplomacy 6, 95; diplomatic correspondence 50, 65; diplomatic gifts 24, 25, 64; elephants 142; giraffes 141; Hulagu Khan 61; lions 50; Mamluk Sultanate 3; medicines 149; al-Muzaffar Yusuf I 39;

Nubian embassies 52; prisoners 134; Qur'an 150; recycled gifts 32; saddles 162; Shahrukh 8
Bengal 9, 29, 46
Berke Khan (khan of the Golden Horde): diplomatic gifts 24; elephants 142; gifts from Mamluk Sultanate 174; giraffes 141; Golden Horde 32; Ilkhanids 62; Qur'an 150; saddles 162; al-Zahir Baybars 28, 169–70
birds *see* animals
Black Sea 61–5
Book of Gifts and Rarities 31, 121
Book of Victories (*Zafarname*) by Yazdi 9, 61–5, 73, 74, 142
Borno 57–9
Byzantium: Christians 6–7; craftsmen 139–40; Fatimids 128; fur 133; gifts 6; gifts to Mamluk Sultanate 129; textiles 152; al-Zahir Baybars 6, 95

camels: diplomatic gifts 53, 54, 123; gifts from Aq Qoyunlus 80; gifts from Dhul Qadirs 81; gifts from Fatimids 129; gifts from Ilkhanids 68, 69; gifts from Morocco 56; gifts from Ottomans 90; gifts from Qara Qoyunlus 78; gifts to Golden Horde 62; gifts to Timurids 73; al-Zahir Barquq 173
carpets 83, 95, 108, 124, 171
cash 47, 73, 80, 104, 136
Castile 6, 95–102
Central Asia 70–6
ceremony: Ayyubbids 127–8; ceremonial garments 158; diplomatic gifts 17; hospitality 11, 13; Ilkhanid envoys and Mamluk Sultanate 68; image 18; Mamluk envoy 113; Mamluk Sultanate 177; Ottoman embassy 88; Ottoman envoy 85; reform 162; tents 125; textiles 152, 154; Venetian embassy 110; weapons 26; al-Zahir Barquq 70
Chancellery 19, 21, 22, 24, xx
Charles VII (king of France) 116, 117
China 6, 9, 38, 126, 134
Christians 49, 50, 51, 103, 140, 147
Cilicia (Little Armenia) 5, 9, 22, 40, 80, 83, 135
Circassian Mamluks 104, 133, 157
Citadel: ambassadors 82; animals 144; celebrations 13; ceremony 83, 110; decoration 171; diplomatic gifts 81; entertainment 76; envoys 15; lodgings 67, 79, 117; magnificence 14; processions 51, 75, 143; reception 88; weapons 165
civet perfume 42, 44, 50, 108, 113, 137
civets 21, 45, 123, 144
Clavijo, Ruy Gonzalez de 12–13, 46, 73, 93, 142
clothes 32, 51–2, 55, 86, 130, 155
Coeur, Jacques 116, 136
Constantinople 6, 7, 28
contents: diplomatic gifts 44–5, 66, 88, 121–2, 123, 130; gifts from Byzantium 128; gifts from Dhul Qadirs 81; gifts from Europe 95; gifts from Ilkhanids 68; gifts from Naples 106; gifts from Timurids 74; gifts to Aragon 99–100; gifts to Cyprus 106; gifts to Fatimids 128; gifts to Florence 113; gifts to France 117; gifts to Golden Horde 62; gifts to Ilkhanids 67; gifts to Qara Qoyunlus 78; gifts to Venice 108

costs: diplomatic gifts 18, 51, 78; hospitality 11–12, 27, 76; Yemeni envoys 42–3
craftsmen 45, 64, 69, 117, 139–40, 164–5
crystal: diplomatic gifts 121; gifts from Aragon 97; gifts from Cyprus 104; gifts from Mamluk Sultanate 51, 100, 169, 175; gifts from Venice 111; saddles 160, 161; Salah al-Din 130; Trevisan, Domenico 110
culture 18, 124–5, 181, 182
Cypriot envoy 104, 106
Cyprus 8, 22, 102–7, 173

Damascus 6, 154
Damietta 153, 174
Dar al-Tiraz: Abu 'l-Fida 156; clothes 64; Damietta 128; embroidery 152, 153; epigraphic textiles 160; gifts 171–2; gowns 77; Jaqmaq 76; Mamluk court 158; physical evidence 155; poetry 155; recession 154–5; robes of honour 70; significance 64, 159; textiles 65, 99–100, 152, 176–7; workshops 154 *see also* Alexandrian textiles
Dawud ibn 'Umar al-Antaki (physician) 59, 147, 148–9
Dawud, al-Mu'ayyad (Rasulid sultan) 40
Dhul Qadirs 9, 22, 27, 31, 80–2, 90
diplomatic correspondence: Alexandrian textiles 154; Aq Qoyunlus 79; brigandine 158; Chancellery 24; diplomatic gifts 18, 21–2, 25, 42, 51, 100; Egypt and Ethiopia 50; gifts from Morocco 56–7; horses 177; Hulagu Khan 61; Inal 78; Malwa Mahmud Shah 46–8; al-Mu'ayyad Shaykh 77; al-Nasir Muhammad 40–1, 96, 99; Ottomans and Mamluk Sultanate 84–5; purpose 173; self-representation 182; Timurids and Mamluk Sultanate 70; Yemen to Egypt 43 al-Zahir Baybars 65.
displays of gifts 19–20, 56, 81
drugs: diplomatic gifts 149; gifts from Mamluk Sultanate 64, 113, 136; gifts to Mamluk Sultanate 44; gifts to Venice 27; requested gifts 48; sugar 149
Dusay, Emerich (Aragonese ambassador) 98–9

East Anatolia 5, 77, 83, 90
economic decline 104, 155
elephants: diplomatic gifts 38, 122, 126–7, 140–5; gifts from India 46; gifts from Mamluk Sultanate 87, 88, 140, 142; gifts from Salah al-Din 130; gifts from Timurids 73; gifts to Eastern Turkestan 124; gifts to Europe 96, 131; gifts to Golden Horde 62; gifts to Morocco 54; Morocco 142; Nubian embassies 52; Rasulids 39, 42; al-Zahir 141
embassies: etiquette 19; gifts 8; to Golden Horde 62; hierarchies 14–15; reception 11; Safavids 82; self-representation 182; Shahrukh 8; trade 15; Yemen 39; al-Zahir Baybars 6
emerald 149–50
emirs 30, 40, 56, 134, 162
entertainment 13, 43, 75, 143

equestrian gifts 163–8
Ethiopia: balsam oil 147; Coptic Patriarch of Alexandria 49; diplomatic gifts 27; Egypt 50; exports 50; gifts 6; giraffes 141; Mamluk artefacts 170; Mamluk Sultanate 49; Qur'an 175
eunuchs: diplomatic gifts 43, 44, 50, 123, 140; gifts from Bengal 29; gifts from Fatimids 129; gifts from India 46; gifts from Ottomans 86, 93; gifts from Yemen 38, 40, 42; gifts to Golden Horde 62; gifts to Ottomans 91; value 133–4
Europe: balsam oil 147; carpets 171; clocks 127; diplomacy 8; diplomatic gifts 18, 122; fur 133; giraffes 141; horses 125; al-Kamil, al-Malik 6; Mamluk artefacts 159; Mamluk Sultanate 95; porcelain 138; portraits 178; tents 124–5; textiles 155; theriac 148, 149; trade 7; al-Zahir Baybars 95–6
Europeans 16, 82, 107
exports: bans 136; crystal 111; Ethiopia 50; Europe 96; Florence 112; horses 172; Mamluk Sultanate 169–76; North Africa 52; sugar 149; trade 170

Fabri, Félix 106, 144, 147–8
fabrics *see* textiles
Faraj, ibn Barquq (sultan) 8, 15, 24, 71–2, 73, 86, 142
Fatimids: craftsmen 139; crystal 111; Dar al-Tiraz 152; diplomatic gifts 32, 41; elephants 143; emerald 150; gifts received 128; giraffes 141; legacy 127–32; porcelain 139; Salah al-Din 131
female slaves: 'Abd al-'Aziz al-Halabi 138; Ahmad ibn Uways 70; diplomatic gifts 50–1, 63, 64, 67, 68, 123; gifts from Dhul Qadirs 81; gifts from Fatimids 129; gifts from Ottomans 87–8, 90, 93; gifts from Salah al-Din 130; gifts from Timurids 70; gifts to Fatimids 128; gifts to Golden Horde 174; gifts to Mamluk Sultanate 139; value 133–4
Ferdinand of Aragon (king of Naples): Aragonese embassy 101; carpets 171; Cypriot succession 105; diplomatic gifts 20, 106; giraffes 142; Qaytbay 16; weapons 173
Florence: animals 126; brigandine 158; Florentine envoy 115; giraffes 142; hospitality 13; Mamluk Sultanate 112–15; porcelain 137
food: diplomatic gifts 123, 125; gifts from Venice 110; gifts to Aragon 100; gifts to France 117; gifts to Golden Horde 63; gifts to Mamluk Sultanate 108; gifts to Ottomans 93; gifts to Venice 108
foreign embassies 15, 23, 25, 51
foreign envoys: Bengal 29; *mihmandar* (emir) 14; protocol 15; Qara Qoyunlus 78; respect 30; robes of honour 74; Safavids 82; Timurids 75; torture 16; Yemenis 37
France 6, 109–10, 115–17
Friedrich II of Hohenstaufen 31–2, 125, 131, 141
fur: Cairo 157; gift selections 181; gifts from Eastern Turkestan 124;

fur *cont.*: gifts from Golden Horde 63; gifts from Ottomans 86, 91, 92, 93; gifts from Timurids 70, 74; gifts to Mamluk Sultanate 75, 111, 133; gifts to Venice 108; al-Zahir Barquq 174

gems 131, 161, 162
Genoa 6, 7, 140
geography 38
al-Ghawri (sultan): 'Ala' al-Dawla 92; Aragonese embassy 101; balsam oil 147; Bayazid II 90–1; death 93; diplomatic gifts 20, 24, 25, 27; elephants 142, 143; gifts from Dhul Qadirs 81; gifts from Ethiopia 51; gifts to Venice 108; hospitality 14; Isma'il I, Shah 82–3; jewels 47; Louis XII 117; Pope Alexander VI 102; porcelain 138; portraits 179; Portugal 109; Qur'an 151; recycled gifts 31; Red Sea 84; requested gifts 32–3; robberies 16; saddles 161; Selim I 30, 92–3; severed heads 135; sheep 145; tents 125
Ghazan (Ilkhanid sultan) 7, 66
Giovio, Paolo 113–14, 142, 179
giraffes: diplomatic gifts 140–5; gifts from Mamluk Sultanate 140–1; gifts to Europe 95–6; gifts to Florence 113–15; gifts to Golden Horde 62; gifts to Morocco 54; gifts to Naples 106; gifts to Ottomans 90; gifts to Timurids 73; Nubian embassies 52
glass: containers 99, 112, 170; craftsmen 45; crystal 111; diplomatic gifts 44; enamelled 169
gold: belts 23, 65, 156; brigandine 158; brocaded silks 115; Chinese gifts 38, 40; clothes 14, 130, 159; coins 73; crown 49; crystal 110, 111; decoration 15, 81, 152, 153, 161, 163; diplomatic gifts 19, 50–1, 75, 90, 97, 122; embroidery 52, 64, 70, 76, 102, 108; fabrics 56; gifts to Venice 112; horses 57, 79, 124, 160; jewellery 47; leather 162; mail shirts 167; Musa I 58; Nur al-Din Zanji 131; ore 123; palanquins 129; processing 59; Qur'an 54; regal barge 13; saddles 55, 68, 78, 86, 91, 106; Safavid gifts 83; Selim I 139; steel 164; swords 44, 89; textiles 16, 62, 67, 88, 174; throne 103; value 128, 146; weapons 48, 53, 165–6; wraps 170–1; Yalbugha 104
Golden Horde: Black Sea 61–5; elephants 142; envoys 13; gifts from Mamluk Sultanate 174; giraffes 141; Mamluk envoy 32; Mamluk Sultanate 62; Qur'an 150; requested gifts 32
gowns: diplomatic gifts 64, 65, 77, 123; gifts from Mamluk Sultanate 88–9; gifts from Ottomans 90, 91; gifts from Venice 110; gifts to Aragon 99–100; gifts to Cyprus 106; gifts to Ilkhanids 67, 68; gifts to Venice 108; textiles 152; *tiraz* 155

Hafsids 24, 53–4; diplomatic correspondence 21; diplomatic gifts 53, 125; envoys 12; tents 57; weapons 24
al-Hakim (Fatimid caliph) 128, 129, 141
Hamza ibn Qara Yoluq (Qara Quyunlu ruler) 79, 151

Harun al-Rashid 19, 122
Hasan, al-Nasir (sultan) 43, 125
helmets 165, 166–7
hierarchies 14–15, 155, 161
horses: Abu 'l-Fida 156; Ahmad ibn Uways 70; diplomatic gifts 52–4, 65, 77, 121, 123, 125–6; gifts from Aq Qoyunlus 79; gifts from Byzantium 128; gifts from Dhul Qadirs 81; gifts from Eastern Turkestan 124; gifts from Europe 96; gifts from Fatimids 129; gifts from Ilkhanids 68, 69; gifts from Mamluk Sultanate 79, 86, 88, 136, 140, 160; gifts from Morocco 55, 56; gifts from Ottomans 85; gifts from Timurids 74; gifts to Aragon 136; gifts to Europe 131; gifts to Florence 113; gifts to Golden Horde 62; gifts to Ilkhanids 67; gifts to Morocco 57; gifts to Ottomans 91, 93; gifts to Timurids 73, 75; publicity 172; al-Zahir Barquq 173
hospitality: al-Zahir Barquq 70; Cairo 75; cooking pots 63; costs 27, 76; diplomacy 11–16; Europeans 103–4; games 46; Ilkhanid envoys 66; Jaqmaq 57, 76; Musa I 58; pilgrims 54; rules 12; security 15; Timur 72; Venice 13
hostilities 61, 73–4, 96
Hulagu (Mongol ruler) 28, 61
human beings 134, 136, 140

Ibn Khaldun, 'Abd al-Rahman ibn Muhammad: descriptions of gifts 55–6; diplomatic gifts 18; Faraj, ibn Barquq 71–2; gifts to Morocco 57; giraffes 142; international relations 53; *Muqaddima* 124; Ottomans 84; threats to Mamluk Sultanate 82; *tiraz* 153, 154
Ibrahim Sultan (Timurid sultan) 73, 167
iconography 124, 176–9
Ilkhanids 8, 13, 61–2, 65–70, 66, 75
image: Faraj, ibn Barquq 73; gift selections 181–2; Mamluk Sultanate 18, 37, 103, 104; Qaytbay 142; Timur 74
importance: Alexandrian textiles 156, 171; animals 132; Aragon 96; diplomatic gifts 18, 28; Jeddah 8; Red Sea 9, 109; textiles 151; *tiraz* 155; Venice 107, 109; Yemen 37–8
imported goods 50, 133, 154, 155, 159
imported objects: diplomatic gifts 122, 125; gift selections 182; gifts to Golden Horde 62; giraffes 141; porcelain 138; recycled gifts 31; Yemen 38
Inal (sultan): balsam oil 146; gifts from Mamluk Sultanate 87, 88; hospitality 16; James 104; Qara Qoyunlus 78; suit of armour 167
India: Bahmanids 89; bamboo 40; Bengal 9, 29, 46; civet perfume 137; Delhi 9, 42; diplomatic gifts 32, 44, 90; elephants 42, 142, 143; embassies 6, 29, 46–8; exotic animals 140, 144; exotica 129, 131; gifts from Mamluk Sultanate 94; Gulparga 9, 46; Indian Ocean 38, 84, 101, 109, 122; indigo 45; jewels 99; Malwa 46, 149;

India *cont.*: rhinoceros 126; silks 147; tents 43; textiles 86; trade 8, 9, 41; weapons 124
inscriptions 165, 168
Iran 7, 9, 21, 69, 70–6, 134
Iraq 69, 77, 78, 84
Isabel of Castile 20, 101
Iskandar 77–8, 135
Isma'il I (Safavid shah) 25, 31, 82, 135
Isma'il, al-Ashraf (sultan) 43–4
ivory: Ethiopian exports 50; gifts from Merinids 55, 56; gifts from Yemen 42; Medici, Lorenzo di 115; Nubian tributes 52; palanquins 129; Qur'an 62

Jahan Shah (Qara Qoyunlu ruler) 78, 135
Jalayirids 65–70
James II of Aragon 96–7, 98, 99, 136, 173
James (illegitimate son of John II of Cyprus) 16, 104–5, 107
Janibak (emir) 47, 48
Jaqmaq (sultan): brigandine 158; carpets 171; Coeur, Jacques 116, 136; diplomatic gifts 24, 30, 165, 169; elephants 142; Ethiopia 51; foreign envoys 16; Foscari, Doge Francesco 107; France 116; gift selections 175; gifts from Morocco 57; gifts from Ottomans 86, 87; gifts from Qara Qoyunlus 78; gifts to France 117; *kiswa* of the Ka'ba 75, 76; marriage 45; Nasrid embassy 100; porcelain 138; Qur'an 150; requested gifts 32; saddles 162; Shahrukh 8
Jawhar al-Qunuqba'i al-Lala (emir) 50, 134
Jengiz Khan 61, 62, 66, 70, 77
jewellery 51, 63, 127, 131, 136, 150
jewels: diplomatic gifts 121; gifts from Aragon 97, 99; gifts from Fatimids 128, 129; gifts from Ilkhanids 68; gifts from Morocco 55–6; gifts to Ilkhanids 67; al-Nasir Muhammad 56, 67; Qur'an 54; saddles 161, 163
John VIII Palaiologos (Byzantine emperor) 160

Khalil, al-Ashraf: assassination 156; diplomacy 7; diplomatic gifts 40; gifts from Aragon 97; hierarchies 156; military insignia 175; military uniforms 155; peace treaty 96–7; saddles 161
Khayrbak (governor of Egypt) 93, 139
khi'la 23, 24, 152 *see also* robes of honour
Khushqadam (sultan) 30, 46–7, 79, 80–1, 107–8
kiswa of the Ka'ba: Abu Sa'id (Ilkhanid) 75; Mecca 74; Shahrukh 8, 16, 76; textiles 54; Uzun Hasan 80
Knight's outfit 160–3

leather: diplomatic gifts 52, 53, 77; gifts from Eastern Turkestan 124; gifts from Mamluk Sultanate 86; gifts from Morocco 55–6; gifts to Fatimids 128–9; gifts to Golden Horde 62; gifts to Ottomans 91; saddles 162
legitimacy 3–4, 8, 9, 18, 41, 84
Levant 6, 7
Little Armenia *see* Cilicia

lodgings 14–15, 52, 55, 67
Louis XII (king of France) 117

Maghrib 6, 52–7, 102, 169
Mahmud Shah (ruler of Malwa) 46–8, 149
Mahmud (sultan of Ghazna) 123–4, 129
maintenance gifts 42–3, 55, 74, 145
Mali 57–9
al-Malik al-Kamil (Ayyubid sultan) 6, 31–2, 49, 125, 131, 141
Mamluk artefacts 159, 170
mamluks: 'Abd al-'Aziz al-Halabi 138; diplomatic gifts 63, 64, 67, 134, 139–40; gifts from Aq Qoyunlus 79, 80; gifts from Dhul Qadirs 81; gifts from Ottomans 90, 91, 92; gifts from Qara Qoyunlus 78; gifts from Timurids 70–1; hospitality 13; Mamluk Sultanate 6–7; Ottoman embassy 88; prisoners 85, 87; status 4; value 133; al-Zahir Barquq 173
Mansa Musa *see* Musa, Mansa
mantle for a statue of the Virgin 158–9
Manuel I (king of Portugal) 126
Mártir, Pedro 14, 20, 101–2, 146
material culture 19, 163
material value 27, 36
Mauss, Marcel: *Anthropologie* 185n35
Maussian gifts 17
Mecca: balsam oil 147; Mamluk Sultanate 5; Ottomans 84; pilgrimage 8, 54; robberies 46–7; Shahrukh 74; Yemen 38
Medici family 12, 138
Medici, Francesco di 33, 149
Medici, Lorenzo di: balsam oil 113; elephants 142; giraffes 142; Ibn Mahfuz al-Maghribi (Mamluk envoy) 113; power 115; Qaytbay 13, 113; sheep 145; tents 125
medicines 137, 146, 148, 149, 150 *see also* drugs
Medina 5, 38, 74, 84
Mehmed II (Ottoman sultan): carpets 171; diplomatic gifts 24, 165; elephants 142; gifts from Mamluk Sultanate 87; Ottoman envoy 88; prisoners 134; raids Anatolia 89
merchants: attacks 109; Christians 102; Coeur, Jacques 116; Egypt 43, 58; embassies 15, 98; Ethiopia 49; Florence 115; France 117; gifts 170; prisoners 103; safety 99; taxation 47; trade 38, 138, 150; Venice 85, 154; Yemen 41, 45
Merinids: diplomacy 55; diplomatic gifts 53, 54, 56, 123; elephants 142; embassies 57; prisoners 134; tents 125
Mesopotamia 9, 77
metalworkers 164–5
Michael Palaiologos VIII (Byzantine emperor) 28
mihmandar (emir) 14, 55, 157
military gifts 163–8
military uniforms 155, 156, 164
'Mirror for Princes' literature: diplomatic gifts 181; gifts from Mamluk Sultanate 179; Mamluk diplomacy 19; royal gifts 18
monetary value of diplomatic gifts 26–31
Möngke (khan of the Golden Horde) 63
Mongols 7, 27, 63, 69
Morocco 54, 55, 142
mosques 15, 69, 192n34

Muhammad, al-Nasir (sultan): Alfonso IV of Aragon 100; Arghun Shah al-Nasiri 134; attacked by Ghazan 66; Byzantium 7; Castile 96; crystal 111; death 75; diplomacy 7; diplomatic correspondence 56–7, 99; diplomatic gifts 21, 23, 25, 27, 39, 54–5; emerald 150; gifts 6, 174; gifts to Aragon 136; gifts to Ilkhanids 67–8; giraffes 142; horses 172; hospitality 13; Indian gifts 46; James II of Aragon 97, 98, 173; jewels 56; Khan Toqta 64–5; marriage 65; marriage requests 68; military insignia 175; military uniforms 155, 156; Musa I 58; prisoners 134; requested gifts 32; rock crystal 169; saddles 161; severed heads 135; tents 125; Yemen 40–1, 42
al-Mu'izz ibn Badis (Zirid ruler of Qayrawan) 128, 141
mules: Florence 115; gifts from Armenia 22; gifts from Byzantium 128; gifts from Dhul Qadirs 27, 81; gifts from Merinids 55, 56; gifts from Seville 96; gifts from Tlemcen 53; gifts from Yemen 43; gifts to Eastern Turkestan 124; poetry 21
Murad II (Ottoman sultan): abdication gifts 88, 89; elephants 142; gifts from Ottomans 86, 87; prisoners 134; Qur'an 150; recycled gifts 32; requested gifts 32
Musa, Mansa (king of Mali) 57–8
Muslim courts 136, 139, 141
al-Nasir, Muhammad (Rasulid sultan) *see* Muhammad, al-Nasir
Nasrids 100, 162, 169
North Africa 52, 53, 123, 172
Nubia 5, 6, 22, 52, 141
Nur al-Din Zanji (ruler of Syria) 125, 130–1

offence: diplomatic gifts 24, 25, 74–5, 82–3; gifts from Europe 96; Mártir, Pedro 101; Ottoman envoy 89
Ottoman envoy 14, 85, 89, 90, 91, 143
Ottomans: battle of Varna 87; carpets 171; diplomatic gifts 169; exotic animals 145; fur 133; Mamluk Sultanate 8, 9–10, 82, 84–94; overthrows Mamluk Sultanate 10; Qur'an 150; recycled gifts 32; requested gifts 33; severed heads 134; textiles 31; theriac 148–9
Özbek (khan of the Golden Horde) 32, 135

Pagani, Z. 14, 84, 110
painters 178–9
parades: giraffes 73, 141; glamour 176; horses 177; musicians 73; spectacles 13; tents 57
patterns of gift giving 121, 135, 174, 175, 181
perfume: diplomatic gifts 19, 121; gifts from Ethiopia 50; gifts from Fatimids 129; gifts from Yemen 44; gifts to Eastern Turkestan 124; gifts to Florence 113; gifts to Venice 107, 108; gifts to Yemen 42; publicity 172; spices 137; value 137
Philip II (king of Spain) 33, 149
Philippe Le Beau (king of France) 25

Pierre of Lusignan (king of Cyprus) 102–3, 153
pilgrimage: Cairo 54; commerce 5; diplomacy 8; elephants 143; Ethiopia 49; Europe 95; from Europe 97; Matariyya 146; Morocco 55; Musa I 57–8
Piloti (Venetian merchant) 85, 154
piracy 7, 96, 109
Pisanello, Antonio 159–60
poetry: Dar al-Tiraz 155; diplomatic gifts 71, 82–3; elephants 144; giraffes 141, 142; horses 177; Mamluk envoy 113; tents 125
porcelain: 'Abd al-'Aziz al-Halabi 138; diplomatic gifts 42, 43, 44, 45, 77, 122; gift selections 181; gifts from Mamluk Sultanate 136, 137–9; gifts from Salah al-Din 130; gifts from Yemen 38, 40; gifts to Cyprus 106; gifts to Florence 113; gifts to France 117; gifts to Golden Horde 63, 174; gifts to Ottomans 91, 93; gifts to Venice 107, 108; publicity 172; sugar 138; suitability as a gift 39
Portugal 9, 109, 126, 138
power 3, 6, 8, 18, 115
prestige: Coeur, Jacques 116; donors 31, 64; Mamluk Sultanate 3, 5, 6; Ottomans 84; saddles 160
prisoners: diplomatic gifts 85, 87; exchanges 134; Mamluk court 107; ransoms 95; release 97–8, 99–100, 116
processions: elephants 143; exotic animals 141; al-Ghawri 161; horses 21, 177; self-representation 176; textiles 198n130
protocol 11, 15, 19, 30, 99, 155
Ptolemy II Philadelphus 141
Ptolemy's Geography 87
Public Treasury 26, 39, 41, 131, 152
Pyramids 13–14, 101

Qalawun, al-Mansur (sultan): al-Ashraf Khalil 7; Constantinople 6; craftsmen 139; death 40; diplomatic gifts 39, 53, 64, 96; embassies 63; gifts from Europe 96; gifts to Golden Horde 174; military insignia 175; Rudolph of Hapsburg 95; saddles 160; textiles 153; *tiraz* 155
Qalawunids 4, 155
Qara Qoyunlus 9, 77–8, 135
Qara Yoluq 'Uthman (Qara Qoyunlu ruler) 24, 25, 77, 80, 135
Qaramanid state 9, 22
Qaytbay (sultan): armour 166; Cypriot connections 107; Cypriot succession 105; diplomatic correspondence 46–8; diplomatic gifts 29–30, 90, 106, 173; elephants 142; Ferdinand of Aragon 16; Florence 13; gifts 111; gifts from Ethiopia 51; gifts to Naples 106; gifts to Venice 108; giraffes 142; Medici, Lorenzo di 113, 115; Palace of Hospitality 15; poetry 113; portraits 179; severed heads 135; sheep 145; suit of armour 167–8; Suwar 81; tents 125; textiles 155; Uzun Hasan 79–80
Qur'an manuscript: diplomatic gifts 54, 66; gifts from Mamluk Sultanate 79, 86–7; gifts from Morocco 55; gifts from Safavids 82; gifts from Salah al-Din 130;

Qur'an manuscript *cont.*: gifts to Golden Horde 62; gifts to Timur 72; Jaqmaq 175; Mamluk Sultanate 69; religious gifts 150; al-Zahir Barquq 173–4
Qutlubugha al-Khalili (emir) 53
Qutuz (sultan) 16, 61

Ramazanoglus 9, 22
Rasulids 22–3, 32, 37, 38, 41, 75
recipients of diplomatic gifts 30, 150, 173, 176
reciprocation 26, 30, 57, 131, 135
recycled gifts: animals 126; diplomatic gifts 31–3, 122, 174; gifts to Ethiopia 51; Nur al-Din Zanji 130–1; self-representation 182; Yemen 38
Red Sea 9, 38, 49, 109
religion 49, 52, 101, 147, 177
religious gifts 150–1
remittances 23, 133, 173
remuneration 17, 30
requested gifts 31–3, 47, 99, 122, 149
robberies 16, 46–7, 91–2
robes of honour: Ahmad ibn Uways 70; ambassadors 30, 81; costs 27; Cypriot envoy 104–5; diplomatic gifts 23, 74; foreign envoys 79; fur 157; al-Ghawri 25; al-Hakim 129; Mamluk Sultanate 152–3; Mártir, Pedro 101–2; Musa I 58; pilgrims 55; self-representation 177; textiles 152–3; Timur envoys 75; Timurid embassy to Cairo 76; Yemeni envoys 42
rock crystal 51, 100, 110, 121, 130

saddles: Abu Sa'id (Ilkhanid) 68; Ahmad ibn Uways 70; al-Ashraf Isma'il 43; diplomatic gifts 160; Friedrich II 160; al-Ghawri 91; gifts from Mamluk Sultanate 112; gifts from Merinids 55, 56; gifts to Golden Horde 62; gifts to Ottomans 86; gifts to Venice 108; Inal 88–9; Jaqmaq 51; al-Mu'ayyad Shaykh 45; al-Mu'izz ibn Badis 128; Pir Budaq 78; prestige 160; Qaytbay 106; Shahrukh 75; significance 175; status 177; symbolism 178; varieties 163; wraps 171; al-Zahir 129; al-Zahir Barquq 174
Safavids 9, 31, 82–4, 92
safety 5, 11–16
Salah al-Din al-Ayyubi 15, 130–1
al-Salih Salih (sultan) 11, 42–3
saqunqur *see* skink
selection of diplomatic gifts 24, 135, 170, 173, 174–5
self-representation 18, 64, 173, 176, 178, 181
Selim I (Ottoman sultan): diplomatic gifts 25; elephants 142, 143; al-Ghawri 30, 82, 84, 91; invades Egypt 92; Khayrbak 93; overthrows Mamluk Sultanate 10; porcelain 138–9; requested gifts 32–3; saddles 161; severed heads 135
severed heads: 'Ala' al-Dawla 92; diplomatic gifts 24; al-Ghawri 135; human beings 134; insults 83; Iskandar 77; Özbek Muhammad Shaybani 82; Uzun Hasan 80
Sha'ban, al-Ashraf (sultan) 14, 149, 153, 155
Shahrukh (Timurid sultan): diplomacy 8, 75; diplomatic correspondence 74–5;

Shahrukh *cont.*: diplomatic gifts 24, 26; gifts from Ottomans 87; gifts from Timurids 74; Iskandar 78; *kiswa* of the Ka'ba 16, 76; requested gifts 32
Shaykh, al-Mu'ayyad (sultan): diplomatic correspondence 77; diplomatic gifts 27, 45, 86; gifts from Ottomans 93; gifts to Venice 107–8; Palace of Hospitality 15; Pisanello, Antonio 160; saddles 162; severed heads 135
significance: animals 173; belts 155–6; diplomatic gifts 18, 22, 24, 27–8, 74, 130; Mamluk envoy 114; saddles 162; silk 153; spice trade 44; textiles 64; *tiraz* 159; value of diplomatic gifts 123
silk 153, 154
silver: Bayazid I 85; Bayazid II 90; belts 155; bowls 112; brass 164; brigandine 158; Coeur, Jacques 116, 117; crystal 111; decoration 166; diplomatic gifts 86, 128; embroidery 100; goblets 124; Murad II 88; Ottomans 93, 169; palanquins 129; saddles 108, 161, 162; Safavid gifts 83; silverware 81; trade 138; weapons 91
skink 48, 64, 149, 190n73, 190n75
slaves: death 145; diplomatic gifts 42, 43, 44, 45, 121, 123; exports 50; female slaves 50–1, 64; gifts from Eastern Turkestan 124; gifts from Ottomans 86; gifts from Salah al-Din 130; gifts to Golden Horde 62; gifts to Ilkhanids 67; from India 46; Jawhar al-Qunuqba'i al-Lala 50; Mamluk Sultanate 19; North Africa 52; Nubian embassies 52; slave trade 6, 140; 'Uthman ibn Idris 59; value 133–4; Yemeni envoys 38, 39 *see also* female slaves
soldiers 104, 134, 177–8
Spain 126, 142
spice trade: importance 37; India 46; Mamluk Sultanate 5, 109, 138; routes 9; significance 44; Venice 107
spices: 'Abd al-'Aziz al-Halabi 138; diplomatic gifts 19, 29, 121, 123–4, 170; gift selections 181; gifts from India 46; gifts from Mamluk Sultanate 136, 137–9; gifts from Portugal 126; gifts from Yemen 38, 39, 42, 43, 44; gifts to Fatimids 128; gifts to Florence 115; gifts to France 117; Mamluk Sultanate 126–7; publicity 172; trade 116; Venetian records 27
status: Charlemagne 19; diplomatic gifts 20; donors 172; Faraj, ibn Barquq 73; gifts 177; Mamluk Sultanate 37, 179; *mamluks* 4; Rasulids 37; saddles 160, 163; textiles 151
sugar: balsam oil 148; diplomatic gifts 149; gifts from Ottomans 88; gifts from Salah al-Din 130; gifts to Dhul Qadirs 45; gifts to France 117; gifts to Golden Horde 63, 64, 174; gifts to Morocco 55; gifts to Ottomans 89, 93; gifts to Qara Qoyunlus 78; gifts to Venice 12, 108; porcelain 138; requested gifts 32; al-Zahir Barquq 174
Surname 43
Suwar, Shah (Dhul Qadir) 80–1

swords: Abu Sa'id (Ilkhanid) 68; Alexander, Tsar Ivan (Bulgaria) 23; Baydara (emir) 156; Berke Khan 62; decoration 163–4, 166; gifts from Ethiopia 50; gifts from India 46; gifts from Merinids 55; gifts from Rasulids 39; Inal 88–9; James II of Aragon 100, 136; Jaqmaq 76, 86; al-Malik al-'Adil 131; Mamluk Sultanate 163; al-Mujahid 'Ali 42; al-Nasir Muhammad 58, 65, 96; offence 25; poetry 71, 83; Qadir Khan (Eastern Turkestan) 124; Qaytbay 48; Qutlubugha al-Khalili 53; Timur 73; Van Ghistele, Joos 106; al-Zahir Barquq 44, 174
symbolism: animals 127; diplomatic gifts 24, 65, 71; Qur'an 150–1; saddles 163, 178
Syria: attacked by Ghazan 66; Crusaders 8; fur 133; Hulagu Khan 61; invaded by Selim I 92; Mamluk Sultanate 5; Ottomans 84; piracy 7; porcelain 139; raided by Timur 8, 71, 104
Tafur, Pero 111, 144, 162
Taghribirdi (dragoman and envoy) 178
tents: diplomatic gifts 66, 122, 123, 124; gifts from Dhul Qadirs 81; gifts to Aragon 136; gifts to Florence 113; gifts to Morocco 57; gifts to Ottomans 91; Ibn Khaldun, 'Abd al-Rahman ibn Muhammad 124–5; as mosques 192n34
textiles: Abd al-'Aziz al-Halabi 138; Ahmad ibn Uways 70; Armenia 22; Dar al-Tiraz 178; diplomatic gifts 19, 20, 31, 53, 65, 121–2; gifts from Bengal 29; gifts from Byzantium 128; gifts from Europe 95; gifts from Florence 115; gifts from Ilkhanids 68, 69; gifts from Mamluk Sultanate 79, 86, 88–9, 136, 151–8; gifts from Morocco 55, 56; gifts from Ottomans 85, 86, 88, 91, 92, 93; gifts from Safavids 83; gifts from Salah al-Din 130; gifts from Timurids 73, 75; gifts from Venice 110, 112; gifts from Yemen 38; gifts to Aq Qoyunlus 80; gifts to Aragon 99–100; gifts to Cyprus 106; gifts to Eastern Turkestan 124; gifts to Ethiopia 51; gifts to Europe 96; gifts to Fatimids 129; gifts to Florence 113; gifts to Golden Horde 62–3, 174; gifts to Ilkhanids 67; gifts to Möngke Khan 63; gifts to Morocco 54, 57; gifts to Ottomans 90, 93; gifts to Timurids 73, 76; gifts to Tunis 53–4; gifts to vassals 23; gifts to Venice 107, 108; imported goods 50; Janus, King 16; *kiswa* of the Ka'ba 54; Levant 7; Mamluk Sultanate 64; Musa I 58; Ottoman gifts 31; from Qara Qoyunlus 78; significance 64; silk 153; trade 116; value 26; al-Zahir Barquq 174 *see also* Alexandrian textiles
theriac: exports 172; gifts from Mamluk Sultanate 146–50; gifts to Cyprus 106; gifts to Venice 107, 108; requested gifts 47, 48
Timur: diplomatic gifts 24, 25–6; gifts from Ottomans 93; giraffes 142; hospitality 12–13; image

74; Jengiz Khan 70; Ottomans 84; raids Baghdad 69–70; raids Syria 8, 71, 104; war with Syria 73
Timurid embassies: attacks 16; diplomatic gifts 74, 158; *kiswa* of the Ka'ba 76; painters 178
Timurids: attacks on envoys 16; disintegrations 9; Iran 70–6; Mamluk Sultanate 8–9; Qara Qoyunlus 77; robes of honour 23; threats 9
tiraz *see* Dar al-Tiraz
Toqta (khan of the Golden Horde) 64–5
trade: balsam oil 146, 147; China 9; diplomacy 8, 96; diplomatic gifts 126; emerald 149–50; Europe 7, 95, 103; exports 170; Florence and Mamluk Sultanate 112; foreign embassies 15; France 115, 116; imported goods 159; India 8; Mamluk Sultanate 5; networks 172; Nubia 52; porcelain 138; ports 8; robes of honour 152; routes 9, 49; Silk Road 7; Yemen 37, 41
traditions 12, 13, 153
transportation 53, 144–5
Trevisan, Domenico 12, 14, 109, 144
tributes 37, 73, 104, 137, 141
Tron, Doge Nicolò 108
tufha see *tuhaf* (marvels)
tuhaf (marvels): Abu Sa'id (Ilkhanid) 67; chronicles 176; descriptions of gifts 121, 127; diplomatic gifts 17, 179; exports 170; Friedrich II of Hohenstaufen 131; Ghazan 21; gifts from Ethiopia 50; gifts from Fatimids 128, 129; gifts from Ilkhanids 66, 68; gifts from India 46; gifts from Khayrbak 93; gifts from Maghrib 53; gifts from Rasulids 39; gifts from Timurids 74; gifts from Yemen 38, 42, 45; gifts to Golden Horde 63; gifts to Timurids 73; literature 18; Musa I 58; Persian literature 19; purpose 77; terminology 173; value 47, 97
Turkmen embassies 22, 27
Turkmens 77–82, 134

'Uthman ibn Idris (ruler of Borno) 59, 87, 150–1
Uzun Hasan (Aq Qoyunlu ruler) 27, 31, 75, 78, 79–80, 135

value: animals 144–5; artefacts 176; balsam oil 146, 147, 172; carpets 171; diplomatic gifts 20, 22–3, 27, 29–30, 123; emerald 150; gifts 12; gifts from Aragon 97; gifts from Byzantium 128; gifts from Ethiopia 51; gifts from France 117; gifts from Ilkhanids 67; gifts from Mamluk Sultanate 65, 92, 174; gifts from Morocco 55; gifts from Ottomans 86; gifts from Salah al-Din 130; gifts from Timurids 74, 75; gifts to Ilkhanids 68; gifts to Morocco 57; gifts to Timurids 75–6; imported objects 31, 125; *mamluks* 134; perfume 137, 172; porcelain 139, 172; recycled gifts 31; spices 172; tents 125; theriac 149, 172
vassals: Anatolia 84, 89; Aq Qoyunlus 151; Cilicia 135; Cornaro, Caterina 106;

vassals *cont.*: Dhul Qadirs 27, 92; diplomatic gifts 23–4, 75, 156; diplomatic relations 77; Faraj, ibn Barquq 73; Nubia 52; Rasulids 37–8; reciprocated gifts 30; status 177; Yemen 40; Zirids 129
Venice: diplomatic gifts 20, 26–7; gifts 11; gifts to Mamluk Sultanate 108; Mamluk Sultanate 13, 107–12; porcelain 137; Portugal 109; reciprocated gifts 30; requested gifts 33; slave trade 140; theriac 148, 149; trade 7, 112; Trevisan, Domenico 12; Venetian embassy 109–10

warfare: diplomatic gifts 25; elephants 143; al-Ghawri 109; piracy 95; poetry 71; prisoners 134
weapons: diplomatic gifts 24, 26, 46, 51, 54, 63; as gifts 134; gifts from France 116–17; gifts from Ilkhanids 69; gifts from Mamluk Sultanate 79, 86, 88–9; gifts from Morocco 55, 56; gifts from Naples 106; gifts from Salah al-Din 130; gifts to Aq Qoyunlus 80; gifts to Aragon 99–100, 136; gifts to Eastern Turkestan 124; gifts to Fatimids 128–9; gifts to Golden Horde 62, 174; gifts to Ottomans 90, 91; gifts to vassals 23; from Mamluk Sultanate 65; offensive gifts 25; production 165; publicity 172; from Qara Qoyunlus 78; swords 163–4; symbolism 65–6
West Africa 57–9
wool: diplomatic gifts 122; exports 112; gifts from Merinids 53, 55, 56; gifts from Nubia 51; gifts from Ottomans 88, 91, 92; gifts from Timurids 70; gifts from Venice 110; gifts to Mamluk Sultanate 129

Yemen: China 9; diplomatic gifts 22, 30, 36, 37–45; emerald 150; exotic animals 140; geography 38; gifts to Mamluk Sultanate 41–2; *kiswa* of the Ka'ba 75; Mamluk Sultanate 5; al-Mujahid 'Ali 21; al-Nasir Muhammad 42; porcelain 137; Portugal 109; trade 9, 41; vassal states 77
Yemeni envoys 37, 42–3, 45
Yusuf, al-Muzaffar (Rasulid sultan) 32, 39, 40

Zafarname see Book of Victories
al-Zahir (Fatimid caliph) 128, 129, 141
zardakhana 165

1 Façade of the hospital of Sultan al-Mu'ayyad Shaykh, temporarily used as a guesthouse.

2 The mausoleum dome of the Emir Jawhar al-Qunuqba'i in Cairo, 1440.

3 Ceramic figurine of an elephant carrying a palanquin with musicians, Syria, thirteenth century.

4 (a, b) *The arrival of a giraffe sent by Sultan Faraj to Timur in Samarqand.* Double page of Yazdi's *Zafarname*, Shiraz, 1436.

و انواع تحف و هدایا از نقود و جواهر و صنوف اقمشهٔ فاخر و سایر تبرکات و تنسوقات آورده بعز عرض رسانیدند و از جمله زرافه

که از بدایع صنع آفرید کار است جل و علا و نه شتر مرغ علاوهٔ سایر نوادر بود و امیرزاده خلیل سلطان که در ترکستان بود توجه نموده

5 Medieval French jug of rock crystal.

6 Brigandine in the name of Sultan Jaqmaq.

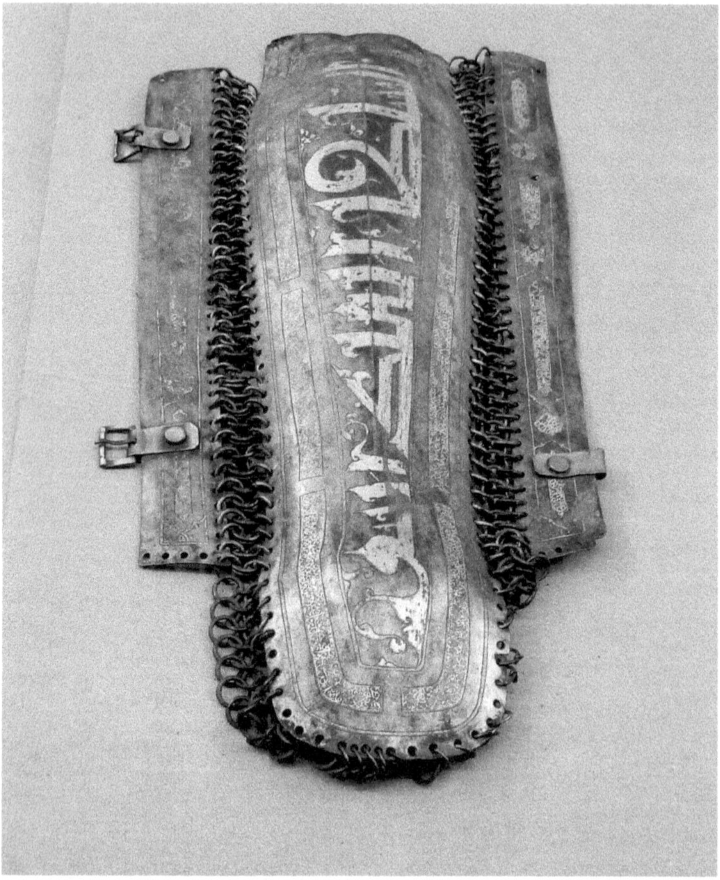

7 (a, b) Elements of Aq Qoyunlu silver-inlaid armours.

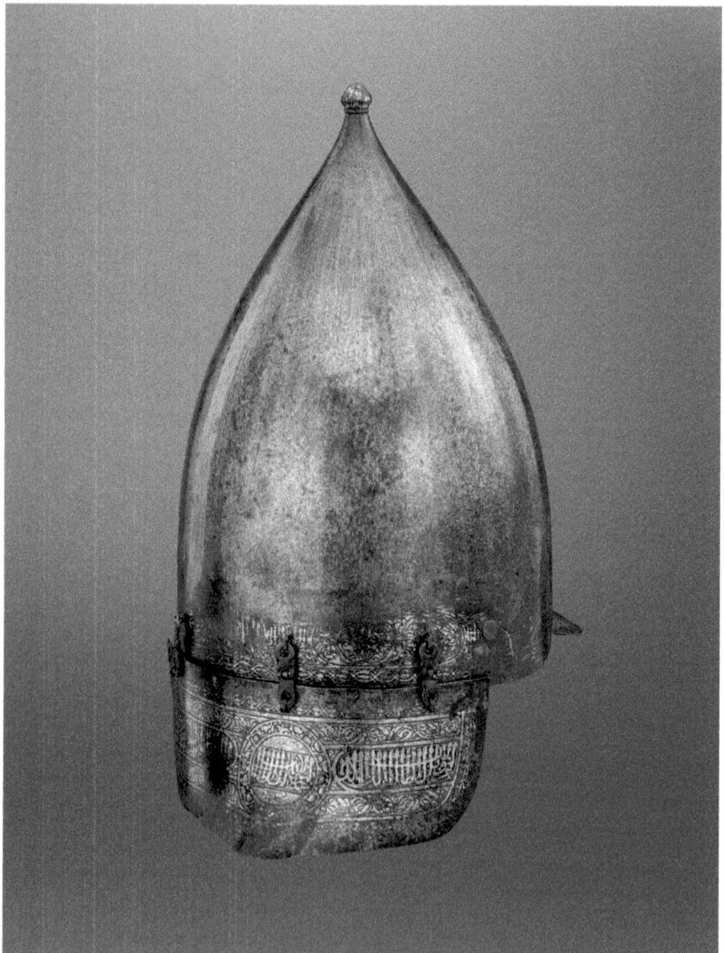

8 (a, b) Helmet in the name of Sultan Barsbay.

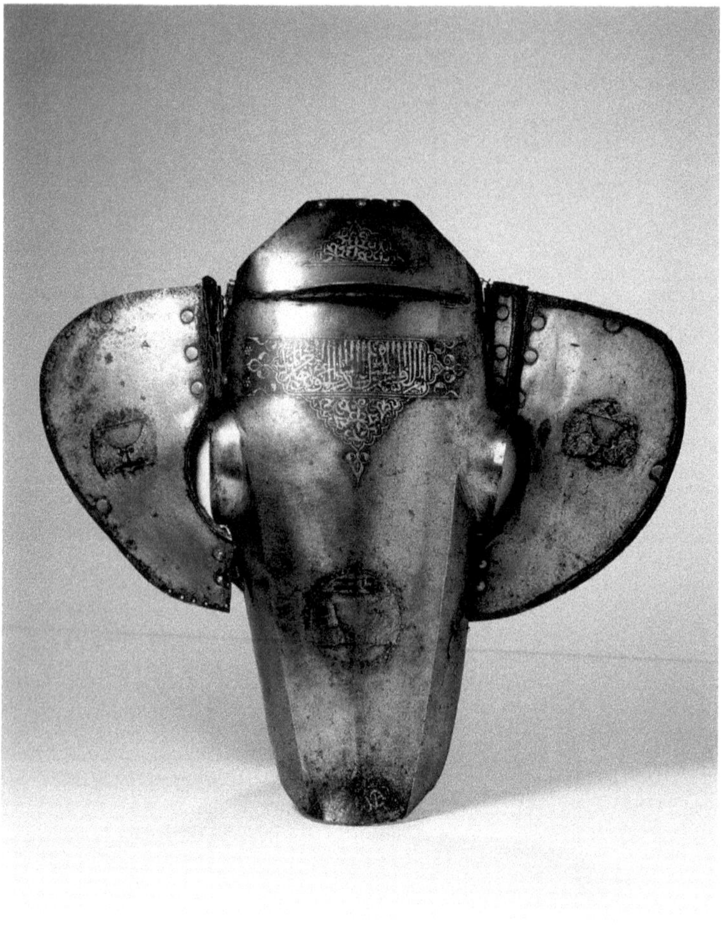

9 Chamfron in the name of Emir Muqbil al-Rumi, early fifteenth century.

10 (a, b) Axe in the name of al-Nasir Muhammad, son of Qaytbay.

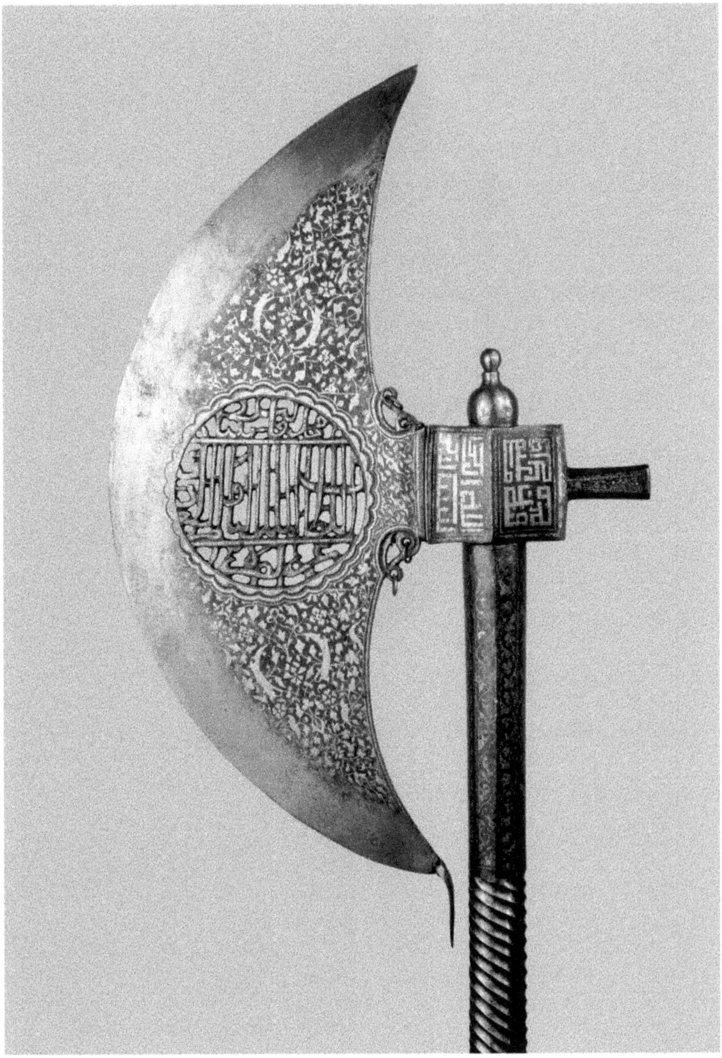

11 Axe in the name of al-Nasir Muhammad, son of Qaytbay.

12 Mamluk axe. Fifteenth century.

13 (a, b) Armour in the name of Sultan Qaytbay, front (**a**), back (**b**) and detail.

14 (a, b) Armour of Emir Sayf al-Din Inal, 1428–43.

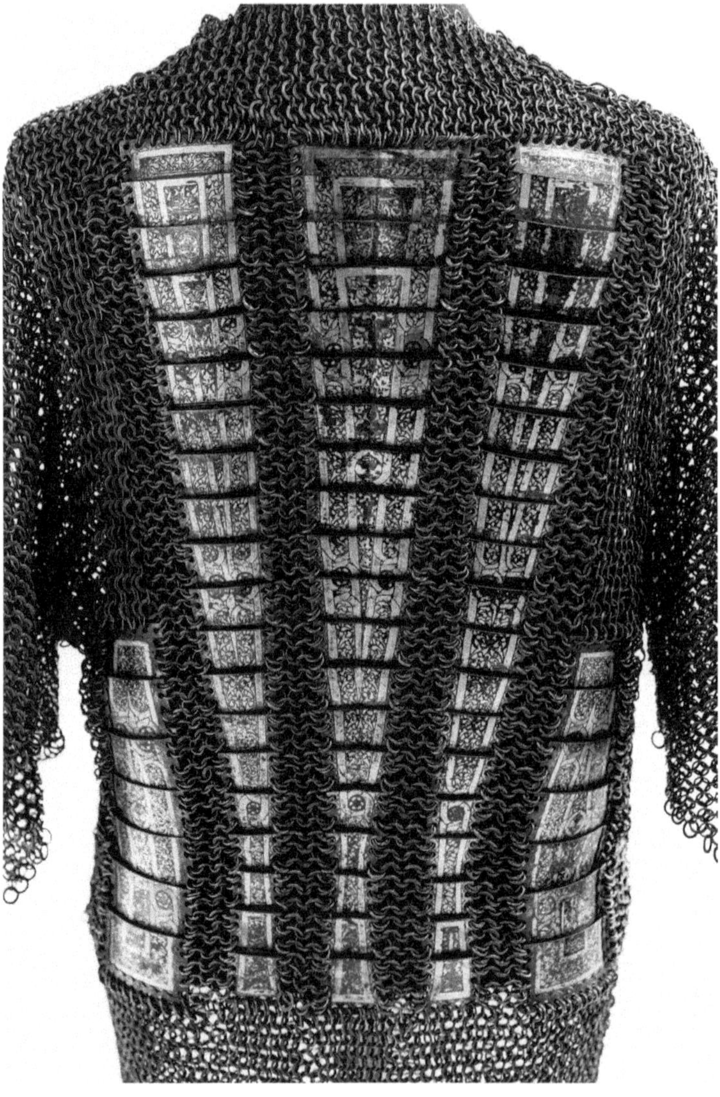

15 *Vulcan and Aeolus*. By Piero di Cosimo, 1490s.

16 *Giraffe with Mamluk groom.* Engraving in Sigismondo Tizio's *Historiae Senenses*, late fifteenth century.

17 (a, b) *Adoration of the Magi* by Bernardino Luini, 1525. Santa Maria dei Miracoli, Sarrono.

18 *Adoration of the Magi* by Bernardino Luini. Cathedral of Como, 1513.

19 *Lorenzo di Medici receiving a Mamluk embassy with a giraffe and other animals.* Painting by Giorgio Vasari 1556–8. Ceiling of Cosimo di Medici's apartment at the Palazzo Vecchio in Florence.

20 *Feast of the gods*. Giovanni Bellini, 1514.

21 *Giraffe led by an African groom*, from a Mamluk manuscript of *Kitab al-hayawan* by al-Jahiz.

22 *Elephant with Mamluk groom.* Fresco by an unknown artist, 1480s. At the courtyard of Castello Sforzesco, Milan.

23 *Capture of an elephant.* Roman mosaics, Piazza Armerina, Sicily.

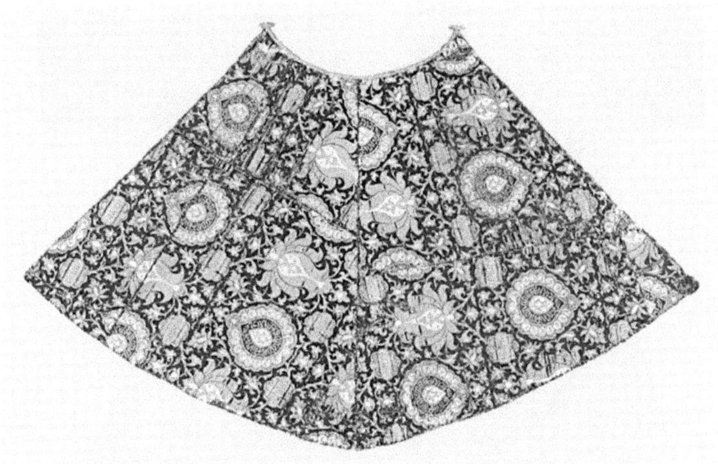

24 Mantle for a statue of the Virgin. Fifteenth-century Mamluk silk.

25 Dalmatic of fourteenth-century Mamluk silk.

www.ingramcontent.com/pod-product-compliance
Ingram Content Group UK Ltd.
Pitfield, Milton Keynes, MK11 3LW, UK
UKHW021831220426
470268UK00007B/118

9 781784 537036